COMIC STRIPS AND
CONSUMER CULTURE
1890–1945

IAN GORDON

COMIC STRIPS AND CONSUMER CULTURE

1890–1945

SMITHSONIAN INSTITUTION PRESS

Washington and London

Copy Editor: Susan M. S. Brown
Production Editors: Ruth Thomson and Robert A. Poarch
Designer: Kathleen Sims

Library of Congress Cataloging-in-Publication Data
Gordon, Ian, 1954–
    Comic strips and consumer culture, 1890–1945 / Ian Gordon.
      p.   cm.
    Includes bibliographical references and index.
    ISBN 1-56098-856-8 (alk. paper)
    1. Comic books, strips, etc.—United States—History and criticism.   2. Popular
culture—United States. 3. American literature—History and criticism.   I. Title.
PN6725.G59 1998
741.5′973′09—dc21
                                                                                    97-25413

British Library Cataloguing-in-Publication Data available

Manufactured in the United States of America
05 04 03 02 01 00 99 98   5 4 3 2 1

♾ The paper used in this publication meets the minimum requirements of the
American National Standard for Permanence of Paper for Printed Library Materials
Z39.48-1984.

Dedicated to my mother, Helen

CONTENTS

ACKNOWLEDGMENTS

In 1983, when I left a public service library job to do my undergraduate degree at the University of Sydney, Marea Terry arranged a part-time job for me in that university's library on the sole proviso that if I should one day publish a book she be mentioned in the acknowledgments. I have not seen or spoken to Marea in many years, but her act of generosity remains with me still as the first of many that eventually led to this book. Lesley Payne's many acts of kindness over twenty years head the list.

This book began as a dissertation. Fellowships from the Swann Foundation for Caricature and Cartoon and the Smithsonian Institution supported my research and early writing. A Graduate Dean's Dissertation Fellowship in the Humanities from the University of Rochester allowed me to complete the dissertation.

I benefited from the intellectual and social companionship of the fellows and curators at the Smithsonian Institution's National Museum of American History. Discussions with fellows sharpened my understanding of consumer culture and the nature of the argument I make. In particular I want to thank Nancy Bercaw, Oscar Campomanes, John Cheng, and Carolyn Goldstein. Charles McGovern, my adviser at the museum, was generous with his sources, knowledge, and time. The staffs of the museum's library and Archives Center, particularly James Roan and Vanessa Broussard-Simmons, helped me locate many an obscure item. I was also lucky to work for and with Fath Davis Ruffins in the Archives Center on completion of my dissertation. Her friendship and understanding of American history have left their mark on this book. In the year I spent researching at the Library of Congress I often spoke with James Gilbert, who provided many words of encouragement. The staff of Michigan State University Library's Special Collections, particularly Randy Scott, whose generosity is matched only by his knowledge of comics, were as always very helpful. Bill Blackbeard, who began preserving comic strips long before anyone else cared, let me roam unattended through his collection. Elsa Nystrom put me in touch with Frances Charman, formerly of Buster Brown Apparel, and I am grateful to them both. In Washington, D.C., I enjoyed the company and community of the house at 1854. The Tuesday night crowd at the Irish Times provided necessary diversions; thanks to Pete, Grace, Joe, Rob, Debbie, and other regulars.

Classmates at Rochester liberally educated me in the ways of America. Their friendship and support made life in a strange land more tolerable. At various times I found a place to stay and solace in the houses of Nancy Baran-Mickle, Mary Chalmers, Rosemary Finn, Cathy Kelly, Dean Kernan, Rex Palmer, Jim Perkins, Chuck Shindo, and Elyse Small. Stephanie Haynes and her family were equally supportive. Monte Bohna, Brian Carso, Steve Dollar, Chris Lehmann, Jenny Lloyd, Morris Pierce, Laura Sebastian, Ben Woelk, and Suzanne Wolk provided necessary corrections to my view of America. Chuck Shindo's and Cathy Kelly's criticism and support improved the quality of my work. In class and on numerous road trips Chuck Shindo taught me much about America and Americans. His parents, George and May Shindo, gave me their hospitality at the start and/or end of several of these trips.

The faculty in the Department of History at Rochester, particularly Robert Westbrook, Stewart Weaver, Mary Young, and the late Christopher Lasch, challenged my preconceived notions of history. My adviser, Robert Westbrook, encouraged me to ask harder questions of my material. His criticism, advice, and support were everything that a graduate student could ask for and more.

I presented parts of this book as papers to the National Museum of American History's colloquium series, annual meetings of the Organization of American Historians, the American Studies Association, and the Cultural Studies Association of Australia. Comments by Michael

Denning, James Gilbert, Janice Radway, Joan Shelly Rubin, and Rebecca Zurier at two of these meetings helped refine my argument. Roland Marchand and I shared information on Buster Brown, and he offered several suggestions, not all of them followed, on converting my dissertation into a book. A portion of this work was published in a different form in the *Australasian Journal of American Studies,* and I wish to thank Ian Tyrrell, Anthony Ashbolt, and two anonymous readers for their comments on that article. Over the years I have received much encouragement and support from Shane White and Richard Waterhouse, both of the University of Sydney's History Department.

Mark Hirsch from the Smithsonian Institution Press guided me through the process of transforming a dissertation into a book. Without his kind words and gentle hints this work may never have been completed. Mick Bell photographed most of the reproduced images. Susan M. S. Brown smoothed out some rough passages in the final manuscript, and Ruth Thomson oversaw the production of the book. My thanks to them all.

The support of my mother; my sister, Sandra; her husband, Evan; and my adult nephew and niece, Mathew and Emma, has helped me stay focused on completing this book. In recent years the trust and faith of Tan Chaity has added to this support immeasurably.

INTRODUCTION

Our world . . . is a world of theme stores and theme parks. A world of cash-ins and tie-ins and endless licensed products. A world where movies become breakfast cereals, where celebrities become board games, where a fast food chain spawns a line of clothing, where the advertising and entertainment industries have merged, where movies contain advertisements and so do public bathrooms, where dead celebrities endorse products that didn't exist when they were alive, where environmentalism is used to sell cars and booze, where radical groups run mail-order businesses.[1]

In 1991, in the Pentagon City shopping mall, the writer Peter Carlson stumbled on the fact that American culture has commercialized "just about everything in just about every conceivable way." Carlson blamed this commercialization on the doubling of media advertising budgets between 1982 and 1990, the increase in product licensing, and the ascent to the presidency of Ronald Reagan, "the only former pitchman ever elected president." Carlson's twelve-page article lists instances of commercialization including the use of celebrity images on dolls, cartoon-character frozen dinners, and comic-book-character breakfast cereals.

One can appreciate Carlson's horror in the north Virginia mall, where he confronted an array of knickknacks distinguished from one

1

another only by the trademarked images splashed across them. But one wonders why these products escaped his notice until 1991. Perhaps it is the sheer volume of licensed products, the market value of which grew from $5 billion per annum in 1977 to $66 billion in 1990, that opened Carlson's eyes to the commercialization of American culture. But an abundance of licensed products, particularly those featuring comic art characters, which account for almost 20 percent of the market, is not a recent occurrence. Indeed it dates from the turn of the century. This book examines the relationship between comics and the commodification of American culture.[2]

I began this study with an interest in the work of Fredric Wertham, a New York psychiatrist whose 1954 book, *Seduction of the Innocent,* railed against comic books and their influence on children. James Gilbert has described Wertham's attack on comic books as a cyclical reaction to a new form of mass culture seemingly beyond the control of cultural elites. Gilbert's description is particularly apt in capturing the demonization of comic books, but it may treat Wertham a tad unkindly. Wertham always maintained that the welfare of children was his prime concern in campaigning against comic books, and his 1973 book on fanzines (magazines published by fans), in which he praises adult comic book fans as engaging in activities "outside of all mass manipulation," suggests he was being truthful. But in *Seduction of the Innocent* Wertham lambasted the whole enterprise, equating Donald Duck and Superman comic books with adult-oriented horror and crime comic books. In this broadside any attempt at genuine discussion of the impact of comics on children was lost in the blaze of publicity, thoughtless reaction, and then counterreaction. *Seduction of the Innocent* has become a cult collectible among comic book fans, who regard its virulence as a form of high camp.[3]

I came to Wertham's most famous work as a longtime comic book reader. Family lore has it that I learned to read through comic books at the age of four. Over the years I read and amassed large numbers of comic books. Unfortunately I periodically disposed of them with little regard to their commercial worth as collectibles. I do not remember when I first heard of *Seduction of the Innocent,* but when I read it in 1988, I shared the fan view of the book as a camp classic and it did not disappoint me. Whatever the merits of his cause, Wertham's book is little more than a 400-page tract. In many ways *Seduction of the Innocent* resembles the comic books it criticized, with Wertham figuring as the superhero capable of driving evil from our midst. It seems that Wertham simplified his message, and sold himself as a celebrity figure, to popularize his cause.

At about the time I reached these observations, Wertham died, and his family appointed a biographer who had sole access to his papers. Without such access it seemed to me that any study of Wertham would be seriously hampered. Moreover a remark of Wertham's had caught my attention and sent me in another direction. In the early pages of *Seduction of the Innocent* he emphasized that his study focused not on comic strips but on comic books. He argued that comic strips were mostly read by adults and subject to censorship from newspaper editors, which protected their readership from the "semipornographic story" sometimes found in comic books. This comment struck me as odd because a number of comic strips, such as Chester Gould's "Dick Tracy," seemed just as violent as the fare offered in comic books. Around the same time I read a 1936 article by John K. Ryan, who, although he regarded comic strips as having a "wholesome and robust vulgarity," worried about the effects of their "steady consumption by an immense public." At this point I decided to study the place of comic strips in American culture, which meant shifting my focus to the late nineteenth century.[4]

Over the last fifteen years historians, along with anthropologists and sociologists, have turned their attention to the development of consumer society in order to comprehend changes in American culture at the turn of the century. At first most of these scholars focused on the emergence of a mass culture of consumption in the last two decades of the nineteenth century. In their accounts shifts in the American economy and society in those decades—notably the development of new technologies and modes of transportation and communication that resulted in large-scale industrial production and craft deskilling, the emergence of national markets and advertising, and the growth of urban centers whose populations had sufficient income to participate in a new leisure culture—produced a culture of consumption. More recently historians have located patterns of consumption in both the late mercantile age and the early industrial era. At the same time other historians have redefined the constituent elements of mass consumer society, stressing commodities' ability to evoke a sense of being American and shifting the arrival of consumer society to the twentieth century.[5]

For all this research there are still good reasons to concentrate on the late nineteenth century as the period when the culture of consumption emerged in America. The two key words here are *culture* and *emerged*. No new mode of living or understanding springs fully formed onto the historical stage. To say that a culture of consumption emerged during the last decades of the nineteenth century is to argue that the way people used goods and services began to define their culture in a new fashion. Existing modes of use were broadened, both demographically and quantitatively, and made subject to the market in a process that led eventually to a mass culture of consumption. Families who had once bought goods in bulk at locally owned dry goods stores began to purchase brand-name items and eventually to shop in chain stores. Furthermore aspects of life hitherto untouched by the market were subject to commodification. Men and women who had understood themselves by the lights of profession, party politics, and religion increasingly defined their character more through the goods and services they purchased, possessed, and used.[6]

The structural changes in the economy of the United States at the turn of the century are generally referred to as modernization and the literary and visual aesthetic the era gave rise to as Modernism. In 1988 Kirk Varnedoe, a curator at the Museum of Modern Art in New York, noted that "the founding premise of Modernism was to call into question the distinction between high and low art."[7] Varnedoe's observation provided the central premise for his and Adam Gopnik's 1990 exhibition and book, *High & Low: Modern Art and Popular Culture*. The book and exhibition subverted established hierarchies of art by reexamining the relationship between "highbrow" and "lowbrow" artistic pursuits at the turn of the twentieth century. In their examination the two curators marshaled the usual suspects. The "highbrow" contenders were modern art masters, such as Picasso, Braque, Gris, and Léger, and in the "lowbrow" corner we found mass-circulated newspapers, graffiti, and advertising. But into this pack of hardened Modernist veterans Varnedoe and Gopnik threw a joker, comic strips. The two regard comic strips as "another kind of modern art" and a form that shared modern art's common desire to establish a "new universal language of art."[8]

For historians interested in the transformation of American society between 1880 and 1920, Varnedoe and Gopnik's conception of comic art as a language suggests fresh ways of using Modernism and modernization as explanatory concepts. To be sure the curators' interest is in the hermeneutics of Modernism and not in American history, but their work parallels historical research on modernization, Modernism, representation, and the establishment of cultural hierarchies along "highbrow/lowbrow" divisions. Recent works on modernization have been accompanied by efforts to grapple with Modernism, which has been described variously as

- a holistic "culture that seeks to know reality" while recognizing that such efforts will always be incomplete
- rejecting Victorian values such as "a moral creed based on repression and rationalism"
- a sensibility "often rooted in hostility to modernization"
- a cultural form that existed in the United States only as a machine aesthetic.[9]

On occasion these analytical strands have come together, perhaps most successfully in Richard Wrightman Fox and T. J. Jackson Lears's edited collection of essays, *The Culture of Consumption.* In that volume Lears, Christopher Wilson, and Jean-Christophe Agnew demonstrate how the ambivalence of a Modernist sensibility undermined attempts at a critical stand against effects of modernization such as the commodification of society. Specifically Lears and his fellow contributors regard the modern condition as a weightlessness brought on by the erosion of a moral creed and the "corrosive impact of the market on familiar values." Into this void stepped the entrepreneurs of mass market amusements and advertisers, who offered visceral, if illusionary, sensations under the banner of "real life." In this ethereal world, where advertising became an all-pervasive if slippery language, Agnew holds that consumers adopted a strategy of "acquisitive cognition," in which commodities were acquired not simply through purchase "but through a kind of all-pervasive knowingness, a thoroughgoing acquaintance with commodities' actual and imagined attributes." Yet even this approach failed to provide a solid foundation since it reproduced "the dislocating dynamic it was intended to reduce because the attributes" constantly changed. Although Agnew limits himself to discussing the appearance of such an "acquisitive cognition" in the work of Henry James, his concept can be applied to the language of comic strips.[10]

The relationship between comic strips and Modernism can be understood through two approaches. First comics can be seen as an outcome of the process of modernization, and second they can be viewed as a humor-based response to the problems of representation faced by a society in transition. As an outcome of modernization comic strips appear as a social phenomenon, in this case one of the first widely consumed commodities produced by the emerging mass entertainment industry. Such an approach helps us locate comic strips within a historical framework, but it is still necessary to describe how comics came to, and could, articulate Modernism. The comic strip mode of representation, particularly the use of sequential panels and narratives without closure, predated bolder Modernist efforts to reconfigure strategies of representation. The art theorist Norman Bryson, in his proposal to read art as codes of social recognition that come together as signs, argues that in the act of creation artists can transfigure existing conventions and project new understandings into social discourse. That is visual representations are not simply metonymical forms but language that can both transform and reflect a culture. Daniel Bell may contest that there was no Modernist culture in turn-of-the-century America save that of the impersonal machine aesthetic, but comic strips gave the machine product a personality and covered the nation by 1908. Comic strips were representations through which an increasingly commodified society saw and constituted itself. In short comic strips helped create Modernism in both its formal art meaning and its broader cultural denotation.[11] My account of the commodification of comic art is an effort to show how cultures are transformed by examining the role of one form in creating a Modernist American culture.

The development of this culture involved wholesale changes in America, too broad to be explained conclusively in a single work, although Jackson Lears has come very close in his *Fables of Abundance*. But the process can be traced in the transformation of a single cultural form into a marketable item. This book examines the mass commodification of illustrated humor in the form of comic strips, comic books, and advertising. Visual images were an important element in the emergence of the culture of consumption. In part their importance derived from the opportunities large cities and towns provided their residents to see and be seen, in public spaces such as streets, mass transit, and entertainment venues, without knowing one another. Visual appearance thus became a factor in demonstrating social standing and character. The rise of visual representation was also fed by the growth of newspapers, which commencing in the 1880s used more and more illustrations, as both news and entertainment. Eventually, in the illustrated humor supplements of these newspapers, the comic strip emerged between 1895 and 1901. By stressing individual characters, the new comic art form lent itself to promotion and marketing because these images provided a means for embellishing commodities with personality. The growth of a visual culture in America is sometimes attributed to the impact of motion pictures on audience sensibilities, or to the earlier widespread distribution of Currier and Ives lithographs. But comic strips were equally important in creating a national market for visual images.[12]

When I began this study very little had been written on comic art. Most of the available works were general in nature, anecdotal histories, encyclopedias, or coffee table books. These books were valuable references even though often marred by lack of, or inaccurate, publication details of the comics they discussed. On the whole they offered a standard history of comic strips. Most comic art historians date the commencement of comic strips from the appearance of R. F. Outcault's "The Yellow Kid" in 1895. These accounts generally acknowledge a European comic strip prehistory encompassing the work of Wilhelm Busch (1832–1908), Rodolphe Töpffer (1799–1846), caricature, the engravings of William Hogarth (1697–1764), and the Bayeux tapestry, and sometimes, for good measure, they include Egyptian hieroglyphics and prehistoric cave drawings. It is generally agreed that comic strips developed in the Sunday supplements of Joseph Pulitzer's *New York World* and William Randolph Hearst's *New York Journal.* These papers added the strips in a drive for increased circulation. Maurice Horn argues that Pulitzer's paper assembled "all the essential elements of the form—the sequential narrative, continuing characters, dialogue enclosed within the picture" but that Hearst brought the form to fruition in the *New York Journal.*[13]

There are, however, two dimensions to this standard history that contribute in varying degrees to the explanation of the American nature of comic strips offered by most works. An aesthetic understanding, such as Horn stresses, argues that the physical makeup of comic strips—panels, word balloons, and continuing characters—distinguished them from earlier graphic forms and made them uniquely American. A sociological approach regards the subject matter of early American strips, particularly "The Yellow Kid," as their distinguishing feature. The proponents of this second position read the content of "The Yellow Kid" as an explanation for the development of comic strips. That is, America produced a class of rough-hewn children, "kids," who found expression in comic strips. In other words, "The Yellow Kid" simply reflected a social reality familiar to residents of American cities. Ergo comic strips are uniquely American.[14]

These different approaches raise methodological questions of how to read comic strips and comic books. Horn argues that comic strips are not a medium of graphic narrative because the story in a strip is conveyed not visually but by both words and pictures. But the relationship between words and pictures in comic strips is complex. Comic strips convey their stories in several registers: the story in words, the story in pictures, the story of the words and the pictures, and stories that are embodied in the ungiven histories of the content and form. The content of a given episode of a comic strip is shaped to some extent by its place in an unfolding and continuing narrative. Horn's argument that pictures and words act in combination only when the text is included in the frame of the graphic simplifies the construction of meaning in comic art. This is not to say that the work of Töpffer and Busch, who did not use word balloons, is qualitatively the same as that of Rudolph Dirk, who did. The point is that Töpffer and Busch, in different fashions, strengthened the link between text and graphic, and Horn's methodology prevents him from seeing their contribution.[15]

The presentation of comic strips as uniquely American because they depicted the reality of American cities is likewise narrow. Comic strips in the United States were the product of a specific set of social relations that ripened in American cities in the 1890s. In a particular time and place comic strips developed a specific form. But it was a form that leaned heavily on the past and that could be transported to, or invented in, other cultures with slight variation as they too achieved modernity.[16] Moreover, such an explanation slides over the diversity of American culture in the late nineteenth century by equating certain cities with the nation as a whole. Comic strips are certainly a national phenomenon today, but behind this status stands a process involving the commercial development of the form and its sale across the country. An associated difficulty with the sociological interpretation is that it generally treats comic strips as a reflection of social attitudes rather than as a constituent element of the culture. Thomas Inge describes comics as "revealing reflectors of popular attitudes, tastes, and mores." Judith O'Sullivan sees comics as "holding an enchanted mirror to American society."[17]

Such approaches, no doubt unintentionally, position comic strips as texts that have little impact on those who read them daily. Furthermore regarding comic strips as a reflection of American culture raises questions of reading strategies given that all comic art embodies some degree of caricature. Reading comics for social meaning requires some understanding of how authors and artists intended their caricatures to be taken and the responses they elicited. In their celebration of comics these aforementioned sociological approaches also ignore other readings of comic strips as uniquely American. For instance, in 1908 *The Nation* labeled comics "a glory all our own" in order to criticize them. And in the 1950s, when Wertham and others lambasted comics, Coulton Waugh described them as "fresh flowers from nature's wonderful hotbed, the people." Both positions regarded comic art as singularly American.[18]

If the importance of comic strips is not that they are uniquely American, how should they be understood? I would argue that comic strips are part of a broader art form, which includes caricature, cartoons, animation, and comic books. This comic art form originated in the eighteenth century, when European artists added linear narrative and caricature to the traditional form of broadsheet graphic narratives. Comic strips are works that employ caricature in a series of drawings to tell a story. They are distinguished from other forms of graphic narrative, stories told through pictures, by their comic element. The comic element is often present only in the form, the style of depiction, and not in the subject matter of the story. Comic strips and comic books developed out of European and American traditions of caricature and cartoon. American illustrated humor drew its form and some of its inspiration from European antecedents.[19] But two factors—the use of continuing characters and their appearance in mass-circulated newspapers—set American comic strips apart from the earlier European form and made them mass market products.

The fact that comic art contributed significantly to the formation of a culture of consumption is by itself not particularly startling, even if no one has taken the time to make such a case. But tracing the process of that contribution both broadens our knowledge of historical change in American society and raises methodological questions about reading, readership, and audiences. The body of this work presents a historical narrative of comic art's role in shaping American society. To make that story I have read comic strips, comic books, and advertisements through a number of practices. In particular I have followed Clifford Geertz's maxim that to understand a joke is to understand a culture. In reading comics then I have sought to understand the audiences comic creators wished to appeal to and the context in which those audiences read comics. Comics as a form attracted diverse audiences, as did individual comic strips and books. From their inception in New York City, American comics had a polysemic character that they retained even as they became icons of an American mythology. In Roland Barthes's conception mythology naturalizes, or suppresses, history. Two histories are suppressed in comic strips: first the strip's relation to the history of the society in which it was created, and second the internal history of a particular comic strip. Recovering those histories allows us to better understand the dimensions of comic art's humor and its place in American culture.[20]

The techniques of comic strip and comic book narratives require readers to fill in the gaps. In comics the narrative flows from panel to panel, but there are quite literally gaps between the panels, which means readers have to interpret the space and comprehend its place in the story. To do so readers have to at various times understand the techniques and structure of comic art, the context of a particular strip, its place in an ongoing narrative, and the likely pace of the story. Reading the nuances of a comic strip then requires a regular and reasonably constant exposure to it. A single episode of a comic strip reveals very little about the overall nature of the undertaking. Comic strip characters' identities are shaped in repetitious story lines and variations on set gags. These formulas call for a recognition of the characters and a suspension of that recognition to let the joke work. Character then is re-created in each instance of a strip in a never-ending construction of identity. But even as readers take the time to assemble their knowledge of comic strip characters, they distance themselves from them. The caricature techniques of comic art, and the often satirical content of strips, set readers apart from the strips. In the distance between the eye and the page, readers come to look on comic humor as a satire on the foibles of a strip's characters and not on the readers' own idiosyncrasies. These two features of comics—the episodic and continuing construction of identity, and a critical distance between subject and reader—lent themselves to advertising strategies that offered goods and services as a means of constructing identity and framed those messages as morality tales. This type of advertising, which increased in the late 1920s and throughout the 1930s, rested in part on Americans' familiarity with comic strip narrative techniques.[21]

Quantifying the readership of early American comic strips is a difficult task. The first comprehensive survey of comic strip readership was taken in the 1930s. Circulation figures for most of the newspapers I examined are available for this period, but they give only an indication of the number of copies newspapers sold; the figures are not a reliable guide to comic strip readership or the composition of audiences. I have therefore concentrated on the potential audience for the comics. I refer to this audience as the market, that is, the population of cities and towns in which comic strips were published. To determine this market I studied the Library of Congress's newspaper holdings for the early years of the 1900s. I examined 152 daily newspapers for 1903, 161 for 1908, and 165 for 1913. In 1900 there were 2,190 daily papers in America, so my sample is by no means complete and is biased in favor of papers from urban centers and larger towns because these are the papers most often microfilmed and collected by the Library of Congress.[22]

This bias reflects important changes in the early years of the twentieth century, when towns expanded their influence on the rural areas around them in part through the medium of newspapers, whose distribution increased with the expansion of mail services and railroads. My figures for potential comic readership are on the conservative side because they do not take into account significant populations in surrounding regions for cities such as New York, Chicago, Boston, and San Francisco, which were served by metropolitan newspapers. Even comparatively small-town newspapers had regional distribution. For instance, the *Memphis Commercial Appeal* of December 1, 1901, gave details of the paper's extensive distribution in Alabama, Arkansas, Kentucky, Mississippi, and Tennessee. As early as 1903 comic strips were enjoyed by diverse audiences, from New York City's cosmopolitan population of 3,437,202 to the Anaconda, Montana, mining community of 9,453 souls.

This study highlights how comic art contributed to the formation and expansion of a culture of consumption and incidentally how this culture shaped a particular ideology of national identity. Comic art in the form of comic strips became a widely consumed commodity. It was also a useful medium for the promotion of other commodities, and the content of comic strips and comic books served as an advertisement for the values and practices of the emerging culture itself. Although I would acknowledge that comic art is often humorous and can provoke aesthetic appreciation, my point here is to show how these qualities have been put to commercial uses in comic strips, comic books, and advertising. These commercial uses came to define comic art to such a degree that comic strip and comic book characters at times seemed less storytelling devices and more ciphers, or business trademarks, that sold a range of products, which incidentally included comic strips and comic books. Moreover these characters became icons of American culture, which if they did not unite all Americans as Americans at least naturalized a conception of defining American identity through the availability, and repetitious purchase, of commodities. When artists devised comic strip characters in the 1890s, they created a form that lent itself to an expanding culture. Comic art played a definitive role in the creation of a mass culture of consumption, which provided a focus for American identity in the twentieth century.

1

FROM CARICATURE TO COMIC STRIPS

The Shaping of Comic Art as Commodity

In 1883 Joseph Pulitzer commenced publication of a Sunday edition of his newly acquired newspaper the New York World. Building on the successes of the penny press the World carried detailed stories about the infamous side of city life, stories that helped shape gossip, rumor, and scandal into a marketable genre: the news. The World and other cheap newspapers were the products of developments in printing technology, transportation, and communication. Their audience was the new reading public of the eastern cities. Close to 90 percent of the urban working class was literate and made significant expenditures for newspapers.[1]

The World led the way for these newspapers. One of its important innovations was the regular use of editorial cartoons, which before the mid-1880s were largely confined to illustrated humor magazines. On October 30, 1884, the World splashed Walt McDougall's "Royal Feast of Belshazzar Blaine" across its front page. This cartoon depicts a bloated James G. Blaine sitting down to dinner with the wealthy of the city while the hungry poor are excluded from the sumptuous repast. In the legends of comic art this cartoon and Bernhard Gillam's equally satirical version of Blaine as a man bearing the tattoos of his corruption, which appeared in Puck, are said to have cost Blaine the 1884 presidential election.[2] Whatever its effect on the election, McDougall's October 30 work certainly established the editorial cartoon as a regular feature on the World's front page.

The increased use of illustrated material in newspapers also con-tributed to the development of comic strips. The first comic strip char-acter to enjoy widespread popularity, Richard Felton Outcault's Yel-low Kid, appeared as an unnamed figure in a series of illustrations in Pulitzer's Sunday *World* in 1895 and 1896. Dubbed "the Yellow Kid" by the newspaper's readers because of the color of his nightshirt, the figure became the center of a craze in New York and nearby cities. The Yellow Kid craze demonstrated that comic strip characters could sell newspapers. By the end of 1895 the Sunday *World* circulation aver-aged half a million copies—almost a 100 percent increase over 1891.[3]

Outcault, Pulitzer, and his competitor William Randolph Hearst recognized the commercial possibilities that the popularity of comic strips and the increased circulation of newspapers offered. Outcault tried to secure copyright protection for his character, presumably in order to license Yellow Kid products. Hearst obtained Outcault's ser-vices over Pulitzer's objection and in October 1896 launched a comic supplement to his *New York Journal* built around the Yellow Kid. Al-though the Yellow Kid was short-lived, other comic strip characters, such as the Katzenjammer Kids and Happy Hooligan, soon followed and en-sured the success of Hearst's newspapers and the comic strip form.

These characters won comic strips an institutionalized place in newspapers, first in New York and later across the country. Artists' de-velopment of popular characters, rather than the graphic form per se, accounted for the strips' success. Indeed artists created mechanisms basic to the comic strip as means of embellishing their characters. De-vices such as panels and word balloons worked to elaborate and ex-tend these characters by placing them in narratives and supplying them with voices. More important, comic strips were the form news-paper proprietors, editors, and artists developed to market distinct comic art characters. Characters laid the basis for widespread distribu-tion of comic strips and development of the formal properties of the art form that later proved useful for advertising.

The Yellow Kid originally appeared in single-panel illustrations. Artists such as Richard Outcault, Rudolph Dirks, and Frederick Op-per created the comic strip art form around this character model. Their early strips primarily represented city life in a form that could be sold through mass circulation newspapers. To understand where these images came from, and how they became commodities consumed on a mass scale, it is necessary to trace the development of comic art in

America. Such a history requires an examination of American illustrated humor magazines and newspaper comic supplements before the development of comic strips.

AMERICAN ILLUSTRATED HUMOR MAGAZINES AND CITY CULTURE

The first American illustrated humor magazine published on a regular basis was *Puck*. Its founder, Joseph Keppler, was born in 1838 in Vienna, where he studied art and appeared on the stage before emigrating to America in 1867. After a stint in a touring theatrical company and two unsuccessful attempts in St. Louis at publishing German-language magazines, including an earlier *Puck*, Keppler moved to New York. In September 1876, in partnership with the printer A. Schwarzman, he launched a new German-language *Puck*. At the prompting of the playwright Sidney Rosenfeld and under his editorship, an English-language edition, using the same illustrations, was issued in March 1877. The English-language edition proved more popular than the German.

Puck demonstrated both the influence of European antecedents and the special, and distinctively American, culture of New York City. The graphic material it published drew its form and technique from European traditions, but except for the occasional nod to Wilhelm Busch, its content was locally inspired by an emerging culture of the cities that the humor magazines not only celebrated but helped create.[4] Keppler's cover illustration for the first issue—"A Stir in the Roost: What Another Chicken?"—showed the influence of the European tradition of representing human action in anthropomorphic symbolism. It depicted *Puck*, freshly hatched from an egg, greeting the rest of the brood, identified as the *Tribune, Herald, Graphic, Leslie's Weekly,* and *Harper's Weekly*. In this brood *Puck* stood out as the only journal to focus predominantly on humor. But it was not simply a copy of its European antecedents *Fliegende Blätter, Charivari,* and *Punch*. Unlike these journals, *Puck* combined social humor with sharp-edged political cartoons. Indeed *Puck* defined a format for American illustrated humor magazines followed by its main competitors, *Judge* and *Life*. Most issues of *Puck* contained a full-page political cartoon on the cover, a double-page political cartoon in the center pages, and a full-page social cartoon on the back cover.[5]

Puck's political cartoons followed the success of Thomas Nast's cartoons attacking the Tweed Ring in New York City, which appeared in *Harper's Weekly*. These cartoons established the effectiveness of caricature as a modern political weapon. And, because Nast's cartoons appealed to an emerging group of urban reformers, they achieved a respectable status in middle-class sensibilities. The single-panel cartoon became a legitimate form of political commentary and action in American society. *Puck, Judge,* and *Life* extended the respectability and appeal of political cartoons to all forms of illustration derived from caricature.

Illustrated humor magazines such as *Puck* fused the rough-and-tumble urban political culture of Gilded Age America with the rich pageant of public entertainment that filled up the leisure hours of thousands of men and women. Leisure time emerged when large-scale industrial production and craft deskilling led to work becoming something one did for a living rather than the way one lived. To increase production and achieve economies of scale, large industrial proprietors sought to exert greater control over the conduct of work. They established new work processes that curtailed an individual's control over a job and created a new class of salaried managers to oversee production. For laborers work became more regimented and rationalized and consequently a chore from which they sought relief. The nonowning managers had less personal stake in the enterprises and spent less time on them than small proprietors had. By the turn of the century leisure was what one did in one's nonwork hours.

As work and leisure split into separate spheres, leisure assumed a growing importance in shaping the class identities of both middle- and working-class Americans. The middle class erected a cultural hierarchy around practices such as the theatrical performance of Shakespeare, which had previously been part of a shared culture. Working-class leisure often involved partaking in activities formerly integrated into the workday. For instance, Roy Rosenzweig describes how owners forced the open consumption of alcohol from the workshops of Worcester, Massachusetts, to saloons. But although owners could regulate the time and place of alcohol consumption, they were less successful in regulating the activity itself. Nevertheless both middle- and working-class leisure swiftly came to be mediated by a culture industry created by entrepreneurs and consumers of professional sports; circuses; minstrel shows; vaudeville; amusement parks; dime novels;

other cheap literature, including illustrated humor magazines, the modern daily, and Sunday newspapers, in which comic strips would appear; and eventually movies.[6]

Precisely because leisure took a greater role in structuring and mediating class identity, it also assumed a greater role in structuring and mediating class tensions. Indeed barrooms, dance halls, vaudeville palaces, and dime novels became contested terrain in the struggle to define urban America. The title of Rosenzweig's book, *Eight Hours for What We Will*, captures workers' determination to control their leisure. This was the trade-off they made for relinquishing control of the workplace. Leisure was obtained through work and was the right of those who worked. The very formation of a self-conscious middle class was bound up in efforts to determine appropriate leisure activities. According to the historian Michael Denning, the middle class defined itself by establishing cultural boundaries between it and the working class following the collapse of the notion of producing class as a mark of social position. Denning's history of dime novels analyzes their conflicting "accents" (different voices for different audiences) in the context of a producerist plebeian mentality reluctantly giving way to an emerging middling mass culture. The revolution in private recreation among the "middle class" between 1880 and 1900, which Francis Couvares describes in his work on Pittsburgh, involved not so much "every leisure taboo [losing] its grip" on an existing static class as a redefinition of social position in the face of changes in the organization of work and the emergence of new forms of entertainment against which taboos had not yet been erected.[7]

If commercialized leisure mediated and structured the tensions between the middle and working classes, it also mediated between the Old World and the New. As did native-born managers and workers, immigrants defined themselves through leisure. In his history of immigrants in urban America, John Bodnar argues that rather than acquiring a set of given traits in a process of Americanization, immigrants shaped their own worlds, drawing on an inherited past in order to meet "the hierarchy of power and resources in urban America." By contrast, Robert Snyder in a history of vaudeville argues that through that medium immigrants fashioned "new ethnic identities formed more from American popular culture than from Old World ways."[8]

But Snyder is not as far from Bodnar as these statements imply. If we take vaudeville as representative of American popular culture, we can see that the latter encompassed a good number of Old World ways. And vaudeville embodied several ambiguities. Originally known as variety, it grew out of the exclusively masculine saloon concert. Changing the name to vaudeville was an attempt to attract a heterosocial audience; the aim was to retain enough raciness to titillate but not to offend the new, broader audience. Moreover, although the syndicate of B. F. Keith and Edward Albee centralized bookings for most of the vaudeville circuit, shows were tailored for specific audiences. Vaudeville appealed to its potential audiences by meeting them in familiar surroundings. The ethnic traditions played out on the vaudeville stage granted immigrant groups a "hyphenated" status, joining ethnic and American identities in a single, if ambiguous, identity. This duality comes out clearly in an anecdote about the Irish American vaudeville singer Maggie Cline. "Once, when she finished the song 'Don't Let Me Die till I See Ireland,' a man in the gallery shouted, 'Well, why don't you go there?' 'Nit!' Cline called back, 'It's too far from the Bowery.' She swaggered off a stage awash in cheers."[9]

Illustrated humor magazines also played on this immigrant American identity. The October 20, 1892, issue of *Life* contained a graphic entitled "The Advantages of an Extensive Repertoire" by Franklin Morris Howarth (see Figure 1). In seven unframed scenes this piece depicts the attempts of a street musician to appease the cop walking the beat. The musician commences his performance with "The Star-Spangled Banner." Howarth probably wanted readers to assume that the cop, lost in contemplation in the background, would not interfere with this display of American patriotism. The joke plays out when the cop demonstrates his intention to put a stop to the performance. The resourceful musician switches to the anthems of Germany and England before striking the right note with an Irish song.

A hundred years later the Irish cop joke appears stale. But the piece did more than contain a stereotypical joke; it offered a vision, shared by artist and reader, of power in the American city. The rapid shifts to German, English, and finally Irish music demonstrate the musician's—and Howarth's—knowledge of urban America. Power—in this case the ability to make, break, and enforce the law—did not belong exclusively to those who regarded themselves as American. It also belonged to German Americans, Anglo Americans, and Irish Americans. But as Howarth suggested, one could never be sure to whom it belonged on any given street corner. As did Maggie Cline, the musician had to

1. Franklin Morris Howarth, "The Advantages of an Extensive Repertoire," *Life,* 20 (October 20, 1892), pp. 222–23.

shape his identity in response to his audience, composed of both immigrant and native-born Americans.

Magazines such as *Life* helped middle-class Americans adapt to an emerging mass culture. The three major illustrated magazines—*Puck, Judge,* and *Life*—combined raucous humor with appeals to respectability. For instance, *Judge* attempted "to make a periodical which no gentleman will be ashamed to read in the family circle." *Life* sold itself as a more genteel version of the other two magazines and probably appealed to a more well-to-do clientele. *Life*'s series of Gibson Girl cartoons, by Charles Dana Gibson, set the standard for middle-class male and female fashion in the mid-1890s. *Puck* often took the side of the workingman against big business but warned against extremism. Although their readership was probably limited to native-born Americans, these magazines acknowledged a shifting and heterogeneous urban population. *Puck, Judge,* and *Life* established illustrated humor as part of the urban scene and set an example for its commercial exploitation.[10]

F. M. HOWARTH AND THE DEVELOPMENT OF COMIC STRIPS

Magazines such as *Puck, Life,* and *Judge* acquainted readers with both a new urban political and leisure culture and a new art form. Franklin Morris Howarth was an important figure in the development of the comic strip. For instance, his "music" emanating from the performer's trumpet in "Advantages of an Extensive Repertoire" was one of the first instances in American narrative comic humor in which text and graphic were combined. Howarth's use of this important feature of comic strips placed him in the forefront of a movement that adapted and expanded Rodolphe Töpffer's and Wilhelm Busch's format for an American audience. As did those two European artists, Howarth narrowed the distance between the textual and the visual to create a comic art form that increased the emphasis on character and narrative by embedding them in the graphic image.

Howarth was one of a number of American comic artists who attempted to yoke narrative humor with graphic illustration. Through the course of Howarth's career a number of artists drew jokes that recast Charles Darwin's theories as a series of highly dubious evolutions,

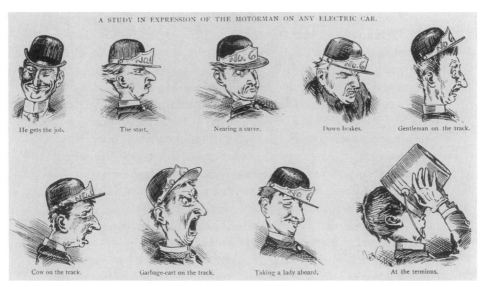

2. "A Study in Expression of the Motorman on Any Electric Car," *Judge*, 23 (September 24, 1892), p. 199.

involutions, and transformations. The visual puns of these illustrations depend on the fusion of people and objects with graphic similarities and on ironic textual juxtapositions. For instance, in "A Thanksgiving Study" a turkey changes into an ax. "The Involution of the Messenger Boy" displays a boy becoming a tortoise. In "The Evolution of the English Sovereign" a bag of sterling metamorphoses into Queen Victoria. And "All Balled Up" features a catcher transformed into a baseball.[11]

Some artists linked the narrative structure of the evolution joke with caricature of city faces and types to comment on the metropolitan scene. "What Will Become of the Men Who Stay Out Late" transforms a dude out for an evening on the town into an owl. Other illustrations depict the expressions of an electric car motorman during a day's work (see Figure 2), and of a man receiving the news, by phone, that his mother-in-law has cut short her visit and left while he is at work. Variations on these types of illustrations include a man who turns into a pig by eating at a lunch counter, a lovers' quarrel illustrated solely by feet, and "Puck's Easy Lessons in Caricature," which shows how to depict any type of face by adding to a basic oval shape. "The Transformation of a Paying Teller," in which a teller changes from a humble servant into an outraged bureaucrat because a customer has endorsed a check at the wrong end, demonstrates the narrative possibilities of these types of illustrations.[12]

Howarth did the most to develop humorous illustrated narratives. He joined *Puck* as a full-time artist in the mid-1890s, during the magazine's reign as the preeminent forum for illustrated humor. Unlike the other artists on *Puck*'s staff, Howarth was not required to draw editorial cartoons. This was an important division of labor, marking the point at which artists and editors separated comic strip art from political commentary. Howarth was one of the first major American comic artists to concentrate on social, or nonpolitical, humor. His work in *Puck* consisted mainly of sequential narratives, occasionally with text underneath, a format borrowed directly from Busch. Howarth's innovation was to block out his work in panels.[13]

Howarth was the leading American proponent of multipaneled comic stories. This feature laid the basis for the creation of comic strip characters because the humor in narrative derives from a dynamic social setting in which the passage of time plays a role. Instead of using the figures as illustrations for gags printed beneath the panels, in these sequences artists created the humor around the figures. Artists such as Howarth gave their figures characteristics attributed to city dwellers and created various types.

Busch's influence can clearly be seen in an early Howarth strip, "The Revenge of the Persecuted Baker," which appeared in *Judge* on July 11, 1891. This pantomime strip, in which two naughty boys steal pastries from an overladen baker, who eventually extracts his revenge by lacing his goods with coal oil, reworked Busch's theme in *Max und Moritz*.[14] Howarth's style, however, was more explicit and conveyed the story without recourse to an exterior explanatory text. For instance, although this strip and "The Advantages of an Extensive Repertoire" were not blocked out with panels, Howarth established a rudimentary frame by changing the positions of the figures. The narrative shifts in both strips also frame the action. In "The Advantages of an Extensive Repertoire," the narrative flows from the "music" coming from the trumpet. In "The Revenge of the Persecuted Baker" the use of depth and perspective help carry the story.

Howarth also borrowed and developed techniques aimed at expanding possibilities for character development. He experimented with graphic methods that captured human feelings and emotions such as pain and anxiety. The last sequence of "The Revenge of the Persecuted Baker" shows the two boys in pain, depicted through contorted facial features, hands clenched to stomachs, and exaggerated sweat beads or tears pouring down their faces. Howarth had used this technique in "The Unexpected," in which an Oriental prisoner about to be beheaded sweat large drops. In "The Advantages of an Extensive Repertoire" the musician's anxious state is depicted by sweat beads. Exaggerated sweat beads became a standard means of displaying anxiety in comic strips, and the credit for them belongs to Howarth. These techniques may seem a matter of little interest. But comic art's ability to convey emotions was important in the development of comic strip characters. Emotions, however crude, offered readers the sensation of intimacy. Moreover, the depiction of these "intimate emotions" in simple, repeatable, easily recognizable forms made them generally accessible, a factor that advertising researchers later concluded was the central appeal of comic strips.[15]

Howarth's use of narrative form and comic art technique allowed him to create new possibilities for comic characters. Rather than illustrate one- or two-line gags straight out of vaudeville, he presented unfolding stories. But as did vaudeville these series of panels worked familiar narrative genres in which the joke lay in the novel solution to a stock situation. Howarth's work made fun of professional photographers and spoiled babies, highlighted the pettiness of fashion and social class, and depicted the numerous frustrations faced by suitors. For instance, in "Love Will Find the Way," he showed a young couple's triumph over a watchful father, while other strips depicted suitors' efforts frustrated by vigilant fathers, jealous rivals, and even uncooperative elephants. These figures and others, such as the overbearing mother-in-law, emerged as stock types, so much so that on occasions Howarth created his humor by overturning expectations. For instance, he drew a strip in which a suitor encountered a cooperative father, and another in which a man's mother-in-law proved a godsend. Nonetheless these stock situations and types remained the mainstay of comic art.[16]

The most important of these pictorial representations of social types in the development of American comic strips was the naughty boy, originally borrowed from Wilhelm Busch's *Max und Moritz*. The first comic strip character, Richard Outcault's Yellow Kid, was developed from this type. Howarth was not the first American artist who borrowed Busch's naughty boys for his comic strips. The leading illustrator of the day, Frank Bellew, and his son "Chip," contributed several such strips to *Life* before Howarth. But neither Frank, who died in 1888, nor Chip, who died at age thirty-two in 1894, developed comic strip work on the scale of Howarth's.[17] His "Revenge of the Persecuted Baker" occupied the whole back page of *Judge* and was in color. When he joined *Puck* the full-page comic strip, combining rhyming text with a graphic blocked out in panels, became his stock-in-trade.[18]

Howarth also regularly drew strips focused on two naughty boys. In addition to "The Revenge of the Persecuted Baker," he featured two boys in strips in *Life* on October 1, 1891, and in *Puck* on May 10, 1893, August 19, 1896, and January 13, 1897. In addition, he and other artists drew numerous strips and cartoons featuring mischievous children. Of these Michael Angelo Woolf's cartoons of the urban street life of children, which appeared in *Life,* stand out as prefiguring the Yellow Kid. Woolf's cartoons featured street urchins speaking the same rough argot later employed by Outcault's Yellow Kid. Furthermore Woolf gave his cartoons titles such as "The Spanish Craze in Mulligan's Lane" and "Gymnastics in Brophy's Alley."[19] These presaged Outcault's "Hogan's Alley."

What separated the early American illustrated humor that appeared in *Puck, Life,* and *Judge* from the comic strip was the lack of a continuing character or cast of characters, the regular use of word balloons, a format that required weekly or daily appearances by these characters in a named strip, and a place in a mass-circulated medium, which made the form and characters consumer staples. But it was the launching of comic supplements to the Sunday editions of the *New York World* and *New York Journal* that set in motion a process leading to the distinct form of graphic narrative that eventually became comic strips.

COMIC STRIPS AND COMIC STRIP CHARACTERS

In 1889 the *World* capitalized on its successful use of illustrated material with the publication of a one-page illustrated humor section, "The World's Funny Side," in its Sunday edition. This section had an appearance similar to that of the humor magazines except it had no color plates. In 1894 the *World* acquired a color press and began a Sunday color supplement. Richard F. Outcault's panel story "Origin of a New

Species, or The Evolution of the Crocodile Explained," published November 18, 1894, was one of the first illustrations to appear in color in the *World*'s Sunday supplement. Before his engagement by the *World*, Outcault worked as a technical illustrator for the Edison laboratories and the journal *Electrical World*. He also sold cartoons to *Judge* and *Life*. "From the Eiffel Tower," probably drawn when he accompanied Edison to the Paris Exposition of 1889, is the only signed example of his early work in the three main illustrated humor journals. It is a poorly executed illustration of a two-line vaudeville-style gag about the size of a hotel bill in Paris.[20] "Origin of a New Species" was a better piece, although it derived its theme from the well-worn genre of gag evolution illustrations. Some historians, such as William Murrell and Martin Sheridan, regard it as the first comic strip because of its panels, layout, and use of color, but Outcault's graphic added nothing to the form. It was not even the first piece of comic art printed in color in an American newspaper.[21]

Outcault's main contribution to the development of the comic strip was that he crystallized a succession of comic kid types into a single character, the Yellow Kid. Between 1895 and 1896 his Yellow Kid defined the artistic and commercial dimensions of comic strips.

On May 5, 1895, the *World* published Outcault's "At the Circus in Hogan's Alley" (see Figure 3). It was the first of a series of large comic illustrations of city kids that appeared in the *World* under the more or less continuous running title "Hogan's Alley." The origin of the title probably lay in the song "When Hogan Pays the Rent," performed by the Irish American Maggie Cline in Tony Pastor's vaudeville theater in 1891. The joke was that Hogan never paid the rent, and this caused a great deal of excitement in his neighborhood (alley) on rent days. In 1893 this characterization was incorporated into "Maggie Murphy's Home," a song for the play *O'Reilly and the Four Hundred*. The song opened with the line "Down in Hogan's Alley." Outcault had adopted this line for "Feudal Pride in Hogan's Alley" (see Figure 4), which appeared in the illustrated humor magazine *Truth* on June 2, 1894.[22]

This Outcault cartoon, and others like it, were almost identical to Michael Angelo Woolf's cartoons of city urchins. Woolf had originated this type of cartoon in the 1870s in *Wild Oats*, an early illustrated humor magazine.[23] In the 1890s Woolf's art appeared regularly in *Life*. A comparison of an untitled Woolf cartoon from 1892 (see Figure 5) and Outcault's "Up to Date" from 1893 shows that Outcault

3. Richard Felton Outcault, "At the Circus in Hogan's Alley," *New York World* (May 5, 1895).

closely followed Woolf's theme, poking fun at fashion, even using the same name for his main protagonist.[24] In Woolf's cartoon a young street urchin named Sally is mimicking the action of a bride making an entrance to the amusement of a crowd of onlookers. In Outcault's "Up to Date" a similar Sally is modeling her new boots, courtesy of the Street Cleaning Department, for her friends. Outcault borrowed his theme from Woolf with little fear of recrimination because it was not possible to copyright themes, types, and situations. But it was possible to copyright characters with distinctive appearances.

The copyright law inspired an Outcault cartoon in the February 9, 1895, "Special Artists' Issue" of *Truth* (see Figure 6). The cartoon satirizes the work of Palmer Cox, creator of "The Brownies," a set of popular illustrated characters that appeared first in *St. Nicholas Magazine* in the early 1880s and then in books, comic strips, and a num-

FEUDAL PRIDE IN HOGAN'S ALLEY.

LITTLE ROSILIA McGRAW—No ; we won't come and play with youz, Delia Costigan. Our rejuced means may temporary necessitate our residin' in a rear tenement, but we're jist as exclusive as when we lived on the first floor front and papa had charge of the pound in the Department of Canine Captivity!

4. Richard Felton Outcault, "Feudal Pride in Hogan's Alley," *Truth* (June 2, 1894), p. 90.

ber of products, including Kodak's Brownie cameras. The joke in this cartoon, "Fourth Ward Brownies," operates on two levels. First, by having "Mickey the Artist" draw the simple features of a "brownie" on a fellow kid, Outcault implied that Cox's work was childish and easily done. Second, the dialogue of the joke plays off this simplicity. Mickey says, "If Palmer Cox wuz t' see yer, he'd git yer copyrighted in a minute," the point being that Cox needed copyright protection because anybody could reproduce his art. In fact Cox's art was reasonably detailed if simple in appearance. But the cartoon turns on the importance of copyright, so Outcault set up Cox's work as easily created.

The appearance of this cartoon in the artists' issue of *Truth* suggests that its message flowed from an ideology of craft pride, which posited that although artists owned the products of their labor and skill, they

Voice from Crowd: CHEESE IT, SALLY, HERE COMES DER WEDDIN' PARTY!
Sally: I DON'T CARE. I WANTS TO SEE WHAT IT FEELS LIKE TO BE A FASHERNABLE BRIDE!

5. Michael Angelo Woolf, Untitled cartoon, *Life*, 19 (April 14, 1892), p. 229.

should not try to control the subjects of their work. If this was Out-cault's intention the cartoon proved highly ironic because one of those admiring Mickey's work was the as yet unnamed Yellow Kid in his first distinctive appearance.[25] This small cartoon was reproduced in the *New York World* the following week. Another Outcault cartoon, "The Fate of the Glutton," appeared in the *World* on February 10, 1895. Shortly after, on May 5, 1895, the jug-eared figure appeared in the *World*'s quarter-page "Hogan's Alley." Unlike the cartoons, the May 5 panel's humor did not rely on a caption under the illustration, and the illustration was in color. On January 5, 1896, in an illustration entitled "Golf the Great Society Sport As Played in Hogan's Alley," this kid's nightshirt was colored yellow, and the Yellow Kid, the first continuing character in a newspaper comic supplement, was born.

6. Richard Felton Outcault, "Fourth Ward Brownies," *Truth* (February 9, 1895), p. 10.

Outcault, it seems, did not deliberately set out to create the Yellow Kid. By all accounts it was the comic supplement audience who named the figure after the color of his nightshirt. Outcault did not refer to the boy as the Yellow Kid during his tenure at the *World*. It was only when he joined Hearst's *New York Journal* in October 1896 that the figure appeared under this title.[26] The title "Hogan's Alley," the vaudeville origins, and Outcault's use of dialect located the comic in New York City, and in some ways the Kid was an archetypical working-class city dweller. Outcault apparently thought the Kid was a type, not an individual.[27] But the Kid was bald, had jug ears and buck teeth, and always wore a nightshirt. Although he was Irish he was so often taken for Chinese that Outcault seized on the visit of Li Hung Chang,

7. Richard Felton Outcault, "Li Hung Chang Visits Hogan's Alley," *New York World* (September 6, 1896).

a Chinese dignitary, to New York to have the Yellow Kid announce that Li was mistaken to think he was Chinese (see Figure 7). These features singled the Yellow Kid out from the other children in Outcault's illustrations and probably account for the feature's popularity. They also singled out Outcault's work as a distinctive representation of the complexity of city life; in his hands comic art transcended stock situations and types to produce an individual character. But the Yellow Kid's meaning and reception often slipped from his creator's control.

The Yellow Kid was immensely popular and figured almost every week in the *World*'s advertisements for the Sunday edition. The "Hogan's Alley" feature itself, however, appeared just eight times in 1895 and on average only every other week in early 1896. Outcault kept no regular schedule for the production of "Hogan's Alley" illustrations up to June 1896. But from June 7 to October 4, 1896, "Hogan's Alley" appeared weekly in the Sunday *World*. The increased tempo of production may have been a response to the *World*'s publication on May 31, 1896, of a George Luks "Hogan's Alley" comic that was indistinguishable from Outcault's work. It is possible that Outcault felt threatened by another artist drawing his successful feature and moved to protect his creation.

In any case, he took action to secure his legal position regarding "Hogan's Alley" and the Yellow Kid. The September 6, 1896, installment of the comic, "Li Hung Chang Visits Hogan's Alley," carried a small box in the left-hand corner that read, "Do Not Be Deceived None Genuine Without This Signature," below which appeared Outcault's signature. On September 7, 1896, he wrote to the Library of Congress seeking copyright for "The Yellow Dugan Kid." He stated that it was not intended as "an article of manufacture but to appear in my cartoons each week in the Sunday World." Outcault was uncertain if the character could be copyrighted, "as he appears in a different fashion each week. His costume however is always yellow, his ears are large, he has but two teeth and a bald head and is distinctly different from anything else." To emphasize his point, Outcault enclosed a sketch of the kid.[28] In the October 4, 1896, "Hogan's Alley," a note attached to the Yellow Kid's arm identified him as Mick Dugan. Whether Outcault took these steps simply to protect his character or as part of a scheme to ensure that he would retain control over it when he left the *World* remains conjecture, but the October 4 "Hogan's Alley" was his last for the *World* before he joined Hearst's *Journal*.

Outcault gave the Yellow Kid singular features as part of his effort to distinguish his work from that of other artists, particularly Michael Angelo Woolf. His jab at Palmer Cox suggests that he thought an artist's worth lay in the novelty of his or her ideas and the ability to render those ideas on paper. If Outcault thought of the Yellow Kid as a type, then the Kid's individuality belonged not to the illustrated figure but to the artist. But as Outcault discovered when Luks imitated his work, such individuality was not only easily reproducible but apt to be copied when it was profitable. The artist's only recourse was to copyright his character.

A letter from the Treasury Department to the *New York Journal* dated April 15, 1897, stated that on the advice of the Librarian of Congress the department held that only the title "The Yellow Kid" and not the Kid's likeness had been copyrighted because of an irregularity in the application.[29] This meant that Outcault could not prevent unauthorized reproductions of the Yellow Kid and so was unable to effectively license his character. Entrepreneurs marketed numerous unauthorized Yellow Kid products, including songbooks, buttons, chewing gum, chocolate figurines, cigars, and ladies' fans. Outcault's copyright difficulties, and loss of income, can be seen in the existence of at least two Yellow Kid chewing gums, the Outcault-licensed Adams' Yellow Kid Gum and the nonlicensed Grove's Yellow Kid Gum.[30]

Outcault's Yellow Kid demonstrated the potential of comic characters to capture the public's imagination and boost newspaper circulation. Both Joseph Pulitzer and William Randolph Hearst saw this potential and waged a battle over the right to publish Yellow Kid comics. Hearst arrived in New York from San Francisco in 1895. He took control of the *New York Journal* and set about emulating Pulitzer's Sunday *World*. To achieve this goal in the shortest possible time, he hired away from the Sunday *World* almost the entire staff at higher salaries. When Hearst decided to publish a humor supplement, it was natural to poach Outcault, especially because his "Hogan's Alley" was the central feature of the *World*'s supplement.

Hearst launched his own comic supplement on October 18, 1896. It was heralded as "eight pages of polychromatic effulgence that make the rainbow look like a lead pipe."[31] A prominent element of the first issue was "McFadden's Flats," which featured the Yellow Kid and the other denizens of Hogan's Alley, who joked, "Say Hogan's Alley Has

Been Condemned By De Board of Helt An We Was Gittin Tired of It Anyway."[32]

Both the *World* and the *Journal* published versions of the Yellow Kid. The *World*'s version continued to appear under the "Hogan's Alley" title because the paper had copyrighted that title as part of its general copyright. The two versions of the character had the same physical appearance because the likeness was not copyrighted. The simultaneous appearance of two Yellow Kids in newspaper strips, and the flood of unlicensed products, diminished the value of the character as a commodity for both Outcault and the publishers. Neither paper could promote its comic strip as an exclusive feature and therefore a reason to buy one paper over the other. George Luks's version of "Hogan's Alley" for Pulitzer's *World* eventually shifted the focus from the Yellow Kid to two new characters, the "yellow kids." When Outcault realized he could not retain exclusive control of the Yellow Kid, he abandoned the character and Hearst but not comic strip characters. Outcault's experience with the Yellow Kid showed him that with the right character, and effective copyright protection, an artist could make a lot of money.

The *Journal* discontinued its version of the Yellow Kid in early 1898, when Outcault left Hearst to rejoin Pulitzer. The *World*'s "Hogan's Alley" folded shortly after. Although he was short-lived, the Yellow Kid established the legal status of illustrated figures as property. When Outcault left Hearst the comic strip had still not taken its definitive form, but the Yellow Kid had introduced comic strip characters as commodities that could be created and sold in the market.[33]

Hearst's *New York Journal* was the most successful medium in the development of these new commodities. The *Journal*'s comic supplement published work by a host of artists in addition to Outcault. Most of this art was similar in content and style to what had appeared earlier in the illustrated humor journals. Indeed many of the *Journal*'s artists—including Archie Gunn, Syd Griffin, Frank Nankivell, and Louis Glackens—were alumni of those periodicals.[34] But none of these artists developed a comic strip character. The first comic strip characters to appear in the *Journal* after the Yellow Kid were in "The Tinkle Brothers" by Harry Greening, which debuted in the *Journal* on September 5, 1897. This strip was an adaptation of Wilhelm Busch's *Max und Moritz*. Although numerous adaptations of Busch's work had appeared in American illustrated humor journals throughout the 1880s and 1890s, "The Tinkle Brothers" was the first to name its characters and appear in a number of episodes. But the strip was short-lived. Only five episodes were published, and it disappeared after October 17, 1897. Two months later, on December 12, 1897, another adaptation of Busch's *Max und Moritz*, "The Katzenjammer Kids" by Rudolph Dirks, debuted in the *Journal*. This feature became one of the most successful comic strips of all time and was still appearing in 1997. But in its early form "The Katzenjammer Kids" had few of the characteristics of the comic strip.[35]

The first episode of "The Katzenjammer Kids," "Ach Those Katzenjammer Kids!" contained six unframed sequences in which three boys played a prank on a gardener with a hose. In subsequent weeks there were only two kids and the feature was drawn in panels. In the initial episodes the action was depicted in pantomime. Occasionally during the first years text was included underneath the panels in the manner of *Bilderbogen* (work like Busch's) and Howarth's work in *Puck*. Dirks did not use word balloons in the strip's first two years. But its cast of continuing characters differentiated "The Katzenjammer Kids" from other comic art. The main characters were the kids, Hans and Fritz, and Mamma Katzenjammer. The basic framework of the strip was the kids' mischief, whose object was usually Mamma. In 1902 Dirks introduced two other regular characters, Der Captain and Der Inspector, who also became victims of Hans and Fritz's pranks.

In 1898, following Outcault's departure, "The Katzenjammer Kids" became the backbone of the *Journal*'s comic supplement. The strip appeared in almost every Sunday edition of the *Journal* up to July 1898, when Hearst temporarily dropped the comic supplement in favor of a series of supplements promoting the Spanish-American War. Following the war "The Katzenjammer Kids" resumed its prominent place. The strip, and its regular appearance, was so important to the *Journal* that, from time to time, artists other than Rudolph Dirks drew "The Katzenjammer Kids."[36]

In one editor's words, "Habit forming [was] the core of newspaper supremacy."[37] Comic strips with continuing casts proved well suited to the task of habit formation. Their attraction lay in their unique and striking characters. To late twentieth-century readers this may seem obvious because we are accustomed to the mass media's creation of new characters, such as Bart Simpson, with sharply defined personalities. But at the opening of the century the construction of such characters was a recent phenomenon. Comic strip artists still, however, had to give their characters voices before those characters could meet the standard of performance required of the twentieth-century personality and thus be able to achieve celebrity status.[38]

The first attempt to give an American comic strip character a voice occurred in Outcault's "Hogan's Alley" published on April 12, 1896, in the *World*. In this single-panel illustration, entitled "First Championship Game of the Hogan's Alley Baseball Team," the Yellow Kid stands in the foreground, mouth open as if to address the audience, his "speech" pinned to his nightshirt. The space on the Kid's nightshirt became Outcault's preferred tableau for conveying his words. On occasion, though, Outcault employed word balloons as means of giving his subjects voice. The *World* of September 15, 1895, carried an Outcault panel entitled "Grand Opening of the Dramatic Season at the North Pole," in which an Eskimo vendor offers theater patrons "Red Hot Tamales and Chili-Con-Carne" through a speech balloon. And on May 3, 1896, in "Hogan's Alley" a parrot exclaimed, "Good Bye, Good Bye," by way of a word balloon. Eventually, on October 25, 1896, in Hearst's *Journal* the Kid himself spoke through a speech balloon. But even on this occasion dialogue was also inscribed on his nightshirt.[39]

The credit for developing word balloons as means of giving comic strip characters voice belongs to Frederick Burr Opper.[40] Before he joined the *Journal* in mid-1899 Opper was an established editorial cartoonist and worked for *Puck*. His first contributions to the *Journal*'s comic supplement were full-page cartoons for its cover. Gradually he began to experiment with panel stories and comic strips. On March 18, 1900, Opper's first comic strip character, Happy Hooligan, made his debut in the *Journal* in a six-panel pantomime story.[41] Between March 1900 and early 1901 Opper experimented with the use of word balloons in "Happy Hooligan" and other comic art features he produced. On December 30, 1900, the *Journal* published an Opper piece entitled "Cupid's Everlasting 'Jolly'": Centuries May Come And Centuries May Go, But This Goes on Forever." This graphic was a comic depiction, in a series of panels, of love over the centuries. Opper used both word balloons and rhyming text underneath the panels to effect his joke. "Cupid's Everlasting 'Jolly'" symbolized the transformation of narrative comic art in turn-of-the-century America. The use of rhyming text and graphics in the manner of the German *Bilderbogen* disappeared with the end of the nineteenth century, and the comic strip complete with characters, panels, and word balloons blossomed. By March 1901 Opper used word balloons in almost all his comic strip work. Moreover the other regular artists on the *Journal*—Rudolph and Gus Dirks, James Swinnerton, and Carl Anderson—followed his lead. By June 1901 comic strips dominated the *Journal*'s comic supplement. And "Happy Hooligan" and "The Katzenjammer Kids" set a standard for the art form. Within a year newspapers throughout America began to carry comic strips in their Sunday editions and the strips became one of the most widely consumed forms of the emerging entertainment mass media.

2 COMIC STRIPS, NATIONAL CULTURE, AND MARKETING

The Breadth of the Form

William Randolph Hearst, the proprietor of the *New York Journal*, more fully utilized comic art's potential to sell newspapers than did Joseph Pulitzer or any other publisher. He outbid Pulitzer for the services of the most popular artists. Between 1896 and 1901 the contributors to the *Journal*'s comic supplement—Richard Outcault, Rudolph Dirks, Frederick Opper, and others—fashioned the comic strip. In particular Dirks in "The Katzenjammer Kids" and Opper in "Happy Hooligan" refined the combination of character, word balloons, and panel layout that define modern comic strips. Hearst used the comic strips produced in New York in his other papers, such as the *San Francisco Examiner*. In 1902 he further offset his heavy costs for comic strips by selling them to newspapers around the country, thus opening a national market for strips. As early as 1903 at least forty-eight newspapers in thirty-three locations carried comic strips, and by 1908 this figure had grown to at least eighty-three newspapers in fifty locations.[1]

Concurrent with the development of a national market for comic strips, Richard Outcault began to license a new strip, "Buster Brown," created in 1902 in the pages of the *New York Herald*, to the manufacturers of a wide variety of products. With "Buster Brown" comic strip characters reached their full potential as marketing tools for other products. The range of Buster Brown merchandise available in 1908 would be envied by more recent licensees of comic art phenomena such as Batman, Teenage Mutant Ninja Turtles, and the Simpsons. The importance of Buster Brown's marketing is that it predated, and presaged, a wholesale shift from text-based to visual, image-centered advertising. Advertisers used Buster Brown as an eye-catching image and as a symbol of qualities to be associated with their product. Buster Brown was a protean type of the form advertising assumed in twentieth-century America's mass culture of consumption. He transcended the comic art form to become a cultural icon. But this success was rooted in the national distribution of comic strips through local newspapers.

THE NATIONAL SPREAD OF COMIC STRIPS

By 1903 newspapers across the country carried comic strip supplements in their Sunday editions. This expansion placed comic strip characters and the art form before a wide national audience, laying the basis for their use in other products. It also provided urban and rural readers with a weekly shared experience and brought together diverse national audiences as markets for mass media products. Apart from the healthy increases in circulation that the New York papers experienced when they introduced comic strips, two factors contributed to the rapid spread of the art form through the nation: the growth of syndication and the consolidation of control by newspaper chains. Both the *World* and the *Journal* organized syndicates to sell comic strip features to other papers. Independent syndicates, which began to supply feature material to newspapers, particularly Sunday papers, in the 1880s developed their own comic supplements that were sold to papers across the nation. Also by 1900 eight newspaper chains existed, the largest of which was the nine-paper chain of Edward W. Scripps.[2]

Hearst was a key figure in the development of both syndicated material and newspaper chains. By 1903 the comic art that originated in Hearst papers appeared in at least seventeen newspapers across the country, and Hearst himself owned six papers in four cities. According to Frank Mott, by 1922 "Hearst owned twenty daily papers and eleven Sunday papers in thirteen of the largest American cities." The consolidation of the production and distribution of comic strips proceeded apace with the centralization of newspapers, news dissemination, and business and industry in general.[3]

Irving Bachellor set up the first successful company to syndicate feature material in 1883. In 1884 Samuel S. McClure established his syndicate, which distributed the stories of Rudyard Kipling, Jack London, Arthur Conan Doyle, and Robert Louis Stevenson. The syndicates sold the bulk of their material to newspapers for use in Sunday editions. Larger Sunday newspapers also syndicated some of their features, with both the *New York Herald* and the *Journal* beginning to do so in 1895. The *World* started to syndicate its material in 1898. In 1897 the *St. Louis Post-Dispatch* began to carry the *World*'s comic supplement, but this was not syndication as such because both papers were owned by Pulitzer. Around this time newspaper owners led by Hearst began to syndicate comic strips. "The Katzenjammer Kids," carried on January 6, 1901, by the *Pittsburgh Post* in black and white as part of its magazine section, is the first syndicated strip I found, but there may have been earlier occurrences. Most likely comic strips did not appear in color outside major cities such as New York, Chicago, and St. Louis in the late 1890s because color web presses would have been a prohibitive capital investment for most publishers.[4]

Hearst was probably the first to distribute a color comic supplement nationally. In 1900 he established two papers in Chicago: the morning *Chicago Examiner* and the evening *Chicago American*. This move gave Hearst three Sunday papers: the San Francisco and Chicago *Examiner*s and the *New York Journal*. The *San Francisco Examiner* first contained a color comic supplement on November 4, 1900. Previously it had carried comic strips in black and white in the magazine section. The supplement in the *San Francisco Examiner* was identical to the *Journal*'s and was either preprinted or reproduced from stereotype matrices. It seems reasonable to assume that Hearst's Sunday Chicago paper began to carry the comic supplement at that time because its inclusion would have required little additional cost. Other papers to carry color comic strip supplements from Hearst around this time included the *Memphis Commercial Appeal*, which first contained a color comic supplement on March 16, 1902, and the *Seattle Daily Times*. In addition newspapers in Denver, Atlanta, Indianapolis, Minneapolis, St. Louis, Omaha, Cincinnati, Columbus, Pittsburgh, Nashville, Richmond, and Spokane carried comic art from Hearst by the end of 1903. And on December 12, 1903, the first issue of Hearst's *Los Angeles Examiner* appeared, giving him four Sunday newspapers.[5]

By 1903 other syndicates had begun to distribute comic supplements nationally. Newspapers in Los Angeles, Chicago, and Minneapolis carried the *New York Herald*'s strips. The *St. Louis Post-Dispatch* and the *Pittsburgh Dispatch* carried the *New York World*'s strips. Additional syndicates that provided comic strips included the World Color Printing Company (unconnected to Pulitzer's *World*) and the T. C. McClure Syndicate, a product of the company founded by Samuel McClure. Papers in Louisville, Baltimore, Boston, St. Louis, Anaconda, Portland, Pittsburgh, Nashville, Knoxville, and Richmond carried the World Color Printing Company's material. The McClure Syndicate's strips appeared in San Francisco, Atlanta, Indianapolis, Topeka, Detroit, Minneapolis, New York, Houston, and Milwaukee papers. Another smaller organization, the C. J. Hirt company, syndicated material to papers in Augusta, Chicago, Indianapolis, Minneapolis, Helena, and Pittsburgh. Two Philadelphia papers, the *North American* and the *Inquirer,* as well as the *Boston Globe,* developed their own comic strips. The combined population of these cities and towns was 11,747,977, or 15.45 percent of the U.S. population. Because some of these papers, such as the *Memphis Commercial Appeal,* acted as regional papers, well over 20 percent of the population at this date had access to comic strips. Thus comic strips were a national and not an exclusively urban phenomenon by 1903.[6]

Comic strips attracted the interest of newspaper publishers because they helped to increase circulation. The *Memphis Commercial Appeal*'s Sunday circulation rose from 29,475 in 1901 to 35,292 in 1902 after the introduction of comic strips on March 16, 1902. The *Topeka Daily Capital*'s Sunday circulation rose from 15,500 in October 1903 to 16,741 in January 1904 after strips commenced on November 22, 1903.[7]

These circulation figures also give some idea of the regional circulation of the papers. In 1900 Memphis had a population of 102,320, and Topeka 33,608. Either one in three people in Memphis and one in two people in Topeka bought these papers or a good part of their circulation was outside the city limits. My data summarized in Table 1 (see the appendix) show that the national aggregate circulation of newspapers with comic strips in 1903 equaled 42.7 percent of the population in the centers where they were published. This figure suggests that most of these papers had significant sales outside their census-defined bases. The establishment of Rural Free Delivery by the Post

Office between 1898 and 1906 boosted urban newspapers' rural circulations. By 1903 newspapers across the country carried comic strips, and the circulation of papers with strips rose, suggesting that comics were a popular feature. Moreover, many of these newspapers carried the same strips.[8]

By 1908 syndicates had brought comic strips to the nation and established methods of distributing their product that continue to the present. Between 1903 and 1908 newspapers in twenty-four locations added comic strips while only two dropped them. Almost 75 percent of Sunday newspapers had strips. The additional locations and the increase in population between 1903 and 1908 added almost 6 million readers to the potential comic strip audience. At the same time twelve more newspapers began to publish strips in major locations, such as Chicago, Philadelphia, Boston, and Cincinnati, where they were already carried by papers in 1903. Both the potential readership and the availability of comic strips to that readership increased notably.[9]

In this period the major syndicates all expanded their coverage of the market. Their growth increased the chances that comic strip readers across the country read the same material. Almost all comic strips originated from six companies, and three (Hearst, World Color Co., and McClure) controlled over three-quarters of the market. For instance in 1908 Hearst strips were available to 66.00 percent of potential comic strip readers and McClure's to 57.79 percent. In short between 1901 and 1908 newspaper publishers and syndicates helped shape the New York phenomenon of comic strips into a shared national cultural artifact. Every Sunday Americans across the country could open their newspapers and read the same strips (see Tables 2 and 3 in the appendix).

The rapid spread and popularity of comic strips provoked a debate over their worth. One contemporary critic of strips regarded the Sunday editions of American newspapers as serving "a single community" but found no place for comic strips in that world. This critic's unsigned 1909 editorial in *Ladies' Home Journal* attacked comics as vulgar and cheap. Other articles that assailed the vulgarity of comics echoed her sentiments. In general these articles, which appeared with some frequency between 1906 and 1912, argued that comic strips eroded the moral fiber of the young by overstimulating their senses. Underlying the thrust of these articles was an uneasiness with a developing mass culture in which "the very element of variety has been obliterated." As one critic wrote in 1908, the comic supplement was for people "who don't care for fine shades of humor, because they can't appreciate them."[10]

In 1903 the literary critic Annie Russell Marble had pointed to a modern society in which sight reigned and surface impressions satisfied "the eyes of our understanding." In her prescient article "The Reign of the Spectacular," she observed "the commercial demand for all grades of illustrations, from classics to crudities." She noted that even scholars and orators were called upon to illustrate their lectures with lantern slides. For Marble this general enthusiasm for illustrations explained why even in "homes refined in other ways" parents gave children the Sunday comic supplement for their amusement. Marble linked the demand for comic strips to a broader consumption of images. She hoped that communities "satiated with the spectacular" would return to "nobler standards" and "rebuke mere affluence and gaud."[11]

But if Daniel Boorstin is to be believed these communities dissipated under the impact of an array of commodities, and new nationwide communities were constituted around their consumption. Boorstin has argued that Rural Free Delivery helped lift rural Americans out of "narrow" communities and put them in "touch with a larger world of persons and events and things." He notes that Rural Free Delivery led to the consolidation of post offices, which in turn destroyed many small towns and the communities based around them and argues that consumption communities appeared in their place. Boorstin's use of the term *consumption communities* retains a connotation of community as a discrete, local entity whose members know and recognize one another. A preferable term is *culture of consumption,* which removes these intimations of "community" while retaining a sense of consumption as an individual act mediated by internal and external factors. Benjamin Rader argues that sport had a similar role in the early twentieth century. He writes that "sport helped give an identity and common purpose to many neighborhoods, towns, and cities which were otherwise divided by class, race, ethnicity, and religious differences. In a larger, less tangible sense, mass sporting spectacles may have been an aspect of a search for city-wide, regional, or even national communities." To be sure, Boorstin was not referring to comics. But it is probable that the experience of reading comic strips created a national audience, or audiences, if not a community, drawn together by the visual images of comic strip characters.[12]

Boorstin's account of consumption communities does not make it clear how they came about. He assigns advertising a central role in their being but is uncertain whether advertisers created or discovered them. In the same paragraph he writes that advertising "aimed at something new—the creation of consumption communities" and that "the advertisement succeeded when it discovered, defined, and persuaded a new community of consumers."[13] The national spread of comic strips shows that the circulation in rural areas of urban cosmopolitan culture—comprising in part newspapers, catalogs, magazines, and books—created audiences of consumers rather than Boorstin's consumption communities.[14]

Newspaper owners decided to publish comic strips because their appeal to readers led to higher sales, not because literary-minded citizens with community-based salons requested their publication. Although purchasers did not directly consume comic strips, the strips established their characters as commodities. The popularity of comic strip characters, and the art form as a whole, suggested broader commercial opportunities to a number of entrepreneurs involved in their production. Richard Outcault's second major comic strip character, Buster Brown, played a key role in the realization of these opportunities and the creation of a culture of consumption around comic strip characters.

COMICS AS COMMODITY AND AGENT OF CHANGE: BUSTER BROWN

A study of the Buster Brown comic strips reveals the amalgam of interests, and techniques, that extended comics' Modernist vision to the nation. Richard Outcault created Buster Brown after his failure to ensure copyright protection of the Yellow Kid. He intended from the start to license Buster's likeness to other products. Buster Brown's physical appearance and manner of dress replicated Victorian representations of childhood innocence. As a visual type he could be described as a Little Lord Fauntleroy. In determining Buster's depiction Outcault hit on the image of a child familiar to many Americans. Commercial lithographers, such as Currier and Ives, and nineteenth-century periodicals such as *Godey's Lady's Book*, made the innocent child a visual staple in the United States. Moreover the Victorian child appeared on thousands of trade cards, a promotion device used by diverse enterprises such as large-scale manufacturers and small-town dry

goods stores. Onto this Victorian icon Outcault layered comic art's urban naughty child themes, creating a strip with diverse appeal by combining two visions of childhood. But he did so employing the formal
attributes of comic strips—sequential panels, continuing characters,
and word balloons.[15]

"Buster Brown" first appeared in the *New York Herald* on May 4,
1902.[16] The title character was a young boy from a middle-class family who played practical jokes and was generally mischievous. Buster's
jokes often backfired. Consequently, he resolved at the end of every
Sunday strip to improve his ways or at least to learn a lesson from his
mistake. The next week he would be back at his old tricks. Outcault
repeated this basic premise week after week. The strip's humor derived
in part from Buster's inability to keep his resolve. The skill with which
Outcault told new stories within the basic framework added to the
strip's appeal. The reader had to appreciate the strip's framework yet
repress that knowledge in order to let the story unfold. Those who
read the strip regularly understood that Buster's mischievous side was
held in check by his practicality. The repetition of the theme assured
readers of the containment of this mischief. Like the Yellow Kid before
him, Buster was a distinct character, yet "he" was simply a pen-and-
ink drawing. Moreover, Buster's characteristics, and copyright status,
made him a "personality" that could be marketed.

The construction of a "personality" occupied many Americans in
the twentieth century. The historian Warren Susman suggested that in
fin de siècle America *character* referred primarily to a person's internal
moral order. Susman saw this vision of self giving way in the first
decade of the twentieth century to a fascination with "personality."
Self-help manuals of the era distinguished between *character* as something one strengthened and *personality* as something one built. Individuals self-consciously created personalities by "paying attention to
others so that they [would] pay attention to you." Susman argued that
both visions of self embodied qualities that could be learned. But the
vision of self embodied in personality addressed personal and social
needs brought on by the developing mass consumer society. According
to Susman, "The social role demanded of all in the new culture of personality was that of performer." Just as novelists and dramatists created fictional characters, people created their own self-images or "personalities." The logical extension of the cult of personality, and one
that reinforced it, was the creation of movie stars by motion picture

studios beginning in 1910. Cultural products, movies, were then marketed through the images and personalities of particular screen players. Susman argued that this led to a new consciousness of personality and a new profession—that of the celebrity—in which any connection between achievement and fame was abandoned. It was possible to be famous merely for being famous.[17]

Susman did not provide a detailed account of the historical creation of a "personality-centered" vision of self. Rather, he saw it as an instance of Philip Rieff's notion that cultural changes alter the types of values that form a person. Susman aimed to show one way in which individuals may have participated in the development of a culture of consumption by creating personalities through leisure activities. To make this point he passed over Rieff's coda, which notes that because people understood themselves, in part, through historical institutions, "even the ignorants of a culture [were bound] to a great chain of meaning," making change both slow and difficult.[18]

Susman overemphasized the ease and continuity of this transformation of character by overlooking a key part of Rieff's analysis. The changes in comic art show one part of this metamorphosis. The long-term factors that gave rise to newspaper comic supplements and comic strip characters formed a visual "chain of meaning" that stretched back to broadsheets of the fifteenth century. The development of comic strip characters with their distinct personalities was the way one tradition of visual representation changed with, and helped shape, mass consumer society. Comic strip characters provide historians with examples of "personality" as celebrity or commodity, but they also show how personality and celebrity took shape. Furthermore, comic strip characters, and the celebrity status accorded them, anticipated Hollywood's creation of movie stars.

Comic strips helped bring a common visual culture to America. In his work on the launching of a commercial culture in New York City, William Taylor has suggested that the success of the Yellow Kid came about through its open-ended humor, which gave the strip "comic significance to those approaching it from different social perspectives." Elsa Nystrom argues that the initial spread of comic strips reflected an urbanization of American culture, or at least a fascination with the urban experience. She suggests that "people were caught by the brash novelty of the Yellow Kid."[19] But that strip appeared only in New York City newspapers; its circulation was never national. When newspapers across the nation began to carry comic strips, artists created works that were less urban in content than the strips that had appeared in New York papers in the late 1890s. They attempted to straddle the urban-rural diversity of American society and embellish their characters with even broader qualities than those needed to appeal to a diverse city audience. By 1903 among the best known and widely distributed strips only "Happy Hooligan" was clearly set in a city. "The Katzenjammer Kids" had a semirural setting and eventually moved to a tropical island. Artists set other strips, such as "Buster Brown" and "Sambo and His Funny Noises," in urban-rural crossroads. Buster Brown, as did his creator, appeared to live in the wealthy semirural countryside of Long Island. But the formal attributes of comic strips remained the same. Buster Brown came to rural folk through the medium of comic strip art, which originated in and owed its nature to urban centers.[20]

The form of these comic strips ultimately may have been more important than their thematic content to the commodification of comic art. But it is necessary to remember that characters are both part of the formal attributes of comic strips and constituent elements of their subject matter. Characters could be removed from their nominal setting in a comic strip and used to market other products. The Yellow Kid craze was just one craze that swept New York City in the 1890s. Others included the "Yachting Craze" of September 1895, brought on by the America's Cup Challenge between Britain and the USA, and the "boy in adult occupation craze" associated with dime novels. But, unlike these crazes that were briefly subjects of newspaper cartoon satire, the Yellow Kid demonstrated that comic strip art sold newspapers and other products.

Outcault wanted to pursue the commercial opportunities the popularity of a comic strip character offered. After abandoning the Yellow Kid in early 1898, when he discovered he could not control the commercial use of the Kid's image, Outcault took four years to find another character with the same licensing potential. He drew a number of comic features for the *New York World, Judge,* and the *New York Herald* until the latter newspaper published the first episode of "Buster Brown" on May 4, 1902. "Buster Brown" was a departure from Outcault's previous style. It was drawn in panels and employed word balloons as the prime means of conveying dialogue. But Outcault retained a familiar feature of his earlier work, a placard, to offer aphorisms in the form of Buster's weekly resolutions.

Frederick Opper's and Rudolph Dirks's work in the *New York Journal* probably inspired Outcault's new techniques. He also drew some of his theme and artistic style for "Buster Brown" from a series of panel drawings entitled "On the Sidewalks of New York" by Louis M. Glackens, which appeared in the *Journal* in 1897. The September 26, 1897, episode of Glackens's series featured a "Bad Boy" confronting a "Good Little Boy" (dressed much as Buster was later dressed) because of the latter's respectability. A "Little Girl" attempted to dissuade the "Bad Boy." A text panel within the borders of the illustration speculated that the "Little Girl" may have been motivated by a desire to grow up and marry the "Good Little Boy" for his money. Glackens's series fell into the school of city kid cartoons pioneered by Michael Angelo Woolf and Richard Outcault, but his use of text within the panel to pose an ethical question and offer alternative readings of the illustration proffered a model for humor with a moral. The trick to this type of humor was to present it in an open-ended fashion so that it had broad appeal.[21]

One mark of Buster's personality was the aphoristic resolution at the end of each strip, which became one of the strip's formal narrative devices. The resolution did not so much close each episode as, through the expectation of Buster breaking his resolve, posit a beginning for the next. Outcault's resolutions opened "Buster Brown" to alternative readings. For instance, during the 1906–12 campaign against comic strips, Maud Summers, a member of the Playground Association, castigated "Buster Brown" as deceitful, whereas an unsigned editorial in the Christian reform journal *Outlook* found the strip to have some redeeming qualities, possibly because Outcault occasionally advocated "Christian" business practices.[22] The resolution also displayed the artist's ambiguous concern with the culture he was helping to create. In one resolution Buster stated that "it must be wicked to go to church on Sunday knowing that you're going to push someone hard for a dollar on Monday."[23] But these sentiments did not stop Outcault from pushing his product before the public for a dollar. Indeed "Buster Brown" may have been so marketable precisely because of this "populist" antibusiness sentiment.[24]

By 1908 "Buster Brown" was a nationally known name that produced considerable revenue for its owner. For instance, Outcault's royalties from a Buster Brown stage show alone came to $44,000 between 1903 and mid-1907. Outcault sought to make the most of his success.

In January 1906, tempted by a lucrative offer, he left the *New York Herald* for Hearst's newspapers. On January 21, 1906, Hearst's *New York American* published its first episode of "Buster Brown." As in Outcault's earlier move of the Yellow Kid from the *World* to the *Journal,* there was a legal dispute over the copyright of the strip. The outcome left the rights to the comic strip title "Buster Brown" with the *New York Herald* but gave Outcault license to draw the characters. A later case established that Outcault owned all other rights to "Buster Brown."[25] The *Herald* hired a succession of artists to produce its own version of "Buster Brown." At the *American* Outcault overcame the problem of not being able to name his strip "Buster Brown" by drawing his characters in the space normally provided for the title. Buster Brown and his dog Tige were so well known, to comic strip readers at least, that their creator could simply ask "Guess Who?" to have the text and the images act as a title.

In 1908 Buster appeared in twenty-four newspapers across the United States. The aggregate circulation of the papers carrying "Buster Brown" equaled only 3 to 4 percent of the country's total population, but it is probable that each copy of these papers had multiple readers, with perhaps as much as 10 percent of the population exposed to the comic strip weekly (see Table 4 in the appendix). But Buster's audience extended beyond the pages of the comic strip.[26] His creator licensed Buster Brown's image to numerous advertisers.

Richard Outcault was not the first to use comic art to sell products. In the mid-1890s Knox Hats ran a number of advertisements in *Life* magazine in the form of two-line gag panels. Other advertisers used celebrity endorsements to sell their wares. Henry Ward Beecher appeared in advertisements for Pears' soap, and Emile Zola pitched Vin Mariani brandy. *Life* even adopted an earlier comic narrative to point out the benefits of print advertising over billboards. In December 1903 Frederick Opper used a "Happy Hooligan" strip to promote a cast-iron Happy Hooligan toy.[27] But none of these examples involved a concerted effort to use the visual image of a comic strip character to market products. Nor did the Yellow Kid craze, for Outcault copyrighted the name only after the phenomenon developed. Buster Brown was the first comic strip character licensed in such a fashion that it constituted a brand name. Buster's diverse use distinguished him from other illustrated characters, such as Aunt Jemima, Sunny Jim, and Phoebe Snow, whose images companies established purely as trademark figures. Buster's celebrity grew out of multiple representations, whereas Sunny Jim and the others were all tied to single products.[28]

According to Robert Lesser, a comic art and memorabilia collector, Outcault licensed his character to a wide variety of manufacturers at the St. Louis World's Fair in 1904. The licensees included the Brown Shoe Company and Robert Ingersoll, the pioneer of inexpensive watches. Ingersoll, looking for new ways to sell watches, struck on the idea of a Buster Brown watch to be given away with a pair of Buster Brown shoes. He was guaranteed a certain number of sales, and the shoe company worked the wholesale price of the watch into the retail price of the shoes. The significance of Ingersoll's marketing scheme was not so much that it used a popular comic strip character to sell a variety of products but that it linked these products in such a fashion that the character constituted a brand name. For instance Ingersoll's first Buster Brown watch carried a direct advertisement for the shoes, but it also acted as an advertisement for the comic strip. Numerous other products—including textiles, harmonicas, a soft drink, coffee, flour, bread, apples, suits, hosiery, and pianos—used Buster Brown as a brand name. Buster Brown dolls, toys, and games, reprints of the comic strip, and the aforementioned touring musical stage show extended the dimensions of Buster's popularity and recognition.[29]

Advertisers who used Buster Brown sought national recognition and distribution for their products. For instance, Ivan Frank & Co., a New York child's clothing wholesaler, distributed a promotional pamphlet that described their audience as extending "from Maine to California." There are examples of children's clothing advertisements featuring Buster Brown from Rhode Island and Washington State, so Frank & Co. probably made good on the claim. The Buster Brown brand name was so successful that Ivan Frank merged his company with an Indianapolis clothing company, and the Chattanooga mill he represented, and formed Buster Brown Textiles Incorporated (see Figure 8). This firm, since bought out by Gerber, still operates as Buster Brown Apparel.[30]

The other major Buster Brown licensee, the Brown Shoe Company of St. Louis, took an advertisement in the *World's Fair Bulletin* of January 1902 proclaiming the United States the "territory of the Brown Shoe Company" (see Figure 9). The ad featured a map showing the territorial gains of the United States on which photographs of Brown's salesmen were superimposed according to their territory. It positioned

8. *Some Frank Con-fess-ions of Buster Brown* (Indianapolis: When Clothing Co., 1906?), p. 16. Warshaw Collection of Business Americana, Archives Center, National Museum of American History, Smithsonian Institution, Collection 60, Shoes, box 9.

Brown Shoes as a company with a national vision. After it bought the Buster Brown name for its shoes, the company expanded rapidly. Between 1902 and about 1907 the physical plant of the Brown Shoe Company doubled from four to eight factories. To promote its shoes, the company ran a national series of "Buster Brown Outdoor Receptions" featuring a nine-year-old boy dressed to resemble the comic strip character. In 1910 J. H. Sawyer, the advertising manager for the Brown Shoe Company, reported in *Judicious Advertising* that Buster Brown, and the touring show, secured the company effective advertising often without cost. The title of Sawyer's article, "Buster Brown Advertises Shoes," gave clear expression to the character's worth as a trademark.[31]

"Buster Brown" was an extensively marketed name brand before name brands and trademarks received the full imprimatur of law in 1905. By 1908 the advertising industry was highly conscious of the importance of brand names. An article in *Printers' Ink* estimated that over 50 percent of that year's advertising existed to "create property in trade marks." These trademarks and brand names contributed to the corporate restructuring of American production and distribution. They helped create a national culture of consumption fixated on images. Michael Schudson, an advertising historian, argues that goods and the sharing of their names help make a culture. The point is, What sort of a culture do they make? The introduction of large-scale production impersonalized the manufacture of many goods. The inauguration of brand names and prepackaged goods altered individual exchanges between retailers and customers. Brand names helped determine the purchase of products. Part of what people then shared was the name, the image of the commodity.[32]

Buster Brown was the crucial link between comic strips and the development of a visual culture of consumption in America. "He" united entertainment and consumer goods. Indeed "Buster Brown" cannot be understood solely as a comic strip. All of his incarnations contributed to the makeup of his character, and each reinforced or advertised the others. Moreover this type of advertising, in the form of entertainment and consumption, allowed Buster's audience to expand their contact with the character by purchasing one of his products. Readers of the strip no longer had to wait for Sunday to get a dose of "Buster Brown." For instance, a 1908 advertisement for the Buster Brown doll in the Sears, Roebuck catalog described it as "a very fine imitation of

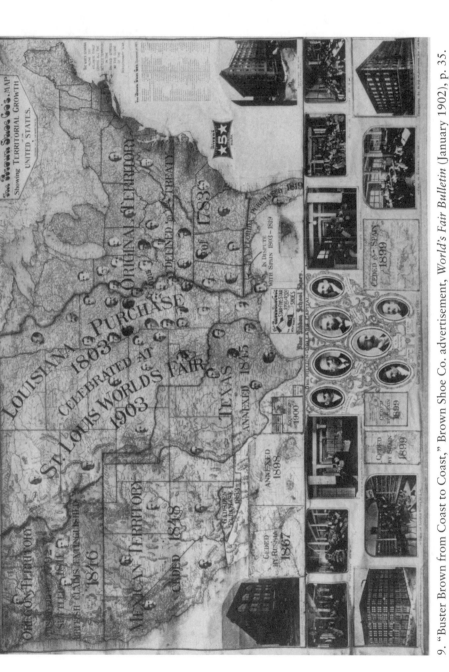

9. "Buster Brown from Coast to Coast," Brown Shoe Co. advertisement, *World's Fair Bulletin* (January 1902), p. 35. Warshaw Collection of Business Americana, Archives Center, National Museum of American History, Smithsonian Institution, Shoes, box 9.

10. Buster Brown Blue Ribbon Shoes advertisement, 1905. N. W. Ayer Advertising Agency Collection, Archives Center, National Museum of American History, Smithsonian Institution, book 402.

the Buster Brown you read about." It added, "This doll will be a delight to the children on account of the popularity of Buster Brown."

And, in the same year the *Daily Oklahoman*, an Oklahoma City newspaper that carried the "Buster Brown" comic strip, contained advertisements for Buster Brown Shoes along with a notice of a live performance by Buster and his dog Tige in a local clothing store. A local bakery ran concurrent advertisements for Buster Brown Bread. In his 1953 autobiography, *Bad Boy,* the crime writer Jim Thompson, who was reared in Oklahoma City at this time, refers to his Buster Brown blouse as a customarily worn item. In this fashion through the purchase of a "Buster Brown" product, a cultural act, reading comic strips, was further tied to acts of consumption and the basis laid for the wholesale selling of a culture of consumption. Moreover in a city such as Oklahoma City, which grew over 500 percent between 1900 and 1910, the consumption of Buster Brown united the inhabitants not as a local community but as participants in a culture of consumption. At the very least these Oklahomans were Americans because they consumed national products.[33]

More than a simple use of Buster Brown's likeness and the techniques of comic art linked comic strips and advertising. Some merchants adopted the maxims expressed in Buster's/Outcault's weekly resolution as advertising slogans. For instance in a March 4, 1906, episode from the *American* entitled "Buster Brown: His Snowman," the resolution read, in part:

> How are you to gain your first idea of a man except by his clothes?
> They are the key to his nature, breeding and taste. Commence at the
> bath tub, and nice stockings and shoes boys.

A later resolution read:

> Clothes are more important than most of us think. What else have you
> to judge a stranger by? . . . *Flashy* attire shows *vulgarity.* Very gaudy
> clothes are worn by vain, cheap people. Since your clothes are your
> best advertisement, try to advertise well, then live up to your advertise-
> ment. . . . Don't advertise *All Wool* and then produce cotton. Don't try
> to fool 'em. It don't pay.[34]

In 1906 Outcault's Chicago-based advertising agency transferred these sentiments into advertisements for W. B. Hutchinson Co., a Seattle clothing store, and a Los Angeles store. A resolution within the advertisement stated "that if you wish to march along you must be clad in the latest. The better your apparel the swifter will be your progress."[35]

In another 1906 strip Outcault expressed his notion of good business practices. The resolution said,

> *Business.* What a lot of trickery and treachery is done in thy name.
> How many so called Christians excuse their meanness by saying

"Business is Business." There's lots better ways of being a good
Christian than going to church—one way is being honest and
generous in business.[36]

In a 1913 advertisement for a Providence, Rhode Island, clothing store
Outcault's agency adapted this sentiment to read, "Resolved. That
people make their good luck by doing the right thing. We have made
ours by giving our patrons the right kind of goods. Square deal always
wins. We want to keep our patrons."[37]

Outcault's advertising agency prepared the advertisements, which
probably accounts for their shared values with the comic strip resolutions. In these instances Buster, an entertainment celebrity, acted as the
spokesman for the company. But he also served as the brand name for
many items. The U.S. Copyright Office in the Library of Congress has,
by my estimate, over 10,000 individual copyright registrations for advertisements using Buster Brown created by Outcault's agency.

Buster's image mediated the reception of the products and gave
them a distinctive, if polysemic, "personality." For instance, it is possible that parents bought Buster Brown shoes for their children out of
regard for the Christian business practices and responsibilities Outcault advocated. The recipients of the shoes, by contrast, may have
wanted them as a form of identification with Buster's youthful rebel-
lion. "Buster Brown Plays Cowboy," published in the *New York Herald* on July 30, 1905, demonstrates the interplay between these two
aspects of "Buster Brown." In his resolution Buster admits to being
wrong in "picking out things to do" and then states, "You can't be
happy unless you are good." But this sentiment is undercut by Tige's
winking comment, "A lot of wise talk from a chap who is always slip-
ping."[38] Outcault also poked fun at the range of "Buster Brown"
products in the December 17, 1905, episode of the strip (see Figure
11). But even this episode can be read as a plug for Buster's trademark,
especially with its resolution extolling the joys of giving.

The structure of Buster Brown's personality made him a figure open
to different and simultaneous interpretations that translated into diverse market appeal. Buster showed that a character-based image
made a wide range of goods and services attractive to disparate audiences. In addition to containing different motivations for consumption, he united the producers of different types of goods and services,
from large-scale manufacturers, such as the Brown Shoe Company, to

11. Richard Felton Outcault, "Buster Brown," *Los Angeles Times* (December 17, 1905). Archives Center, National Museum of American History, Smithsonian Institution.

small shopkeepers, such as F. E. Ballou of Providence. This unification may have helped to contain tensions produced when localized economies were subjected to national market forces. But more to the point, Buster's diverse usages represent the gradual transformations that took place as a locally oriented producerist society became a centralized consumer society. Hal Barron, a historian of rural America, recently discovered a seemingly paradoxical use of Buster and Tige in a series of antimail-order advertisements run in the Upper Midwest and West in 1916. As Barron notes, Buster was "a paragon of national mass popular culture" and a familiar figure to local communities through the shoes that "were sold only by local retailers and were not available by mail order."[39] In this case Buster Brown literally represented the process of transformation where new cultural forms overlay, interact, and flow out of the culture being displaced.

Inevitably when I mention my work on Buster Brown to Americans, someone will recall having had a pair of Buster Brown shoes as a child. Everyone it seems has a story to tell about a Buster Brown product. Indeed the African American diva Marian Anderson recalled in her autobiography owning a pair of Buster Brown shoes. Perhaps this is not surprising since according to John A. Bush, the president of the Brown Shoe Company in the 1950s, the company had spent $30 million on advertising the shoes by 1959. The ads seem to have been particularly successful. In 1996 the historian Michael Barton could still remember the adaptation of Langston Hughes's poem "All God's Chil-

12. Buster Brown mask, Warshaw Collection of Business Americana, Archives Center, National Museum of American History, Smithsonian Institution, Shoes, box 9.

dren Got Shoes" for a Buster Brown Shoes radio commercial in the 1950s. And it is even now possible to buy Buster Brown clothing for children and Buster Brown Shoes in places such as the Buster Brown Shoe Shop on Philadelphia's South Street.[40]

My examination of Buster Brown suggests that the culture formed around these products was neither imposed by manufacturers nor created by the populace out of a desire to participate in a democracy of manufactured goods. Rather consumer culture was created in a struggle to assign meaning and values to a variety of products and to lives changing under their impact. Singling out Buster Brown as a representative component in the long transition from a producerist society to a modern culture of consumption points to the multifaceted causality that brought on this change. The modern era was not constituted simply by an increased and universal consumption of goods and services but involved the extension of commodity status to, among other things, ideas and symbols and the development of intellectual property.[41] Comic art was one of the subjects, objects, and agents of this change.

Comic strips not only transformed comic art, by stretching its commodity value but also transformed the culture. The simple, repeatable, easily recognizable form of comic strips made a Modernist aesthetic generally available. By the mid-1910s Americans across the country could open their newspapers and see the same strips. They could also buy an array of products branded with the image of one of the most popular comic strip characters. Ill at ease and hesitant, Americans began to recognize these comic strips and their characters as part of their daily lives. Around such recognitions America became a national culture of consumption.

3 COMIC ART AND THE COMMODIFICATION OF AFRICAN AMERICAN TYPOGRAPHIES

The Limits of the Form

I have shown that between the 1890s and the 1920s comic strips transformed a particular type of urban imagery into a national commodity. In this process artists and syndicates reshaped the rough-edged humor of the illustrated journals and the early comic strips. Notably artists toned down the ethnic jests and dialogue gags that underpinned many of the early strips. Syndicates tended to limit the distribution of comic strips premised on ethnic humor, such as "Abie the Agent," to larger cities. Such maneuvers suggest that the sense of an American culture created by comic strips was fragile and open to challenge by humorous depictions of the diversity of that society.

Ethnic humor had a place in American culture but usually as a reference point to some "other" that lay outside the culture's acceptable norms. Based in cities, with rapidly changing ethnic compositions, illustrated humor journals and early comic strips challenged these norms, expanded the acceptable, and established comic art as both a cultural form and a commodity. The expansion of comic strips from an urban to a national phenomenon revealed the art form's limitations as transformative agent. For instance, Rudolph Dirks, having shaped the dimensions of comic strips with his "Katzenjammer Kids," had to move the strip offshore to maintain its anarchic tendencies and dialect jokes.

Dirk's relocation of his strip was a technical solution to the difficulty of maintaining the strip's humor as its readership expanded beyond city dwellers who shared an understanding of diverse ethnic identities. Richard Outcault made a similar response with his multidimensioned Buster Brown, which allowed him to expand the city urchin into an American type. Such adjustments were necessitated by the commercial drive of newspaper syndicates, but they also expanded the commodity values of the strips and characters. Comic strip humor then represented a negotiation among artists, syndicates, and readers over commerce and over identities and their construction. But if this understanding seems to have granted the process of commodification a too generous character, it is instructive to look at who and what was excluded from the negotiation.

As we have seen, American comic art took shape in the polychromatic cultures of large cities, particularly New York City. The artists and staffs of the illustrated journals and comic strip supplements came from many ethnicities. Their art boisterously satirized their own and one anothers' backgrounds. It mediated a shifting sense of identity in which an American component played an increasingly important role. But artists regularly allied these emerging identities against black Americans. Until George Herriman passed, or was allowed to pass, as white there were no artists of black heritage working regularly in the field.

There are few thematic surprises in white artists' depictions of blacks in the early illustrated humor journals. Joseph Boskin argues that representations of African Americans have largely adopted a single stereotypical image, of Sambo. Drawing on Walter Lippmann, Boskin argues that by treating African Americans as overgrown children, given to the impetuousness of childhood, white Americans created "a form of perception" that regarded all African Americans as comic performers. By the midnineteenth century such an outlook held the status of common sense. For Boskin the figure of Sambo was the unified whole of a multipart stereotype. Moreover these representations of African Americans fit prevailing European conventions for depicting blacks. Humorous presentations of African Americans in late nineteenth-century illustrated journals then would have been commonplace.[1]

In the 1880s and 1890s comic artists generally poked fun at African Americans by drawing on a range of typographies, such as Zip Coon and minstrelsy's Tambo and Bones. Two *Puck* cartoons amply demonstrate the prevailing style. The first panel of a two-panel cartoon by Edward Kemble that appeared in *Puck*, March 21, 1888, shows two well-dressed black figures paying an Irishman twenty-five cents to lay

a board down for them to cross a muddied curb. The black gentleman
Mr. Breathwait says, "Put him righ' down dar Irish; an' doan spen' dis
yar twent'-five cen's fer booze!" The second panel shows the Irishman
splashing the black pair by dropping the plank directly in the mud and
commenting, "It's not a McKackin av shligo thot'll be gineraled be a
coon!" Whereas F. M. Howarth's "Advantages of an Extensive Repertoire" (see Figure 1) offered a variegated view of power in the city,
Kemble's cartoon makes it clear that the lowliest Irishman outranked
any African American.

Frank Nankivell's full-page six-panel illustration for *Puck*'s back
page of August 6, 1896, shows his indebtedness to minstrel shows.
Two seated figures, Mr. Johnson and Miss Jackson, approximately
replicating Tambo and Bones, engage in conversation. Mr. Johnson,
having asked Miss Jackson if she likes the circus, is taken aback at her
enthusiasm for side shows, lemonade, peanuts, and minstrel shows,
and he extracts himself from a costly venture by remembering he will
be out of town and unable to take Miss Jackson. The accompanying
drawing employs thick-lipped, wide-eyed caricatures of the black figures against an otherwise realistic setting. Given that by 1896 the conventions of panel illustrations included extracting humor from the
combination of text and graphic, this piece associates a voracious ap-
petite for excitement and limited generosity with black women and
men respectively.

Both of these illustrations can be read as comedies of manners and
as such as commentaries on appropriate social behavior. Artists directed their messages in the form of humor at their white readers, not
at their black subjects. Kemble's cartoon relies on a hierarchy of caricature in which the Irish stood above African Americans. Kemble re-
minded readers that, whatever fun could be had with caricatures of
the Irish, they were not, and I suspect he thought at least they were
not, black. Nankivell could have substituted white figures for black
and the text of his cartoon would still have worked. But the conventions of American humor derived from minstrelsy ensured that the
joke obtained its full force through black figures. These cartoons then
were instances in which whites defined their identity against blacks.[2]

The use of stereotyped caricatures was a common feature of the art
in illustrated humor journals. When comic strips began to take shape
in these journals, and more rapidly in newspaper comic strip supplements, these kinds of typographies opened up a little, partially because

of the need for appeal to mass audiences but also because of the way broader audiences read the strips. Outcault's Yellow Kid is an example of how an audience could perceive a character as a particular ethnicity through a reading other than the creator intended.

Mostly audiences' ability and willingness to read characters in multiple fashions added to a comic strip character's commercial worth, but the relative absence of black comic strip characters, especially leading characters, suggests the reluctance of creators and audiences to grant African Americans even the little more complexity of character that a polysemic comic strip figure required. Given that advertisers frequently used representations of African Americans drawn from minstrelsy's stereotypes—the best known being Aunt Jemima, the Cream of Wheat Chef, and the Gold Dust Twins—the lack of a black comic strip character with equal staying power is puzzling at first. But the constraints of well-established stereotypes shut off this option for black figures and so limited their value as comic strip characters. The limits faced by black comic strip characters demonstrate the importance of polysemic characters in ensuring comics' success. Furthermore they show how the deracination of black stereotypes created broader scope for comic humor.

TOWARD AFRICAN AMERICAN COMIC STRIP CHARACTERS

The first discernible attempt to develop a black comic strip character occurred when Richard Outcault left Hearst's *New York Journal* in early 1898 to rejoin Pulitzer's *World*. On February 13, 1898, two Outcault features appeared in the *World*'s comic supplement. One of these, "Here's the New Bully," a single-panel illustration reminiscent of the artist's early "Hogan's Alley" work, presented the title character, a tough black boy. The New Bully, described by his mother as "ma own coon," carried a cutthroat razor and held sway over the Casey's Corner Gang, who with the exception of the bully were all white. The following week's feature made it clear that the New Bully was the boss of the gang. A poster in the panel proclaimed, "De Casey's Corner Gang has got a new captain an we hereby gives warning ter Old-Red Neck Dooley de fresh cop dat he don't own this corner."

Outcault's creation of a black figure leading a white gang may at first seem a radical step, what today might be called the creation of a role model, but the New Bully had nothing to do with progressive social engineering. Rather this character reproduced a vision of African Americans as the possessors of brute strength and behavior. The New Bully dominated the Casey's Corner Gang through muscle, not intellect. Most likely Outcault was experimenting with the form in search of a new feature possessing the commercial potential of the Yellow Kid rather than seeking to break down stereotypes. For instance, his one-shot, four-panel feature published in the *World* on February 27, 1898, shows his willingness to use a range of stereotypical images. In this illustration a black valet impersonates a nobleman, giving Outcault plenty of opportunity to engage in Zip Coon humor, which deemed African American aspirations to high culture ludicrous.

It is difficult to determine how readers responded to the New Bully and whether or not they granted him the polysemic interpretations they had given the Yellow Kid. It would seem the feature was not popular because it lasted only a month. Outcault, however, continued to draw black figures. In 1900 he created for *Judge* a series of cartoons set in the fictitious rural community of Possumville. He depicted African Americans as superstitious, lazy, violent, and shiftless individuals who loved to eat watermelon, wielded razors, and had pretensions to refinements such as religion and Shakespeare, in short, a cavalcade of stereotypes drawn from minstrelsy. Beyond Outcault's racism, which to note in passing is not to diminish, his *Judge* cartoons stand out from the rest of his work because they lack a central character and feature adult bodies.[3]

By the time he created the Possumville cartoons, Outcault had developed a standard format. His cartoons and comic strips combined illustration and text through an arrangement of placards within the image. Outcault developed his style as a means of delivering humor without the necessity of gag lines under the illustrations. Text helped center the large "Hogan's Alley" comic pages by providing a voice for the feature. Eventually these aspects of Outcault's work were unified in the Yellow Kid in a process that had more to do with readers' construction of the Kid than with a conscious maneuver by the artist. Certainly Outcault choose to work the kid genre of cartoons and comics, and he initiated the use of text in the body of comic illustrations through placards, but the Yellow Kid was an accidental creation. Whether or not Outcault understood the centrality of a character to comic strips at this stage of his career is unclear.

In any case his work for *Judge* was in a different medium and of a different form. The cartoons were the creations of a professional comic artist working a humor genre. In this context the lack of a distinctive character can be attributed in part to the medium. Although comic strips developed from the illustrated humor of journals such as *Judge,* there were differences between the two, particularly in regard to the media in which they appeared. *Judge* was more respectable than the *New York World* or *Journal,* and its lack of comic strip characters marked this status. At the same time the distinction between cartoons and comic strips was not so fixed in 1900 that a series of cartoons, such as Outcault's Possumville illustrations, could not have developed into a character-based comic strip in the right medium; that after all is how the Yellow Kid came about. However, the fact that Outcault's Possumville work appeared in *Judge* and not in a newspaper probably had a great deal to do with its subject matter.

Individual distinctive characters were central to comic strips. If we regard the elements of comics as constituting a language, or at least a set of symbolic codes, we can see that the polysemic characteristics of comic strip characters produced a series of problems for artists wishing to represent African Americans. Artists were not so freely able to shape a representational language that gave African American characters a polysemic nature. Unlike those of the newly arrived immigrants in New York City, the typographies surrounding representations of African Americans had developed over two hundred years. Moreover they had become codified in the set pieces of minstrelsy and in the politics of post-Reconstruction America. The clearest understanding of the limits facing comic artists can be found in an examination of the only two sustained attempts to create African American lead comic strip characters before 1915. That both characters were children comes as no surprise.[4]

"PORE LIL MOSE"

Richard Outcault's "Pore Lil Mose" commenced publication in the *New York Herald* on December 2, 1900. Lil Mose originally appeared in a large-scale panel with two small inset panels. The strip was an outgrowth of Outcault's earlier work for *Judge*. On his debut Outcault described Mose in the following terms:

> Et ur wus a lil boy—a cur'ous lil coon:
> He comed fum some whar—I dunno—I spee it de man
> He never had a bit ob luck, dis funny lil mose,
> He never had a thing to wear exceptin' only clothes,
> He never had a thing to eat but jest three meals a day,
> He never had no work to do but only jest to play,
> De only place he had to sleep, was in his lil bed,
> De pillow was de only place he had to lay his head,
> His mammy was de bestest friend that lil Mosey had,
> She'd allus pet and cuddle him whenever he wus bad,
> An so he ate an drank and slept an laughed fum morn till night
> It's sad to think of any one in lil Mosey's plight.[5]

The notion that most African Americans lived in some version of an Arcadian paradise and wanted for nothing not only fit the racist notions of the post-Reconstruction era but also treated blacks as simple and childlike in their needs and aspirations. "Pore Lil Mose" fused Outcault's *Judge* cartoon style with his newspaper comic strip work, which after the Yellow Kid always featured a distinctive juvenile character.

For the first six months of its existence, "Pore Lil Mose" repeated all the racial stereotypes of Outcault's Possumville series. For instance, in the episode of January 6, 1901, the artist had Mose daydream of being a millionaire. Mose's vision of the high life includes his entire family clad in the style of Zip Coon, and a family coat of arms composed of a straight razor, a set of dice, and a slice of watermelon. Outcault placed Mose's desire to own "the first auto-mobile in coontown" at the center of his dream. This style of strip, which basically consists of what Boskin calls "Negro jokes" with illustrations, continued until mid-June 1901, when Outcault sent Mose to New York City.[6] In moving the strip to New York, Outcault mostly abandoned the "Negro joke," probably because of that trope's primary association with tales of black rural life. But the relocation only marginally altered the artist's conception of his character. In his urban incarnation Mose became an innocent abroad and the focal point for a range of tomfoolery.

The relocation to New York saw Outcault shift from telling his story through a text box containing doggerel verse to using letters from Lil Mose to his mother. Mose's "letters" consist of the same dog-gerel verse, but such a rhetorical device allowed the artist to suggest greater authenticity for his efforts at capturing a black dialect. The move also provided Mose with greater depth of character because the letter gave him a voice beyond that of a figure whose actions an external narrator described. Also when speaking through Lil Mose, Outcault mostly abandoned derogatory terms such as *coon*. Nonetheless he continued to use commonplace representations of African Americans. In an episode published on January 5, 1902, Lil Mose buys his mother a hat from a Fifth Avenue store. Both the text and illustration show that Mose's mother normally wears a bandanna and cares little for style. On receipt of her new hat, however, she puts on airs and graces in keeping with Zip Coon humor.

From mid-1901 to his demise in 1902, Lil Mose served primarily as Outcault's instrument in poking fun at the habits of New Yorkers. In this guise the strip revisited some of the Yellow Kid's subjects and revealed Outcault's deep-seated ambiguity toward modernization. For instance, on June 23, 1901, Lil Mose visited Coney Island, allowing Outcault to remark on the brutishness of barkers, the swarm of humanity, and the cheap, noisy quality of the endeavor in general. Shortly after, on August 18, 1901, Outcault raised the same themes by having Lil Mose take a ride on a trolley car. An additional jibe at advertising read:

> You ought to see the funny ads dey haf in all de cars,
> 'bout things in packages an cans, in boxes an in jars.
> Deres "Fifty Seben Vaudevilles" and "Folks ob Speckled town,"
> An some ones "Bestest Chocolate," of bery great renown,
> An things to make de blind ter hear, an make de lame ter talk
> An make der bald ter see an make de def an dum ter walk . . .

In late 1901 Outcault's targets included Jewish tailors on Baxter Street, in whose fine clothes Lil Mose looks "redic'lous"; housing development in Harlem employing Italians ("sceeckin dagos"); and the "Chings" of Chinatown, with whom Lil Mose "hit de pipe." Even Outcault's former employer Thomas Edison came in for some stick on September 15, 1901, when the artist depicted his laboratory in theatrical terms, complete with "Stage Door." Urban noise and meanness were constant themes. Against the hubris of the city the only alternative Outcault raised was a return to a more contemplative culture. In one of his trademark placards within a panel of the October 20, 1901, episode, Outcault proclaimed:

All the Latest Books
Even Shakespeare and
Uncle Tom's Cabin
Buy a Book and Read
It Just To Keep In Practice

Given the episode's complaints about elevated railroads, ticket scalpers, crooked cops and politicians, and a general unwillingness to act against such matters, it would seem Outcault wanted to pose a standard of a more genteel society.

In "Pore Lil Mose" Outcault used available and familiar typographies of African Americans to create comic humor. That he spoke in the voice of Lil Mose for almost a year of the strip's existence represents no particular advance in the depiction of African Americans. He had to give Lil Mose voice to meet the emerging convention of distinguishable characters in comic strips. The demise of "Pore Lil Mose" in mid-1902 probably resulted from Outcault's desire to experiment with his format. Lil Mose's evolution as a social commentator on the New York scene was largely accidental, and although the innocent abroad routine worked well enough, Outcault did not give Lil Mose the didactic moral tone that became one of Buster Brown's features. I would suggest that he could not introduce such a tone directly because an African American character could not sustain the burden of being innocent and sagelike at the same time. African American characters could have been wise fools, but for them to have been knowingly so would have suggested too much complexity of character and shattered too many typographies. The accidental quality of black wisdom was the central feature of a later strip: "Sambo and His Funny Noises."

"SAMBO AND HIS FUNNY NOISES"

In 1905 the T. C. McClure newspaper syndicate began to distribute "Sambo and His Funny Noises," a half-page comic strip created by William Marriner. Marriner had begun publishing cartoons in *Puck* and *Life* in the late 1890s. He swiftly became adept at the kid cartoon genre, which became a feature of his work for *Puck*. As did many other *Puck* illustrators, Marriner tried his hand at comic strips working on a freelance basis for the *Philadelphia Inquirer,* the Hearst papers, and the *New York World* before finding a more permanent base with McClure.[7]

Marriner's comic strip stories generally involve Sambo, a young African American boy later named Samuel Johnson, in a confrontation with two young white boys, Mike and Jim Tanks. More often than not Sambo apparently comes out on top. The first Sambo strip I found, which appeared on April 2, 1905, in the *Detroit News,* reworked a standard kid cartoon theme. Numerous illustrated humor journal cartoons of the 1890s depict kids enticing older gents to kick seemingly light objects, such as hats, that contain bricks or other hard items. The humor of these cartoons comes from both the unexpected pain that follows such action and the fact that adults should know better. In the first Sambo strip, Sambo's head is the hard item in the hat, and the humor lies in working the genre. That is, the strip poses a joke question, "When doesn't a head belong in a hat?" the answer being, "When it's a black head, because it is as thick as a brick." To be sure, violence was endemic to cartoons and comics, but the point here is that stereotypically the thick head belonged to a black American.

Sambo's fate in his encounters with whites mostly seems the result of luck, or displays his "natural" cunningness and ability to absorb pain. Rather than shattering stereotypes most of Sambo's victories reassert them because they result from either dumb luck or childlike innocence. On April 23, 1905, Sambo won the egg-pecking contest by having eggs cracked on his head. When a chicken popped out of one of the eggs, Sambo grabbed it and ran. His hardheadedness saved him again on May 21, 1905; set up by the Tanks brothers to have his backside butted, Sambo turned around and head-butted the goat. On June 4 Sambo acquired grapes after the Tanks boys broke a barrel on his head. Again, on July 23 the hardness of Sambo's head saw him obtain fruit while the Italian vendor chased the Tanks brothers. A variation on this theme on October 1, 1905, had the Tanks brothers coat Sambo's head with maple syrup, which attracted flies. Consequently a grocer paid Sambo to attract all the flies in his shop and lead them away like, in Sambo's words, "dat pie-eyed piper ob Hamlin."

It would be easy to portray the Sambo strip as simply an example of racism in America. William Marriner could be held up as a virulent racist or a man of his times, little worse if no better than his contem-

poraries. But the important point here is that Marriner drew and relied on contemporary stereotypes and the conventions of comic strip
humor. The October 1, 1905, Sambo strip might seem particularly
horrific given that the Tanks brothers thought the maple syrup they
poured on Sambo was gasoline and intended to set him alight, but
when set against the similar outrages the Katzenjammer Kids regularly
inflicted on the Captain, it becomes only one more instance of comics'
anarchic humor.[8] Given the nature of comic strips, Sambo's hard head
is more horrific than a story about setting him alight, because it replicated and naturalized stereotypes. Moreover, whereas the diverse
audiences for, and commercial possibilities of, other comic strip characters resulted in artists making their characters polysemic, the stereotypes associated with African Americans closed off such possibilities
for Sambo.

Still on many occasions Sambo seemingly outwitted the white boys.
On May 7, 1905, he asked the brothers for a ride on their bicycle and
offered a banana in exchange. The boys demanded that Sambo give
them the whole bunch of bananas, which he willingly did because he
"jest got to have dat ride." As Sambo departed an Italian fruitier
grabbed the Tanks brothers and accused them of stealing his bananas.
The brothers responded that "de nigger done it," but to little avail.
The episode can be read in two ways: Sambo set the Tankses up or he
was lucky to have swapped the bananas for a ride. In either case
Sambo's actions conform to a stereotype. In the first he displayed "typical" cunning in displacing blame; in the second he benefited from
dumb luck.

Marriner portrayed multiple instances of Sambo's dumb luck, which
taken together suggest that the artist consciously worked this stereotype for all it was worth. For instance on September 10, 1905, the
Tankses persuaded Sambo to "hide" in a gentleman's grip in the hope
of getting rid of "de moke." To their dismay the man entered a theater
and Sambo saw the show. Sambo's luck held on January 7, 1906,
when the boys set him on a toboggan ride in which he skittled an old
lady and a grocery boy, collecting the lady's dog and the boy's basket
before knocking a man on top of him for the remainder of the ride.
Landing outside the railroad station, Sambo collected a dollar from
the man, who otherwise would have missed his train. He announced
his expectations of further payments from the lady and the grocery
boy to the Tankses, who commented, "Wot's de use?" The Tanks

brothers doubted the usefulness of their attempts to harm Sambo because his dumb luck always held out.

To be sure Marriner's "Sambo and His Funny Noises" follows the formulaic device of most comics in which stock characters repeat a similar scenario week in and week out, and in which the humor and entertainment lie in the artists' abilities to conjure new ways of telling the same story. But in Sambo's case Marriner inevitably drew on a stereotype. In the July 26, 1908, episode Sambo picks flowers for his girlfriend, Phoebie Snow. The Tanks brothers sabotage his gift with red peppers that cause Phoebie to sneeze. But the sneeze is only the penultimate moment. Marriner's punch line has Sambo chased by his straight-razor-wielding "brudder in law," who exclaims, "Yous dun sulted my sister!" The name of Sambo's girlfriend too involved a pointed joke at African Americans, since Phoebe Snow was a trademark character created by Earnest Elmo Calkins's advertising agency to publicize the cleanliness of the Buffalo & Lackawanna Railroad with the slogan her "dress stayed white, along its road of anthracite."[9]

Even when Sambo's victory over the Tanks brothers seemed unequivocal, Marriner undercut this outcome with a stereotypical image. For instance, in the July 11, 1909, episode the Tanks brothers steal Sambo's clothing when he is swimming. Sambo dons a scarecrow's garments, whereupon a generous woman is outraged that he has to wear such rags. In the penultimate panel she says that Sambo will "have the most becoming suit I can buy you." The final panel shows him kitted out in the manner of Zip Coon, in a ridiculous hat and bow tie. Once again the strip's humor lay not in any particular circumstance but in Marriner's notion of African Americans.

In the ten years that Marriner produced the Sambo strip (1905–14), only five episodes clearly drew their humor from a source other than stereotypical notions of African Americans. The contrast can be seen by comparing episodes with similar themes. On July 15, 1906, December 9, 1906, and January 4, 1914, Marriner reworked Mark Twain tales with Sambo getting the better of the Tanks brothers. These three episodes were dissimilar to other Sambo strips, in which Marriner presented Sambo's cunning in distinct racial terms. In the July 15, 1906, strip Sambo cons the Tanks brothers into carrying a heavy load to the junk dealer's for him. In the title panel Sambo is singing, "I'se got a white man workin' foh me!" Here the motive is at least partially racial. By contrast in the 1914 episode in which Sambo has others shovel snow for his profit, just as Tom Sawyer had others whitewash a fence, the gag is not specifically racial. In another episode, on May 3, 1908, the joke was on an Irish policeman who saved Sambo from the Tanks brothers for the price of a drink.

Two other strips that stand out were probably created by Marriner's assistant because their art style is different. On February 23, 1913, Sambo and the Tanks brothers conspired together against their school-teacher. On June 15, 1913, Sambo proceeded to school, despite invitations from various other boys to join them in play, only to find it shut. These episodes are particularly surprising because they are the only occasions in the strip's history that Sambo is treated as an equal by white boys. Even more surprising in the latter episode is the multiracial group of boys playing baseball. I cannot recall another instance between 1890 and 1945, outside the African American press, in which a black character's persona was so little stereotypical.[10] Nonetheless these particular episodes have to be read in the context of all the others, and their absence of discernible racist stereotypes balanced against the strip's overall content. And Sambo's character remained stereotypical in these strips because comic strip art reduces visual representation to caricatured stereotypes.

The two extraordinary 1913 episodes that are different in style were probably drawn by Pat Sullivan. Born in Australia in 1885, Sullivan was an opportunist looking for his main chance. He supplemented work for Marriner with postcard production. Perhaps less inclined to employ racist stereotypes in his work than Marriner, Sullivan would nonetheless have been well aware of the conventions; minstrelsy was an international form of popular culture well known to Australian audiences.[11] Sullivan drew a number of Sambo strips because Marriner's intemperance left him incapacitated. The strip folded shortly after Marriner burned himself to death in a house fire lit in a drunken rage on October 9, 1914. Prophetically the strip that week had Sambo comment, "Dere ain't no room on dis earth fo' dem white boys an' me" (see Figure 13).[12]

More than Marriner's demise, however, led to Sambo's disappearance from the funny pages. When the McClure company first syndicated "Sambo and His Funny Noises" in 1905, comic strips were a relatively new phenomenon. In the years between 1905 and 1914 many strips came and went, and a ten-year run was an exception. Comic strips, such as "Buster Brown" and "Katzenjammer Kids," that survived for

13. William Marriner, "Sambo and His Funny Noises," *Indianapolis Star* (October 11, 1914).

ten or more years generally had strong central characters and appeared in newspapers across the country. Moreover their creators found ways to broaden their appeal and to either remain fresh or achieve iconic status.

That Sambo survived for so long was an indication more of the centrality of African American stereotypes to American culture than of Marriner's skill. The strip had never had a wide circulation. In 1908 "Sambo and His Funny Noises" appeared in only 13 of the 83 newspapers I have identified as having had comic strips. In 1913 this had shrunk to 7 of the 114 newspapers with comics. By 1913 the *San Francisco Chronicle* was the only large city paper that contained Sambo. In June 1914 the *Chronicle* dropped the strip, leaving it running only in relatively minor newspapers. Sambo never broke the shackles that stereotyped African American characters. But this did not mean that the characteristics making up those stereotypes could not be reanimated in such a way that they became available for broader comedic and commercial purposes. Ironically as long the stereotypes defined black characters, the appeal of those qualities was limited by their "blackness." Once they were deracinated their attraction was considerably wider. The career of Pat Sullivan subsequent to his work on the Sambo strip is a case in point.

Shortly after Marriner's death Sullivan established an animation studio. Between March and December 1916 Sullivan's fledgling business produced and released nine *Sammy Johnsin* animated cartoons. In everything but name Sammy Johnsin was identical to Sambo (aka Samuel Johnson). Although these cartoons enjoyed some success, Sullivan abandoned the character, first to do Charlie Chaplin cartoons and eventually to develop Felix the Cat, the first ongoing, successful animated cartoon character. As the historian John Canemaker notes, the Sammy Johnsin cartoons contributed to the development and look of Felix.[13]

It would be too bold and too reductive a step to regard Felix as purely a deracinated and anthropomorphic version of Sambo. Nonetheless it is instructive to note that Felix's adventures often involve the same sort of dumb luck that Sambo enjoys. In *Felix Strikes It Rich,* an animated short released in July 1923, Felix is forced to dig his own grave at gunpoint only to strike oil and win a reprieve. The September 14, 1923, Felix comic strip for Hearst's King Features Syndicate repeated this gag (see Figure 14).[14] As with Sambo the penultimate panel

14. Pat Sullivan, "Felix," *Boston American* (September 14, 1923). © King
Features Syndicate. Reprinted with special permission of King Features
Syndicate.

contains the gag, in this case striking oil. The final panel comments on Felix's nature. Felix had gotten himself into trouble in the first place by eating pet goldfish. His reward for striking oil was a large fish presented to him in the last panel by his would-be executioner. The final panel reminds readers of the strip's conceit in attributing human qualities to a cat. Nothing is more natural than for a cat to eat fish. Likewise the Marriner strips "naturalized" Sambo's dumb luck and stereotyped character.

The structural conventions and commodity nature of comic strips established in their first twenty years meant that in them an anthropomorphic cat had a more complex nature than an African American and hence was more salable. Pat Sullivan's grasp of this situation seems to have developed through producing animated cartoons, and he may even have understood it in these terms. Others who copied Sullivan's success as an entrepreneur, such as Walt Disney, may not have understood the origins of their characters, but anarchic, funny animal characters became a mainstay of American animation, and in Disney's case the foundation of a media empire. The ironies of funny animal figures, whose characteristics owed something to stereotypes of African Americans, may have been other more than humorous for George Herriman, who created "Krazy Kat" for the King Features Syndicate.

GEORGE HERRIMAN AND "KRAZY KAT"

George Herriman's "Krazy Kat" has long been a favorite of the intelligentsia. Jay Cantor's 1988 novel *Krazy Kat* figures Krazy as the key to the latter half of the twentieth century. In 1924 Gilbert Seldes described Herriman's work as "the most amusing and fantastic and satisfactory work of art produced in America today." e. e. cummings in the 1940s found Krazy Kat's capacity for love an illimitable transcending force indicative of true democracy, which is fulfilled only when "society fails to suppress the individual." Recently Kirk Varnedoe and Adam Gopnik have described Herriman as liberating "the sublime landscape from the decorum of high seriousness." Seldes found "Krazy Kat" a delicate mixture of sensitiveness, irony, and fantasy. Varnedoe and Gopnik regard the strip as "Arcadia without nostalgia" and Herriman's style as prefiguring Surrealism, which used some of his devices.[15]

"Krazy Kat" was all these things and more. Underpinning the luminous beauty that most critics find in it was the strip's basic running gag: Ignatz Mouse throws a brick at Krazy Kat, who, oblivious to Ignatz's intense dislike, takes the brick as a sign of love. A third character, Officer Pupp, does his best to uphold the law and prevent Krazy being hit. "Krazy Kat" began as a set of extraneous characters at the bottom of Herriman's daily "Dingbat Family" comic strip. The mouse first beaned the cat in this strip on July 26, 1910. By 1913 a daily "Krazy Kat" strip appeared in the *New York Journal*. The daily strip was slapstick physical comedy in which Krazy almost inevitably received a brick in the head. So well established was this theme that when the strip still ran underneath "The Family Upstairs" (the strip's title changed on August 1, 1910), Herriman could play with the joke to have Ignatz miss when he used balls at a circus, and again when he used a boomerang. The Krazy Kat of surreal landscapes and witty patois arrived in the Sunday version of the strip, which appeared in the arts section of Hearst's newspapers when not omitted by the local editor (see Figure 15).[16]

Beyond the basic gag it is difficult to ascribe typical qualities to a "Krazy Kat" strip, but the November 26, 1916, episode is at least indicative of Herriman's style. Ignatz has his portrait painted by "Mr. Michael O'Kobalt, artist, painter of portraits, signs, fences, and interiors, mender of sinks, keys, and shot rifles, buyer of 2nd hand false teeth, and popular purveyor of katnip, and lavender to the royal family." O'Kobalt arranges for Krazy to deliver the framed portrait to Ignatz. Ignatz observes Krazy and unbeknown to the kat hitches a ride on the frame. Stopping for a rest, Krazy observes of the portrait, "L'il Ainjil, how netural he looks, almost I could observe a quiva in his whiska." As Krazy speaks Ignatz beans him, whereupon Krazy exclaims, "Netural, oh so netural—even unto his hebits—sweetniss." Ignatz then has to conceal himself as "Offissa" Pupp arrives on the scene. The strip concludes at midnight, with Ignatz still in hiding as Pupp bemoans the duration of his shifts.[17]

The basic premise of "Krazy Kat" was no less violent than that of the average Sambo strip. What tempered its humor then, and now, was that the characters were animals. It would be easy enough to weave a story of Krazy Kat as a metaphor for black existence in white America. Krazy's constant uncertainty of gender, his/her attempt to become blond in one episode, Herriman's lines "we call him 'cat,' we call

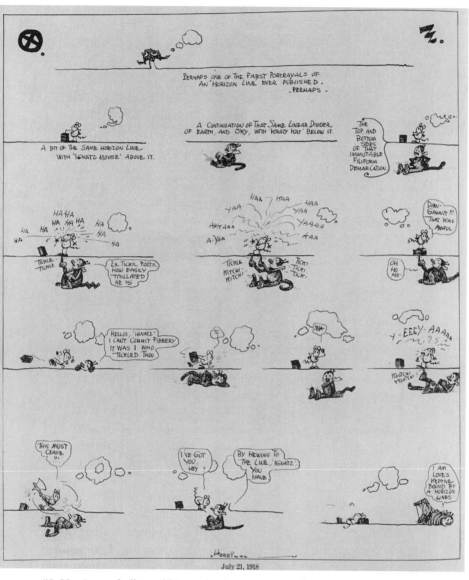

15. Herriman challenged his readers' conceptions of time and space. George Herriman, "Krazy Kat," *New York American* (July 21, 1918). © King Features Syndicate. Reprinted with special permission of King Features Syndicate.

him 'crazy' yet is he neither," and Herriman's own ambivalent identity offer tempting possibilities.[18]

George Herriman's identity has always been a bit of a puzzle. He gave various accounts of his background, telling his daughter that his parents were French. Among his comic strip pals Herriman was known as the Greek, dubbed thus by Tad Dorgan because, as Dorgan recalled, "we didn't know what he was." Herriman also confided to a friend that he might have some "Negro blood." Indeed his New Orleans birth certificate described him as "colored," and the 1880 census designated his parents "mulattoes." Patrick McDonnell, Karen O'Connell, and Georgia Riley de Havenon's *Krazy Kat: The Comic Art of George Herriman,* from which this information is gleaned, notes that the Creole society of New Orleans consisted of two groups: those of "entirely French or Spanish descent" and those who "referred to themselves as 'colored' Creoles." The latter were of mixed ancestry, mostly had not been slaves, and spoke primarily French but also English and a dialect.[19] To describe Herriman as an African American then reduces the richness of his identity and heritage. But it was probably just these kinds of reductions in post-Reconstruction New Orleans that caused Herriman's parents to seek better opportunities in Los Angeles. In Herriman's observation to his friend, and in Dorgan's comment, there is just a hint that the artist and his colleagues knew of his background and colluded in its obscuration.[20]

Fascinating though it may be, the story of Herriman's hidden cultural heritage finding expression in Krazy Kat is not my tale. Nor do I want to suggest necessarily that Krazy Kat is an anthropomorphized African American; rather I want to hint at Krazy's connection to stereotypes of blacks. Krazy may be not crazy or a cat, but neither is this character human. Krazy's heritage is that of the world turned upside down, a tradition with both symbolic and holistic magical associations. For instance, an oft repeated world-turned-upside-down motif of ox-driving peasants has at least two meanings. First the metaphorical linking of, say, the shared stubbornness of ox and peasants, and second the holistic relationship between ox and peasant, who depend on each other. This holistic link is probably clearer in traditions of role reversal, common to both European and African societies, in which peasants become kings for the day and vice versa. The holistic nature of the society and shared, even if stratified, obligations are magically ensured through the enactment of inversion. These traditions had long found expression in popular broadsheets and engravings from which comic strips derived. Such anthropomorphic associations gave rise to a genre of early gag cartoons that played with Darwinian theories of evolution (see Chapter 1). In America these cartoons helped give birth to comic strips.[21]

Krazy Kat belongs to this tradition. Herriman once described Krazy variously as "a sprite, an elf" and "a spirit—a pixie—free to butt into anything."[22] Krazy's illimitable love has a childlike innocence and Krazy's speech more than a hint of dialect jokes. Freed from any direct association with African Americans, these devices of racist stereotyping gave comic art its first funny animal character and helped establish a vein of humor later strip-mined by Walt Disney with his derivative Mickey Mouse. Deracinated, uncertain of gender, impossibly loving and innocent, Krazy is the essence of comic strip humor.

Krazy Kat may well have been the favorite of middle- and highbrow intellectuals, but the character had a limited following, and Hearst's lowbrow editors constantly dropped the Sunday version from their papers. In his Sunday pages Herriman experimented with the comic strip format and pushed against its limits. He established an aesthetic benchmark for comics, a fact witnessed by Bill Watterson's recent usage of similar techniques in "Calvin and Hobbes." Herriman's experimentation with the basic form of Sunday comics, which delivered a gag's punch line over twelve panels, probably accounts for his strip's lack of popularity. The story goes that only Hearst's love for the strip assured its continued presence from 1916 to 1944. But perhaps the success of the daily strip, and the industry practice of running Sunday versions of successful daily strips, accounts for its longevity. Herriman's major achievement in terms of the commodity nature of comics was to show that funny animal comics could use techniques and themes generally associated with stereotypes of African Americans without the potential limit to sales posed by black characters. In the 1920s and 1930s Hearst's King Features Syndicate had great success with two funny animal comic strips, the aforementioned "Felix the Cat" and a strip version of Disney's Mickey Mouse.

4 COMIC STRIPS AS CULTURE

From National Phenomenon to Everyday Life

In 1921, when Richard Outcault retired, Buster Brown was the only extensively licensed comic strip character. Other comic strip characters had been used as subject matter for stage adaptations and toys, but only Buster Brown sold products such as shoes and bread. Moreover, only Outcault's Chicago-based advertising agency used comic art with any regularity in its advertisements. But beginning in the 1920s, and culminating in the 1930s, the promoters of goods and services used comic art more extensively to capture the buying public's attention. These entrepreneurs recognized that they could profit from the high readership and popularity of comic strips. Their activities helped establish the comic art form as a part of everyday life in the United States.

Doll and toy manufacturers were among the first to use comic strip characters to sell their products. For these businesspeople the characters' attraction was their widespread national recognition, derived from the broad distribution of comic strips. Broadway entrepreneurs and sheet music publishers also attached themselves to the popular comic strips by producing works that focused on favorite characters. Although these adaptations of comic strip characters were important in expanding the use and acceptance of comic art, they were mostly an extension of the late nineteenth-century, city-based "craze" phenomenon. Toys, Broadway shows, and song sheets added quantitatively to the use of comic strip characters but did little to expand the use of the comic art form as a method of commercial communication.

Not until the early 1930s, in response to the restricted market brought on by the Depression, did many advertisers realize the potential of comic art to sell products. In 1931 comic-strip-style advertising began to appear frequently in the Sunday comic supplements of William Randolph Hearst's papers. Two advertising historians, Stephen Fox and Roland Marchand, argue that this increase was a result of the interest advertising agencies showed in the newspaper surveys conducted by George Gallup, a former professor of advertising and journalism at Northwestern University. Gallup's surveys revealed that the most popular and most frequently read part of a newspaper was the comic strip page. Gallup himself went to work for the Young and Rubicam agency, but his studies influenced the newspaper, magazine, and advertising industries across the board. Following the lead of Hearst's papers, the color comic sections of most Sunday newspapers opened their pages to advertising rendered in a comic art style. Furthermore, advertisements in this style began to appear in general periodicals, such as *The Saturday Evening Post* and *Ladies' Home Journal*. In addition to Young and Rubicam, other large agencies, such as J. Walter Thompson and N. W. Ayer, produced comic art advertisements.[1]

The popularity of comic strips among adults, demonstrated by Gallup and others, suggests that by the 1930s the strips had become an ingrained feature of American life. Moreover, if comic strips were the most frequently read part of newspapers, then reading, for most Americans, involved understanding graphic as well as textual content. Advertising agencies may not have understood this change in the reading process, but they knew enough to cast their messages in the form of comic strips.

Comic-strip-style ads helped shape a new aesthetic of advertising. One of the advantages of the comic strip style was that it allowed advertisers to create graphic narratives, through the sequential panels that demonstrated visually the supposed benefits of using their products. Through these images advertisers attributed therapeutic value to their products, and a product's "image" became less the way it looked and more the intangible qualities it was thought to embody. Also, by incorporating text into graphics through the use of word balloons, the comic strip style transformed advertising copy from salesmanship in print to seemingly disinterested commentary or testimonial. More important, the use of comic art in advertising strengthened the links between leisure, entertainment, and consumption.

Comic strips were always a commercial undertaking. Publishers introduced them to newspapers to increase circulation and profits. But newspapers presented strips as entertainment, and their public consumed them as such. Comic strips were one way newspapers began to provide entertainment as well as information. Indeed, one historian argues that the newspapers of the two progenitors of comic strips, Joseph Pulitzer and William Randolph Hearst, discovered "news" as an entertainment concept.[2] The comic-strip-style advertisements used the entertainment quality of the form to sell goods and services. In doing so they transformed advertising in part from an element in the reader's consumption of a newspaper or magazine as information to a form that offered a possibility of entertainment. Such advertising provided a seamless experience for those who consumed newspapers as entertainment.

DOLLS, BROADWAY SHOWS, AND COMIC STRIPS

Buster Brown was the most extensively licensed comic strip character and until the 1920s the only one used as a name brand for products. But starting in the early 1900s the copyright holders of other comic strip characters licensed their use for a number of products. The most common of these were comic strip reprint books published by Cupples & Leon in New York and F. A. Stokes of Philadelphia.[3] More important, comic strip characters extended beyond the printed page when toy and doll manufacturers, and Broadway producers, began to use their likenesses. This expansion was a slow and uneven process, but by the 1920s entrepreneurs had emblazoned comic strip characters on a wide range of goods and services. The increased use of these characters took place as a nascent American toy manufacturing industry tried to establish itself against imported and homemade playthings.

Until 1914 imports from Europe accounted for over 90 percent of the toys sold in America. Moreover, until the 1920s most children played with homemade rather than manufactured toys. Bernard Mergen, a historian of childhood, has noted that manufactured dolls constituted a small percentage of playthings used by children until well into the 1920s.[4] Nonetheless the American toy trade was sufficiently lucrative that in 1902 the McCready Publishing Company of New York began to publish *Playthings,* a trade journal for the industry. A 1920 editorial in that journal noted that "certain far seeing men" had observed "the purchasing power" of American children after their tenth birthdays and thereafter kept step with these consumers until their college years and beyond.[5] To attract and maintain the loyalty of this market, individual manufacturers, particularly the makers of dolls and figurines, sought to distinguish their products. By the 1920s they regularly turned to comic strip characters for marketable images.

From the 1890s to the early 1900s, manufacturers and retailers increased their use of advertisements for name brand or novelty dolls, as opposed to generic dolls described by their material composition. The September 1889 issue of Butler Brothers' mail-order catalog offered Washable Dressed Dolls, French Bisque Dolls, Kid Body Dolls, and Solid China Dolls. In addition it advertised Baby Dolls and Talking dolls. The 1894–95 Montgomery Ward catalog included a similar range of generic dolls and dolls with "Patent Indestructible Heads." By 1903 the use of a brand name became an almost universal feature in advertisements for dolls. In that year Butler Brothers listed Kestner dolls, United States Emblem dolls, Rattle Head dolls, Matlock washable dolls, Model washable dolls, and Marvel kid body dolls.

Name brand dolls served two purposes. First, a name brand protected a doll from imitation under copyright and, after 1905, trademark laws. Second, manufacturers could promote named dolls more easily than generic dolls, an important consideration when children were still likely to have homemade rather than manufactured dolls. Doll makers sought to distinguish their products by manufacturing them in the likenesses of well-known characters. For instance, Little Red Riding Hood was one of the most popular names in the doll-making trade because a red hood and a cape could be added to any doll. But because the name Little Red Riding Hood could not be copyrighted or patented, any doll maker could produce a doll bearing this name. By contrast, artists copyrighted and licensed their comic strip characters.[6]

The high national visibility of comic strips and their easily recognizable characters made them useful to doll manufacturers and others wishing to sell their own goods. As already noted, the first comic strip character, R. F. Outcault's Yellow Kid, appeared on a number of products including a doll. Outcault's second main character, Buster Brown, also appeared as a doll. Various other comic strip characters materialized as dolls, including the Katzenjammer Kids, Moon Mullins, and Little Orphan Annie. The Live Long Toy Company's 1926 advertisement for its line of comic strip dolls in the trade journal *Playthings* demonstrates that at least one company consciously sought to associate itself with the popularity of comic strip characters to ensure a healthy business. The advertisement noted that artists such as Harold Gray ("Little Orphan Annie"), Sidney Smith ("The Gumps"), and Frank Willard ("Moon Mullins") had "created characters which are known and loved the country over through Comic Strips in the Nation's leading newspapers. And Live Long Toys, by personifying these characters into attractive, lifelike dolls, have added to the fame of the artists and have established the firm itself, on a lasting foundation of national popularity." The company said it put the artist's "idea in practical, usable form."

Based in Chicago, the Live Long Toy Company derived all its comic strip character dolls from the strips of the *Chicago Tribune–New York Daily News* syndicate. Schoenhut, another American doll manufacturer, produced wooden dolls based on George McManus's "Bringing Up Father" and Billy De Beck's strip "Barney Google," which ran in Hearst newspapers. German and Japanese manufacturers also produced a large number of toys based on comic strips, apparently as aware as their American compatriots of the profits to be made from putting comic strip characters into "practical, usable form."[7]

These dolls were but one manifestation of merchandisers' efforts to take advantage of the popularity of comic strips. Comic strip characters also appeared in short live-action movies as early as 1902. And the first animated feature was Winsor McCay's comic strip "Little Nemo in Slumberland," which McCay himself animated in 1910–11. The popularity of comic strips was so great that even the burgeoning amusement park industry got in on the act with a Katzenjammer Castle and Toboggan Park erected in St. Paul, Minnesota, at the turn of the century. As usual, when it came to comic strips, William Randolph Hearst led the way. Hearst's Kinescope company produced many of the short features based on comic strips. Hearst had published sheet music in his comic strip supplement from the outset; on November 8, 1896, he published music for a song about the Yellow Kid. Other publishers followed suit, and at least three versions of Yellow Kid songs appeared in the late 1890s. Throughout the first years of the twentieth century, Hearst's papers carried music supplements that often featured comic strip character sheet music. The theater historian Mark D. Winchester has noted that as early as 1898, beginning with the Yellow Kid in McFadden's Row of Flats, Gus Hill produced musicals based on comic strip characters. In 1914 Hill adapted McManus's "Bringing Up Father" for a new musical. Hill's productions continued throughout the 1920s. In 1921 and 1922 John Murray Anderson and John Alden Carpenter staged two productions of Carpenter's Krazy Kat Ballet Suite in New York City, based on the "Krazy Kat" comic strip by George Herriman.[8]

The popularity of doll and Broadway manifestations of comic strip characters suggested that the strips had the potential for other profitable applications. But the dynamic between a comic strip character and works and objects based on it was not simply that of authentic original art and a derivative commodity manufactured for commercial gain. Certainly the popularity of a comic strip and its national distribution helped sell dolls. But at the same time the existence of commodities derived from a strip broadened its appeal and strengthened the status of the art form. In this way a comic strip "character" could move beyond a daily or weekly appearance in a newspaper to a dimension where these appearances competed with other items as just one representation of the character. This process allowed comic strip characters to assume a multiplicity of meanings, which appealed to diverse audiences and so helped unite and contain diverse features of American culture. In other words a commercial creation became a cultural icon of mythological dimensions. Not only did the control and marketing of these icons became a lucrative trade but the advertising industry appropriated the comic art form itself, often without the presence of recognized comic strip characters, to sell a wide range of goods and services.

EARLY SURVEYS OF COMIC STRIP READERSHIP

George Gallup's surveys in the early 1930s revealed that more people read "the best comic strip in a newspaper, on an average day" than read the front-page banner story. Gallup's initial publication of his findings appeared in 1930 on the front page of *Editor & Publisher.* Gallup directed his article at newspaper editors wishing to save money by cutting back on features. The majority of the piece concentrated on his "scientific" methodology for determining the readership of given features. The purpose was probably to advertise Gallup's services. Consequently his comments on the readership of comics, although summarized in a box on the front page, only surfaced at the end of the piece, on page 55. Based on 4,000 cases, drawn evenly from surveys of six metropolitan newspapers, Gallup made a number of observations that had important ramifications for the direction of advertising. He wrote:

- Comics are more popular with women than with men although a majority of both sexes usually reads them.
- A new comic or continuity strip, no matter how good or how well promoted, attracts its following slowly.
- Continuity strips today have greater following than comic strips.
- ankers, professors, doctors, farmers, and lawyers read comic strips as avidly as truck drivers, waiters, and day laborers.

Finally, Gallup noted that the only parts of a metropolitan newspaper consistently "read" by over 40 percent of both women and men were pictures and comics.[9]

Gallup was not the first social scientist to discover that comic strips had a broad appeal. A survey of children's play activities in Kansas conducted by Harvey Lehman and Paul Witty in the mid-1920s revealed that "looking at the Sunday 'funny' paper" was "the one activity most frequently engaged in by children [of both sexes] during all seasons of the year, and Negro and white children alike manifested an inordinate interest in it." In 1924 readership rates among city-dwelling girls and boys between ages eight and sixteen did not drop below 84 percent, with slightly more girls than boys reading the strips. Even in rural areas, readership did not fall below 55 percent for any one age-group and was as high as 82 percent. Furthermore, comic strip reading was one of the most popular activities for rural children, even though it was not as predominant in rural as in urban areas. Lehman and Witty speculated that fewer rural children read the comic strips because of the "relative inaccessibility" of the comic sheet.[10]

Published in the obscure *Journal of Applied Psychology,* Lehman and Witty's study received no attention from advertisers or newspaper

proprietors. If their survey demonstrated the almost universal importance of comic strips to children and adolescents, this fact seemed to
be of little commercial importance because publishers and advertisers
understood newspapers and other products as adult purchases.
Gallup's survey not only showed that most adults read comic strips
too but came at a time when newspaper owners and advertisers sought
more effective ways to market their goods and services.

According to Fox and Marchand, advertising executives and the advertising trade journals did not pay attention to Gallup's work until, at
the earliest, the middle of 1931. Advertisers' failure to notice, or understand the significance of, Gallup's work in 1930 may have been because his focus was on selling his services to newspaper proprietors.
Although Fox and Marchand cite Gallup's work as the causal factor in
the initial expanded use of the comic art style, it is possible that it simply acted as a "scientific" explanation of why comic advertising worked.

Advertisers had experimented with comic-strip-style advertisements
before Gallup's survey received public attention. As Marchand notes,
Rinso published advertisements in the *Chicago Tribune* on June 14,
1929, and October 19, 1930, which used word balloons to give their
photographed subjects voices. The *American Weekly,* a Sunday supplement to Hearst's papers, published a similar ad on January 12,
1930. A Lifebuoy advertisement that had some of the features of a
comic strip appeared in the *Chicago Tribune* on June 18, 1929. The
September 1930 issue of *Ladies' Home Journal* also contained a full-
page Rinso advertisement in the manner of those in the *Tribune.* Furthermore, Wrigley's chewing gum published comic strip advertisements in Hearst's comic supplement several times in the 1920s. And of
course thousands of advertisements from 1904 to the 1920s featured
Buster Brown.[11]

In early 1931 the Hearst organization informed advertising clients
of its decision to open its Sunday comic section to advertising on a
trial basis, but ad agencies only paid attention to the selling power of
comic strip advertisements when they had direct proof of their success.
The item that provoked the rush to comic-strip-style advertising in the
1930s, General Foods's "Suburban Joe" advertisement for Grape-Nuts
cereal, which appeared in Hearst's comic supplement on May 17,
1931, included an encoded reply coupon for a free sample. The use of
encoded coupons to ascertain whether advertising was read dated
from the publication of Earnest Elmo Calkins and Ralph Holden's

Modern Advertising in 1905.[12] Probably because of the number of responses to the coupon, General Foods ran six more full-page comic-
strip-format advertisements for Grape-Nuts in Hearst's comic supplement between June and November 1931. The ads reversed declining
sales figures. Before 1931 sales had been falling at a rate of 15 percent
a year. In the first six months of 1931 they fell 13 percent. After the
comic strip ads appeared Grape-Nuts sales for 1931 picked up and exceeded 1930 sales by 13 percent with no additional advertising expenditures. Early in 1932 General Foods ran advertisements for Postum
and Jell-O in the comic supplement.[13] But even if Gallup's surveys only
lent "scientific" credence to advertisers' use of the comic strip format,
they demonstrated that comic strips had pervaded all levels of American society. And, with the certainty of Gallup's "scientific" evidence
behind them advertisers further expanded their use of such ads.[14]

In the 1930s newspaper and magazine editors began to use Gallup-
like surveys to follow trends in American life. For instance, the editors
of *Fortune* instigated a quarterly survey in 1935 that they hoped
would serve as the basis of "the New Technique in Journalism." After
two years of the survey, the magazine editorialized that they had
gained "a better knowledge of the U.S., of the points at which section-
alism is stubbornly distinct, where class consciousness is persistent and
articulate, and those other points at which both boundaries of opinion
break down and merge into a national sentiment that speaks with
one voice."[15]

Fortune's survey confirmed Gallup's findings about adult readership
of comic strips and regarded them as an instance in which the nation
almost spoke with one voice. *Fortune* stated that syndicated comic
strips most likely had a "wider intellectual influence" than newspaper
editorial pages. The *Fortune* survey showed that only 30.4 percent of
U.S. adults regularly read a columnist, whereas 51.4 percent had a favorite comic strip. Of the ten most favorite comic strips, the Hearst
and *Chicago Tribune–New York Daily News* syndicates accounted for
four apiece. As had Gallup, and Lehman and Witty, *Fortune* found the
readership of comic strips to be widespread, with a majority of adults
following them in every part of the country save the South and Southwest and some small towns.[16]

Gallup's work also inspired an ongoing survey of newspaper readership by the Advertising Research Foundation. Conducted from 1939
to the mid-1950s, this survey provided page-by-page and column-by-

column breakdowns of readership. The 1950 summary of 137 such surveys revealed that comic strips had a uniformly high readership across the country. Between 1939 and 1950, in cities with populations under 50,000, between 53 and 94 percent of men, with a median of 82 percent, and 50 and 92 percent of women, with a median of 80 percent, read comics. In cities with populations of over 500,000, between 60 and 91 percent of men, with a median of 75 percent, and 58 and 86 percent of women, with a median of 77 percent, read the strips. Nowhere in the country did the median of comic strip readership fall below 75 percent. Likewise a breakdown of the statistics according to occupational groupings revealed the lowest figures, for professional men and women, as 70 and 68 percent respectively. Among all occupational groups a total of 79 percent of men and 77 percent of women read comics.[17]

Clearly by the 1930s comic strips, and the techniques of communication they employed, were embedded in American daily life. When Gallup's survey, and the response to General Foods's Grape-Nuts advertisement, showed the popularity and selling power of the comic strips, advertisers hastened to speak in this newly acknowledged American voice.

COMIC-STRIP-STYLE ADVERTISING

Advertisers did not use comic strip techniques extensively until the 1930s. Richard Outcault's Buster Brown appeared in thousands of advertisements but was limited to a single illustration rather than a series of panels. The change in advertisers' use of comic strips in the 1930s —that is, the shift from the employment of comic strip characters to sell products to the deployment of the art form itself—marked the changed position of comic strips in American life. They were no longer a singular phenomenon resulting from the popularity of particular characters but a form of communication understood by the majority of Americans.

Use of comic strips in advertising before the "Suburban Joe" Grape-Nuts advertisement of 1931 had mostly involved well-known comic strip characters, such as Buster Brown, "endorsing" products.[18] For instance, the Wrigley's P.K. chewing gum advertisement that appeared in Hearst's comic supplement of September 19, 1926, used Maggie and Jiggs from George McManus's "Bringing Up Father," Hans and Fritz from Harold Knerr's "Katzenjammer Kids," Barney Google and Spark Plug from Billy De Beck's strip of the same name, Frederick Opper's Happy Hooligan, and Jimmy Murphy's Toots and Casper. The ad featured the characters in a series of individual panels drawn by their regular artists and at first glance was indistinguishable from the other strips in the supplement. This advertisement, and others like it that appeared throughout the 1920s, was a string of simple character "endorsements" in sequential panels but without narrative.[19] Advertisements did not use the comic strip format to create images and tell stories about their products until 1931. The Rinso advertisements of 1929 and 1930, although arranged in sequential panels with word balloons, were, strictly speaking, not comic strip style because they employed photographs rather than drawings.

General Foods's "Suburban Joe" Grape-Nuts cereal advertisement set off a tidal wave of comic-strip-style advertising in the 1930s. In 1931, after "Suburban Joe" and several other Grape-Nuts advertisements had appeared, Rinso revamped its campaign and published "Goodbye Blue Monday," the first of a series of half-page comic-strip-style advertisements signed by C. A. Voight (see Figure 16), a pioneer daily comic strip artist, in the Hearst comic supplement on September 20, 1931. A half-page Lifebuoy advertisement employing a similar style generally accompanied each of these Rinso advertisements.[20]

On November 8, 1931, the Vick Chemical Company published a comic-strip-style advertisement in the Hearst supplement to launch its two new products: Vicks [sic] Medicated Cough Drops and Vicks [sic] Nose & Throat Drops. The Hearst organization persuaded Vick to use comic art rather than a display advertisement. According to Hawley Turner, a Hearst executive, in a speech to a J. Walter Thompson Agency meeting, sales exceeded Vick's expectations by 15 percent. One Thompson copywriter suggested the ad would have appeared more natural if it had shown the man about to lose his job because of ill health rather than simply suffering from a cold. Turner agreed but explained it had been a rush job.[21] All these ads used pen-and-ink-rendered sequential panels to tell a story that centered on their product. The Grape-Nuts, Rinso, and Vick's advertisements used word balloons to give the figures in the panels voices. The Lifebuoy ad used narrative text within the panels to clarify the story told in the illustrations. Between 1932 and 1933 these advertisers were joined in the Hearst

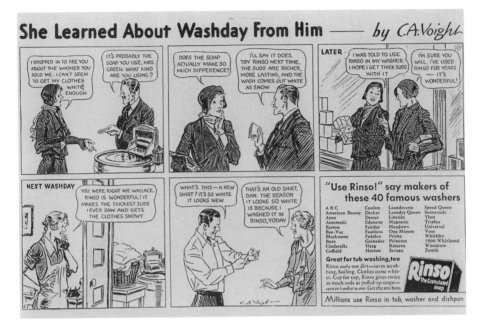

16. Rinso advertisement, *New York American* (April 10, 1932), comic sec.
Courtesy of Lever Brothers Company.

comic supplement by Postum, Jell-O, Ovaltine, Cocomalt, Listerine,
Aunt Jemima, Lux, Groves Laxative, Kruschen Salts, Lionel Electric
Trains, R. J. Reynolds (Camel), and Parker fountain pens.

The Hearst corporation recognized the advertising revenue to be
gained from comic strip advertising and in July 1932 took out a nine-
page advertisement of its own in *Printers' Ink*, an advertising trade
journal. The ad touted the success of the supplement's advertisers and
noted the high response to coupon offers.[22] The *Printers' Ink* advertisement, and others like it in 1933, helped the Hearst corporation expand its comic strip supplement advertising pages from two in 1932 to
at least three in 1933. In 1933 the price of a full-page advertisement
was $17,300 for the back page, $16,000 for an inside page, and
$9,000 for a half page. By 1934 most advertisements in the comic sup-
plements occupied only half a page. For instance, the April 8, 1934, issue of Hearst's *Puck* supplement contained a full-page Ovaltine, and
half-page Rinso, Lifebuoy, Royal gelatin, and Postum advertisements.
The number of advertising pages expanded from eleven in 1931 to

ninety-one in 1933, generating $1,280,000 extra revenue for Hearst at a time when advertising appropriations declined.

Other newspaper publishers opened their comic supplements to advertisements, but none could match the combined circulation of the seventeen Sunday Hearst newspapers.[23] In 1934 the Hearst corporation published a twelve-page advertisement for the comic supplement in *Printers' Ink*. This ad outlined the success enjoyed by advertisers in Hearst's *Puck* and stressed it as the most cost-effective medium to reach consumers. Hearst not only reached 72 percent of the women and 68 percent of the men who read Sunday newspapers but offered "the extra bonus . . . [of] the great and growing market of youngsters coming of age." The Hearst corporation highlighted the national appeal of its comic supplement. In 1938 Hearst ran two advertisements in its competitor's paper the *Chicago Tribune*. These ads, in comic strip form, pointed to the "coast to coast" standard of the supplement, and its almost 13 million adult and 7 million "juvenile" readers.[24]

According to the Hearst corporation, one of the selling points of advertisements in their comic supplement was the profitability of basking in "the reflected light from" stars such as Barney Google, Jiggs and Maggie, Mickey Mouse, and Toots and Casper. Hearst likened their comic strips' array of talent to that of a radio program featuring major stars. Just as the stars of early radio did not plug sponsors' products directly, the stars of Hearst comic strips did not appear in the advertisements in the comic supplement.[25] When personalities appeared in comic strip advertisements they were generally of the flesh and blood type, although not necessarily more complex than two-dimensional comic strip characters. Dizzy Dean pitched for Grape-Nuts, Jimmy Durante "nosed around" for Royal gelatin, and numerous sportsmen attested to the smooth taste and health-giving properties of Camel cigarettes.[26]

Given the earlier success of Buster Brown, it is uncertain why comic strip characters were not featured in the 1930s advertisements. Hearst's Hawley Turner suggested to the staff of the J. Walter Thompson Agency that use of established characters detracted from the product being sold, but he offered no evidence for his assertion.[27] Comic strip artists, trading on the popularity of their work, may have gained control of the subsidiary rights to their characters as Outcault had done with Buster Brown and resisted their use in advertisements, or demanded fees that advertisers found prohibitive. Or the absence of comic strip characters from comic-style advertising may have been an attempt to imitate early radio's use of sponsorship and thus establish the comic supplement as a respectable advertising venue on a par with radio. The widespread licensing of toys and other products based on comic strip characters in the 1930s lends credence to this argument. One Thompson executive made this link. He noted that "the comic section has values in some respects like that offered in radio advertising. Entertainment and humor develop a frame of mind that makes the reader susceptible to advertising much the same as radio."[28]

The important point is that in these advertisements the comic art form showed that it was an effective method of communication even without the characters who made it a popular entertainment. And advertisers, of course, did not have to pay fees to use the format. Assured of the effectiveness of comic-strip-style advertising, agencies began to place such copy in general periodicals.[29]

Although *Ladies' Home Journal* published a Rinso advertisement that used word balloons and panels in 1930, comic-strip-style advertising did not appear regularly in general periodicals until 1932. By 1933 such advertising had boomed. For instance, a spot check of the September issues of *The Saturday Evening Post* and *Ladies' Home Journal* from 1929 to 1933 showed that there were no comic strip advertisements in the former in 1930 and 1931 and only one for each year in the latter, both times for Rinso. In September 1932 *The Saturday Evening Post* contained one half-page, and two quarter-page comic strip advertisements; *Ladies' Home Journal* published one full-page, one quarter-page, and three half-page advertisements in the comic strip style. In September 1933 *The Saturday Evening Post* published the equivalent of ten and a half pages of advertisements that used one or more of the features of the comic strip style; *Ladies' Home Journal* held the equivalent of seven and three-quarters pages.

Most of these advertisements used all the features of comic strip art. They had sequential panels containing pen-and-ink figures and backgrounds, and text or speech delivered through word balloons. But some simply used word balloons as a means of providing photographed subjects—whether animal, human, or inanimate—with voices. By September 1933 talking ducks, thermometers, and toothbrushes had become commonplace, so much so that an article in *Printers' Ink* berated advertisers for stretching credibility.[30] But word balloons excited advertising executives because they allowed the incorporation of advertising copy and illustrations in such a way that the copy seemed disinterested commentary. The J. Walter Thompson Agency referred to this style as the "conversational technique," which they regarded as "more credible than indirect discourse." Writing in 1939, the copywriter Jesse Thompson commented that the word balloon style meant copy was "working full blast—*selling.*"[31]

Advertisers also turned to word balloons, and the comic art form as a whole, in response to the Depression. They used this new form of advertising in a determined attempt to maintain and expand market share for their products in the face of contracted consumer spending. In some ways this adoption represented an appropriation of an existing, popular art form for commercial purposes with little regard to the form's technical properties. But at the same time, for some manufacturers the use of comic art was a stage in a long-term struggle to individualize their products and so distinguish them from the competition.

The dimensions of this process can be seen in the advertising copy of the Hygienic Products Company, manufacturers of Sani-Flush and Hy-Pro, which until 1940 simply adopted the convention of word balloons for their advertisements, and the Atlantic Refining Company, which in the 1930s used the comic art form to create a distinctive image for their products. Both companies were clients of the N. W. Ayer Advertising Agency, and the archives of that agency, held by the National Museum of American History, contain reasonably comprehensive files of their advertising from the 1920s to the late 1930s. It could be suggested that basing this part of my argument on the work of one agency is reductive. But my case is simply that these two accounts demonstrate early efforts at introducing to advertising some of the features the comic strip technique later allowed. At one level the use of the comic strip style represented progress in the technical aspects of advertising, the integration of illustration and text. The J. Walter Thompson Agency also understood comic-strip-style advertising in these terms. One Thompson executive described these ads as "the swiftest and the most compelling way to tell a story in print."[32]

The Hygienic Products Company of Canton, Ohio, manufactured Sani-Flush, a chemical compound designed to clean toilet bowls without scouring, and Hy-Pro, a bleach. The advertising for Sani-Flush varied little from 1912, when the company first sold it, until the mid-

1930s. The standard ad for Sani-Flush consisted of a quarter- or eighth-page column-width piece that combined a pen-and-ink illustration of Sani-Flush being poured into a toilet bowl by a woman, accompanied by a block of copy testifying to the product's effortless cleaning properties. The heading "Immaculately clean!" topped the 1929 version (see Figure 17). It was a very ordinary advertisement.

In the mid-1930s N. W. Ayer tinkered with the basic formula by incorporating the heading and the illustration. On most occasions Ayer did this by means of a word balloon or a similar layout. These too were ordinary advertisements; their sole distinction was the seeming disinterestedness of their central message. The word balloon style gave statements an air of objective commentary because the text appeared to emit from the figure in the ad. For instance, a 1938 advertisement featured a woman pouring Sani-Flush into a toilet bowl while commenting, through a word balloon, "Toilet stains and rust vanish" (see Figure 18). But, as a glance at *The Saturday Evening Post* for 1933 confirms, the use of word balloons was a commonplace feature of advertising by the mid-1930s.

Ayer's advertising for Hy-Pro bleach was more inventive. The Hy-Pro advertisements reworked the conventions of headings and word balloons so that they were indistinguishable. In 1938 N. W. Ayer produced a series of advertisements for the Hygienic Products Company that sought to teach rural consumers the many uses of Hy-Pro. Ayer laid out the ads in four distinct parts: two panels of illustration and text, a product blurb, and an illustration of the product itself. In the first two panels the illustrations were laid over three words in large text surrounded by a border. The text explained the illustration but in such a way that the words seemed to come from the character in the illustration. For instance, above an illustration of a woman looking at a tablecloth scorched by her hot iron the text read, "Scarred by Scorch." The next panel showed the woman holding up the scorch-free cloth under text that read, "Saved by Hy-Pro."[33]

The Hy-Pro advertisements were not the only ones to play with word balloons. Westinghouse did something similar in a September 1933 advertisement in *Ladies' Home Journal*, but Hy-Pro was the most inventive. As well as their balance of text and illustration to tell a narrative of housekeeping redemption, the Hy-Pro ads employed alliterative text, also a convention of comic strips.[34] Titles in the series included "Ruined by Rust," "Stained by Steps," "Doomed by Dirt,"

Immaculately clean!

YOUR toilet bowl can be sparkling white . . . safe from germs . . . sanitary. And it needn't be scrubbed and scoured and labored over. Sani-Flush will clean it easily.

Just pour a little Sani-Flush into the bowl, following directions on the can. Then flush. Marks, stains and incrustations vanish. Odors disappear. The toilet bowl is left spotless.

Sani-Flush reaches the hidden trap —cleanses the whole toilet system. And it's harmless to the plumbing. Use it frequently. Always keep it handy.

Buy Sani-Flush at your grocery, drug or hardware store, 25c. In Canada, 35c.

Sani-Flush
Reg US Pat Off
Cleans Closet Bowls Without Scouring

THE HYGIENIC PRODUCTS CO.
Canton, Ohio

Also makers of Melo . . . a real water softener

17. Sani-Flush advertisement. N. W. Ayer Advertising Agency Collection, Archives Center, National Museum of American History, Smithsonian Institution, book 577.

TOILET STAINS AND RUST VANISH

Try sprinkling a little SANI-FLUSH in the toilet bowl. (Follow directions on the can.) You don't scrub or rub. Don't do any unpleasant work at all! Just flush the toilet and watch the porcelain become snow-white and glistening. SANI-FLUSH is *made* to do this job. It cleans the trap or invisible outlet.

Buy a can of SANI-FLUSH from any grocery, drug, hardware, or five-and-ten-cent store — 25c and 10c sizes. It cannot injure plumbing connections. SANI-FLUSH *is also effective for cleaning out automobile radiators.* The Hygienic Products Company, Canton, Ohio.

Sani-Flush
CLEANS TOILET BOWLS WITHOUT SCOURING

18. Sani-Flush advertisement. N. W. Ayer Advertising Agency Collection, Archives Center, National Museum of American History, Smithsonian Institution, book 577.

"Blemished by Blots," "Gray from Grime," "Marred by Mildew," "Spoiled by Spots," and "Disfigured by Fruit." Hy-Pro's borrowing from the comic art form did not extend beyond this combination of word balloons and alliterative titles. But it demonstrates that advertisers could put to use consumers' familiarity with comic strips.

In the 1930s the Atlantic Refining Company made fuller and more extensive use of the comic art form in its advertising. Atlantic's 1930s ads represent the fruition of earlier efforts to develop a distinctive image for their products. The company's advertisements between the early 1920s and the late 1930s served a number of purposes. In the 1920s they sought to build up consumer loyalty to the Atlantic brand name by promoting an aura of reliability and convenience. For instance, under a drawing of a car motoring through the week and the caption "Atlantic Gasoline is always uniform," a 1920 advertisement invited motorists to put the same trust in Atlantic gasoline, day in, day out, "that you would in a lifelong friend." A 1921 ad linked reliability and the Atlantic brand name more explicitly by showing a consumer choosing motor oil from a portable tank pump clearly marked with the Atlantic emblem. A sidebar to this black-and-white illustration instructed consumers to look for the Atlantic colors (blue and red) when choosing motor oil (see Figure 19). Bids to establish consumer brand name loyalty were standard advertising fare of the 1920s, but Atlantic's ad went beyond basic formulas and attempted to introduce disinterested commentary and a visual narrative.[35]

Two 1922 Atlantic motor oil advertisements offer the clearest example of the N. W. Ayer Agency's early effort to establish an objective voice in their copy. Both advertisements link a large block of text with the image of a gas station worker. In one the worker raises his left arm as if to lean on the block of text. This depiction ties the text and the image together in such a fashion that one can view the text, "There is no finer motor oil than Atlantic Medium," as a statement by the worker. In the other ad the image of the worker is laid over a text block to achieve a similar effect. The worker's arm is extended to a portable Atlantic Motor Oil tank pump as if to show where a man should go for oil (see Figure 20). The remainder of the text in both advertisements stresses the reliability of Atlantic motor oil. These statements reinforce the message already displayed through the combination of image and text, and show that gas station workers considered Atlantic the finest motor oil. Further, the ads combine a new, image-based form of advertising with the old, text-based form.[36]

Look for the Atlantic sign, or the blue and red Atlantic portable tank-pump, at garages and other dealers where pride is taken in selling you the best motor oil obtainable.

Look for refinement when
choosing a "medium" oil

Asking definitely—insistently!—for Atlantic Medium is the finest guarantee of smooth-working health you can give your motor—the surest way of getting an oil that *remains* "medium" under the operating conditions of the motor.

It is very easy to give an oil a medium-bodied appearance as it pours from the can or measure. But it is *refinement*—that intangible essential hidden away in the multifarious processes of manufacture—that gives an oil the stability needed to resist the terrific heat of the cylinders, as well as the fluidity necessary to reach the close-fitting cooler surfaces of the bearings.

This book, "The Story of Motor Oils", will give any man a better understanding of the requirements and differences in motor oils—and of the vital importance of *quality*. Your copy is waiting for you. Simply write or 'phone for it, to The Atlantic Refining Co., 1211 Chestnut St. PHILADELPHIA

Atlantic Medium

is the product of the highest degree of refining skill. Its "body" is permanent—as permanent as body in oil can be. After use, even though diluted by the absorption of the fuel vapors and contaminated with the foreign matter found in the crank case, Atlantic Medium can be restored to its original condition—showing that the character of the oil is not appreciably changed by use.

Atlantic Medium consists of the best crude-oil hydrocarbons, refined to a purity that means definite stability, definite quality—definite assurance that your motor is always efficiently lubricated.

ATLANTIC
MOTOR OIL
Keeps Upkeep Down

19. Atlantic advertisement. N. W. Ayer Advertising Agency Collection, Archives Center, National Museum of American History, Smithsonian Institution, book 581.

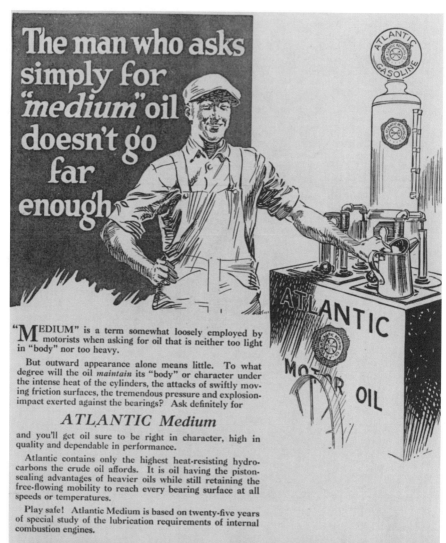

The man who asks simply for "*medium*" oil doesn't go far enough

"MEDIUM" is a term somewhat loosely employed by motorists when asking for oil that is neither too light in "body" nor too heavy.

But outward appearance alone means little. To what degree will the oil *maintain* its "body" or character under the intense heat of the cylinders, the attacks of swiftly moving friction surfaces, the tremendous pressure and explosion-impact exerted against the bearings? Ask definitely for

ATLANTIC *Medium*

and you'll get oil sure to be right in character, high in quality and dependable in performance.

Atlantic contains only the highest heat-resisting hydro-carbons the crude oil affords. It is oil having the piston-sealing advantages of heavier oils while still retaining the free-flowing mobility to reach every bearing surface at all speeds or temperatures.

Play safe! Atlantic Medium is based on twenty-five years of special study of the lubrication requirements of internal combustion engines.

ATLANTIC MOTOR OIL

20. Atlantic advertisement. N. W. Ayer Advertising Agency Collection, Archives Center, National Museum of American History, Smithsonian Institution, book 582.

In the same year Ayer introduced the concept of obtainability to Atlantic advertisements. The agency depicted Atlantic's widespread distribution and uniform quality as other measures of its reliability.[37] To sell this concept the agency prepared ads that focused on traveling. Linear movement through time and space is an inherent aspect of travel, and in 1923 the Atlantic advertisements turned to multipanel illustrations to denote this passage. These ads had an unrealized narrative quality that invited their readers to fill in the details of a motoring trip that necessitated a gas purchase. In 1923 Ayer also prepared a six-part series of advertisements on "things that count in buying gasoline." These ads used a storytelling technique about Atlantic gas stations and their employees that concentrated on their "courtesy, convenience, accuracy, cleanliness, safety, and promptness." Here the agency attempted to locate Atlantic's goods and services in cultural settings familiar to consumers. At the same time the advertisements sought to shape those settings, at least as far as gasoline products were concerned, in Atlantic's image. To this end Ayer also produced a number of localized advertisements depicting neighborhood gas stations. But all these ads used a large amount of text to further explicate the message of the illustration.[38]

Toward the end of the 1920s, Ayer began to experiment with simpler advertisements that used striking images and little text. These ads coexisted with others that used comparatively large amounts of text, but they demonstrate Ayer's interest in simplifying ads by abandoning text. In the 1930s these narrative trends and illustrative experimentations blossomed into comic-strip-style advertising.[39]

In 1930 Ayer placed several full-page comic advertisements in general automobile magazines. Most of the text in these advertisements was contained in word balloons, but they consisted of only one panel.[40] These advertisements were closer in kinship to the cartoons in *The New Yorker* than to comic strips. In the early 1930s this type of advertising was mostly limited to automobile magazines, but in 1934 Atlantic began to publish cartoon ads in newspapers. The highly stylized advertisements featured three identical men in top hats.[41] They presented Atlantic's themes of convenience, uniformity, and dependability in a stripped-down version (see Figure 21). From the volume of advertisements featuring these three characters, it appears that Ayer sought to make them a ubiquitous symbol of Atlantic gasoline. One ad even commented on the characters' omnipresence to make a favorable comparison with the availability of Atlantic gas.

21. Atlantic advertisement. N. W. Ayer Advertising Agency Collection, Archives Center, National Museum of American History, Smithsonian Institution, oversize box 51.

In 1936 Ayer adopted the comic strip format for Atlantic's advertisements. The first series of comic strip ads, published in April, used a realistic style to give Atlantic's products a cost-cutting and performance-enhancing image. These advertisements sold the importance of using Atlantic gas, oil, and lubrication to achieve the results obtained by cars in a road test. Atlantic's three top hatted men appeared in the last

22. Atlantic advertisement. N. W. Ayer Advertising Agency Collection, Archives Center, National Museum of American History, Smithsonian Institution, oversize box 52.

panel (see Figure 22). In September 1936 Atlantic began a second series of comic-strip-style ads. Ayer rendered the ads in a more comic style. The message of the second series was the same as that of the first: the "scientific" results of a road test could be repeated by using Atlantic's products.[42]

In this second series Atlantic portrayed a total image. The ads linked the company's three major consumer products, not just in the results of the road test but through the placement of their names on the little men's hats. Atlantic's three little men became the symbol and voice of the company. For instance, their series of comic strip advertisements carried a block of text signed by "Atlantic's 3 Little Men." Both series contained a plug for the radio show *The Atlantic Family,* thereby link-

23. Atlantic advertisement. N. W. Ayer Advertising Agency Collection, Archives Center, National Museum of American History, Smithsonian Institution, oversize box 53.

ing diverse instances of the company's advertising. Atlantic's advertising in the 1930s sought to draw customers to their products through entertainment. Ayer designed the printed media cartoons, comic strips, and the three little men to capture readers' attention, amuse them, and sell the product in easily digestible form.

In the beginning of the 1940s, the three little men were eased out of Atlantic ads as advertising adopted a more serious tone during the Second World War.[43] After the war Atlantic returned to advertisements that used comic art and word balloons but not the three little men or the comic strip format (see Figure 23).

The advertising N. W. Ayer prepared for Atlantic and the Hygienic Products Company in the 1930s shows how advertisers adopted the comic strip format and techniques to sell their goods and services. Advertisements that used comic art turned the process of consumption—advertisement, purchase, and use—into entertainment. By associating products with distinctive personalities, such as Atlantic's three little men, or by giving products voices through word balloons, advertisers bestowed personalities on inanimate commodities. The purchase of goods and services became then a matter of deciding which personalities to share one's life with. In this way comic strip art, with its emphasis on personality and voice, participated in the development of a consumer culture.

5 ENVISIONING CONSUMER CULTURE

"Gasoline Alley" and "Winnie Winkle,"
1920–1945

At a 1930 camp for teachers of high school English, the 400 participants from across the United States recognized one of their number as
bearing a striking resemblance to Walt Wallet, the central character of
the "Gasoline Alley" comic strip. One of those present, Julian M.
Drachman, was so stirred by the occasion that he wrote a prospectus
for American mythology arguing that comic strip characters were
"real national heroes" because, unlike the president's or Ralph Waldo
Emerson's, most Americans recognized their visage. Drachman attributed the appeal of the comic strip characters to their timelessness and
"vulgar," popular subject matter.[1]

This story demonstrates that in the 1920s comic strips became part
of everyday life in America. Americans incorporated the strips into
their daily existence simply by reading them, as well as through the
widespread licensing of characters and the use of the art form in advertising. Comic strips tied their audiences together as national communities of readers and familiarized them with the language of the art
form. Comic strips gave these readers a shared visual culture. Moreover comics depicted appropriate ways of incorporating a growing
number of commodities into their lives.

Although most of the pioneer comic strips had disappeared by the
1920s, a new crop of popular strips took their place. The longevity
of these strips, which included "Gasoline Alley" (1918), "Winnie

Winkle" (1920), and "Blondie" (1930), suggests not only that they appealed to a wide variety of readers but that, starting in the 1920s, those readers assimilated the strips into their daily routines. Furthermore in the 1920s Americans elevated some comic strip characters to the pantheon of folk heroes. For instance, newspaper editors who attempt to drop long-running features, such as "Gasoline Alley," meet fierce opposition. When the *Washington Post* redesigned its comic strip pages in 1991 and dropped "Gasoline Alley," it set up a special phone line to handle the several thousand calls it received. The level of engagement with comic strips displayed by the *Post* readers can be explained in part by the longevity of some strips.[2]

In the 1920s comic strip artists created a vision of America as a predominantly white, middle-class, consumer society. Most of the strips that adopted American society as a subject dealt with middle-class themes. Some strips, such as "Gasoline Alley," were clearly middle class; by contrast, "Winnie Winkle" dealt with working-class aspirations to middle-class "lifestyles." Other strips, such as "Polly and Her Pals," "The Gumps," "Tillie the Toiler," and "Fritzi Ritz," all held to the middle-class image. Although strips such as "Moon Mullins" and "Barney Google" offered a risqué vision of American life, their humor derived from, and was cast as, a transgression of middle-class values. William Henry Young argues that during the 1930s comic strips focused on middle-class mores to put the Depression at a distance and to suggest that an ordered society and individuals could overcome the threat the Depression posed to stability. By and large comic strips ordered society through an ethos of consumption.[3]

For this study I read every "Gasoline Alley" strip from 1918 to 1960 and every "Winnie Winkle" strip from 1920 to 1961. I also read numerous other strips from the period. The most popular strip of the 1920s and the 1930s, "The Gumps," frequently commented on appropriate means by which to acquire and use commodities, although in a more raucous style than either of the strips I discuss in detail. Compared with the content of "The Gumps," Frank King's focus on automobiles in "Gasoline Alley" puts the use of commodities into sharp relief. Likewise Martin Branner's "Winnie Winkle" offers the clearest expression of an artist's ambivalence toward the developing culture and the limited possibilities for criticism. The *Chicago Tribune–New York Daily News* syndicate distributed both strips, but their origins and subject matter were noticeably different. "Gasoline

Alley" began in the respectable *Tribune,* whereas "Winnie Winkle" started in the more down-market *Daily News,* a tabloid paper. It is possible, but not provable in the absence of comparative readership statistics, that these strips' syndication and appearance together in newspapers across the country gave comic strip pages a heterosocial character. The comics page then had the broadest appeal possible and individual strips broad enough appeal that their proximity to other strips offended no one.

"Gasoline Alley" and "Winnie Winkle" remarked on the increasing commodification of American society in the 1920s. The strips themselves signified that process. Not only were comic strips commodities but they often served as advertisements for the values and practices of consumer culture. By the mid-1930s there was a striking reciprocity between advertising, which used comic art to sell commodities, and comic strips, which displayed a vision of American life shaped by those commodities.

"GASOLINE ALLEY": THE DEPICTION OF A MIDDLE-CLASS CONSUMER "LIFESTYLE"

Frank King's "Gasoline Alley" first appeared in the *Chicago Tribune* on November 24, 1918. King and the editors of the *Tribune* conceived the strip as a humorous commentary on the growing use of automobiles by the paper's wealthier readers. But as the automobile industry grew, and the ownership of cars expanded beyond the wealthiest 5 percent of Chicago's population, the strip's focus shifted from gags about upper middle-class suburban males and their fetishization of cars to a general story line about middle-class lives that entailed the use of automobiles and other commodities.[4]

During the 1920s the automobile industry became, as the historian James Flink has noted, "the backbone of a new consumer-goods-oriented society and economy." By the mid-1920s the industry ranked first in production value; factories sold cars with a wholesale worth of over $3 billion. Flink states that Americans spent $10 billion in operating expenses to travel 141 billion miles in 1926. The manufacture and consumption of automobiles spurred the growth of the petroleum, steel, plate glass, rubber, and lacquer industries. The construction of streets and highways also contributed to economic growth. Martha

Olney, an economist, has demonstrated that annual expenditures on automobiles grew from $22.53 per household in the decade 1909–18 to $80.15 per household in the decade 1919–28. Comparative expenditures on furniture, the next largest category of spending, were $21.83 and $43.90 respectively.[5]

The *Tribune* both benefited from and promoted the growth of the auto industry. "Gasoline Alley" and the automobile section were part of the *Tribune*'s active support for the expanding automobile industry. For instance, the November 24, 1918, automobile section contained an article by George C. Diehl, chairman of the American Automobile Association Good Roads Board, who argued the need for a national highway system. Diehl contended that the construction of a highway system was a national planning priority and made sound economic sense because it would offer employment to those discharged from the army and war industries. The unstated assumption was that the automobile industry itself would continue to expand. The revenues from the growing number of advertisements for automobiles and related products probably accounted for the *Tribune*'s support for the automobile industry. The paper tried to capture as much of this market as possible through its regular Sunday automobile section and special supplements on major automobile shows.[6]

In the early 1920s there was a widespread growth in the amount of automobile industry advertising, particularly in papers directed at middle-class readers. Both the *New York Times* and *New York Herald* both increased their already considerable advertising linage for cars between 1921 and 1922. In Chicago the *Tribune* carried advertisements that promoted the automobile both as a plaything and as the triumph and lifeblood of American capitalism. For instance, a 1919 Standard Oil advertisement celebrated car ownership as providing "the means of satisfying one of [man's] most primitive instincts, a desire to venture forth like a true adventurer and enjoy the freedom of the country." A 1920 Continental Motors Corporation ad depicted the motorcar industry as "as much a part of America as the ground upon which we walk," a status achieved through individual stock holdings in auto firms, consumption, the application of scientific management and the techniques of mass production, and the romance of the industry's rapid development. In the early 1920s the *Tribune* also carried stories and advertisements about the construction of "a great hotel in the Loop for automobiles," the shortage of new Ford cars and trucks, and the growing use of cars as transportation to and from work for Chicago's "army of toil."[7]

"Gasoline Alley" was a product of, and a comment on, the growing significance of cars in American life. In its early incarnation the strip was one of several panel cartoons published together on the front page of the *Tribune*'s "Editorial-Automobile" section every Sunday. The initial episode was typical of the humor of the first year's panels. A group of men gathered in their rear alley garages comment on the problems associated with maintaining an automobile. In this episode each has a different solution to Doc's difficulty in starting his car. The number of solutions offered and the conviction behind the advice imply either that automobiles are troublesome machines prone to multiple failures or that none of the men truly knows what the problem with Doc's car is so they offer bloated and false certitudes. Both interpretations of the joke suggest that the maintenance of a car requires a qualified, or at least a knowledgeable, mechanic. The didacticism of this message, leavened as it was by humor, fit the strip's location in the automobile section, which provided consumer tips for motorists. For instance, car owners looking for better advice than that offered Doc could turn to the "Motordom" column in the same issue, which contained advice on cold weather engine efficiency.[8]

"Gasoline Alley" outgrew its Sunday panel format and became a daily comic strip in August 1919.[9] By this stage King had begun to develop a cast of characters, which included the couples Avery and Emily, Bill and Amy, and the bachelor Walt, in addition to Doc and his wife, Hazel. In the daily panels these characters flourished, and King constructed the strip's humor around their "personalities." The occupants of "Gasoline Alley" were middle class, and their creator conveyed this status in the commodities they purchased. In the early 1920s King depicted the characters as members of the upper echelons of the middle class. For instance, with the exception of Doc, who was indeed a medical doctor, none of the characters seemed to hold a job or engage in any occupation. A number had servants, and Walt Wallet advertised for a chauffeur in late 1920. The clearest symbol of the characters' social position was that they all owned cars.

Not only were automobiles the initial subject of the strip but they often provided the language through which the characters understood the world. In the November 16, 1920, episode Walt and Bill, on a downtown shopping trip, discuss the need for a set of sidewalk traffic regulations. Bill couches his regulations in terms of those governing the use of automobiles, thereby equating the laws governing the use of cars with desirable conduct on a shopping trip. On February 18, 1921, Doc examined Skeezix, a baby boy left on Walt's doorstep. King surely meant Walt's description of the baby as "that new acquisition of mine" and as possessing a "chassis and universal joints" to be humorous, but it transformed the terms of consumption, and the elements of a particular commodity, into an appropriate language to describe human life. King also showed Walt engaged in animistic conversations in which Walt told his old car that, just as an old horse would, it shed, growled, and had bad teeth.[10]

King was not alone in developing a metaphorical language about consumption and commodities. Throughout the 1920s the *Chicago Tribune* carried Christmas season advertisements for the Marshall Field department store that celebrated the "Cathedral of All Stores," comparing shopping at the store to having a religious experience. The *Tribune* also sang its own praises as a purveyor of a society whose sumptuous commodities surpassed those depicted in the Arabian Nights tales. *McCall's* magazine attempted to personalize its million and a half readers as the "residents of McCall Street" to sell that audience to national advertisers. As did King, these advertisements utilized customary forms of language and experience to represent the mass consumption of commodities. But King also reversed the convention and showed a commodity shaping the ways people thought and spoke.[11]

The depiction in "Gasoline Alley" of a relationship between the ownership of automobiles and social position, and the strip's demonstration of the way that commodity shapes language, conveyed an image of life as a style built around the consumption of commodities. The dynamic of the strip's history followed the construction of personality around a commodity. Walt and the other characters were shaped by the feature's original focus on automobiles. Their relationships to cars defined their selves and social positions. The personalities of the strip's characters were so tied to the consumption of automobiles that Walt Wallet's social position declined in rough proportion to the increased availability of cars. By 1928 King's story lines had depleted Walt's finances to the point where he took a job for the first time. Walt became a sales manager for a furniture company, and eventually the general manager, which allowed him to retain his middle-class status although at a less secure level.[12]

As King developed his characters, the strip shifted from gags about male fixation on automobiles to more socially oriented humor about the ways and means to consume commodities. This metamorphosis can be seen in the contrast between panels from 1919 and 1921. In the first panel, from January 5, 1919, when the feature appeared only on Sunday in the editorial section, anonymous women look down on a group of men gathered in an alley. The men are discussing the operation of automobiles and ignoring their wives' demands that they come inside to dinner. The second panel, a daily from February 5, 1921, shows Emily, Amy, and Hazel discussing their chances of persuading their respective spouses to purchase new cars. King framed the panel so that the women look out at their husbands, who are discussing Walt's new car. Rather than disparaging their husbands' interest in cars, the women are now interested in acquiring newer models. There is a suggestion of the status the women seek from car ownership in Doc's wife saying, "I want an enclosed car but Doctor is afraid I'll want him to dress up as my chauffeur!" This comment suggests that a closed car was more prestigious than an open car and so required a chauffeur as an appropriate mark of class position. Sinclair Lewis made much the same point in *Babbitt*: "In the city of Zenith . . . a family's motor indicated its social rank as precisely as the grades of the peerage determined the rank of an English family." A closed car designated top rank. This type of commentary on consumption became a mainstay of "Gasoline Alley."[13]

"Gasoline Alley" did not simply reflect the growing importance of consumer goods. Nor did it urge readers to consume with a single-minded passion. Instead the strip commented on consumption, delineating the appropriate ways for the middle class to consume. In late 1920 King drew a number of episodes that comment directly on behavior associated with the consumption of commodities. Most of these strips deal with the need to purchase gifts for others at Christmas. On December 12, 1920, Walt discovered that all his ideas for gifts had already been purchased for their intended recipients by other friends. In the December 16, 1920, strip Walt and Doc discuss the gifts the Gasoline Alley wives seek from their husbands.

Both these strips depict the exchange of purchased gifts as an appropriate practice at Christmas. They also show a richly commodified society and knowledgeable consumers. In the first episode Walt and his friends can choose from an array of products, including sweaters, automobile tools, spare parts and accessories, toy cars, and driving gloves. In the second episode Emily wants a new dining room set and Amy a fur coat. Doc's wife, Hazel, a more canny consumer, wants cash so that she can make her own purchases at the post-Christmas sales. Although consumption is important to the humor of both these strips, it is a given against which the joke is played out. In the first strip, Walt is able to guess what Emily is buying Avery for Christmas based on the purchases of his other friends. The joke is Emily's shock at the prescience of Walt's guess. In the other episode the joke turns on the way wives dictate patterns of consumption and Walt's relief that he is not married.

This latter episode may seem to be a critique of consumption as a feminizing activity. But other installments of the strip make it clear that King accepted consumption as a given and was mostly concerned with the means, and appropriate ways, of consuming. On December 18, 1920, Bill, Walt, Avery, and Doc gathered in a garage and reminisced about Christmases past. With its nostalgia about the domestic production of gifts, this episode might also be read as a critique of consumer culture, but the force of the strip is directed not at the purchase of gifts per se but at the high cost of those goods. This meaning is made clear in Avery's statement that "now'days you buy 'em and the war tax on what you get is as much as the presents themselves used to cost." Doc adds, "My father used to come home with four dollars worth of dress goods and make a hit. If I get by this year without a bond issue I'm lucky!" Bygone days could be recalled fondly. But the issue at hand was the cost of commodities, not a return to domestic production.[14]

King also commented on the qualities of consumer culture by contrasting the behavior of his characters. For instance, he depicted Avery as a miser who rarely made a purchase. One of the first daily episodes of the strip shows the other characters discussing Avery and Emily.[15] The consensus is that Avery is "close with his coin at times," "a nickel looks as big to him as a manhole cover," and Avery and Emily "can afford lots more" than those present. Avery's stinginess became a recurring joke in "Gasoline Alley." On January 28, 1923, Walt and Skeezix came across Avery at the automobile show, sitting in the most expensive car on display. Avery derived his pleasure not from the contemplation of new car ownership but from his estimate of the money he saved by running his old car, some $41,000 over twenty years. The expression on Walt's face in the final panel indicates that he thinks Avery's notion of pleasure through thrift is ill-conceived.

Walt spent his money freely. On July 12, 1921, he purchased a whole new wardrobe for a road trip to Yellowstone Park. On July 24, 1921, he spent sixty dollars on a calf because his adopted son, Skeezix, could not be parted from it. On November 15, 1921, King depicted Walt's house complete with a phonograph cabinet well stocked with records. The March 4, 1923, episode shows Walt with a new radio and Skeezix with an ample collection of toys.[16] King played on the contrast between Avery's stinginess and Walt's willingness to consume for the strip's humor. Avery's behavior transgressed that expected from members of the middle class, who the strip suggested should denote their class position through consumption of commodities. Although Walt made inappropriate purchases, such as his road trip outfit, which his friends laughed at, it was the particular items, not the act of consumption, that were the objects of humor and derision.

King occasionally expressed his unhappiness with features of modern society, but, as with those about domestic production, these comments most often took the form of nostalgic resignation rather than critical engagement with the direction of society. In the Sunday, November 13, 1932, episode, Walt and Skeezix discover that the country road on which they used to take their hikes has been replaced by a concrete road complete with billboards, hot dog stands, and a gas station. Walt states that "the old meandering lanes were charming but they must make way for progress. . . . but you can't help feeling a bit sorry that they're disappearing."

Two earlier installments of the strip made it clear just what King meant by progress. On July 28, 1929, he showed Walt reminiscing about his childhood and its lack of modern commodities. After Walt lists the things he did not have as a child—including movies, sodas, ice cream cones, automobiles, electric lights, telephones, vacuum cleaners, electric fans, and toasters—Skeezix asks if Walt knew George Washington. Walt's response is surprise. Skeezix's casual manner—he has his hands in his pockets and at eight years old is too young to be sarcastic—suggests that the question is a reasonable one for a child to ask. Walt's surprise, indicated in comic art style by his hat popping off his head, is at the question's appropriateness. To Skeezix, and to Walt when he thinks about it, a time without those commodities is as ancient as Washington's lifetime. The October 18, 1930, episode, in which Walt and Skeezix enjoy shop window displays, is further evidence that King understood progress as an abundance of commodities. He believed the charms of the countryside had to be sacrificed to this progress because it represented a social advance.[17]

King's single, and somewhat tentative, criticism of consumer culture was that it encouraged speculation. In December 1928 Walt, acting on a tip from Bill that the price would soon increase, purchased stock in the Rubber Keyhole company on margin. On December 16 Walt worried that if the stockbroker called his margin he would be finished. By December 21 the price of the stock had increased enough for Walt to buy expensive Christmas presents for the whole family. The company's stock improved steadily into 1929, and on January 10 Walt and his wife, Phyllis, discussed buying a new dining room outfit and a dressing table, even though two days earlier Walt did not have four dollars in cash for a kitchen mixer Phyllis wanted. (Walt and Phyllis had married on June 24, 1926.) Although the profit Walt expected had not yet been realized, Phyllis was determined to shop around. Shortly after, the stock slid from a high of 28.5 points to 17.0 points before Walt could sell.

On January 30, 1929, Walt figured the 11.5 points difference between the stock's high point and his selling price as a loss, but Doc pointed out that, because Walt had originally purchased at 15.0 points, the loss was only on paper. Doc, who had bought high and sold low, spoke of his own loss as "real money . . . not money chalked up somewhere on somebody's books but money I've earned, fingered and had a personal acquaintance with." Not altogether convinced by Doc's argument, Walt stuck to the notion that he had lost money (see Figure 24). The next day he discovered the true cost of his speculation when Phyllis revealed she had bought a bedroom set on time payment. In these episodes King presented stock speculation as promoting a false conception of wealth, which led to inappropriate expenditures. Both Walt and Phyllis risked their family's well-being by anticipating the profit to be had from speculation.

Phyllis's irresponsible purchase of a commodity on time payment may seem incidental to the broader message about the foolishness of playing the stock market, but the need to make payments was the only encumbrance the Wallets bore following their speculation. Given the

24. Frank King, "Gasoline Alley," *Chicago Tribune* (January 30, 1929).
© Tribune Media Services, Inc. All Rights Reserved. Reprinted with permission.

melodramatic quality of extended comic strip story lines, which re-warded virtue and punished wrongdoing, the time payments can be read as a form of penance.[18] Furthermore, King presented time pay-ment itself as an unwarranted speculation. When Phyllis made the arrangement to purchase the bedroom set, she too gambled on the in-secure prospect of wealth.

King made his condemnation of time payment as an imprudent means of consumption explicit in a story line featuring the adolescent Skeezix. In December 1938 Skeezix gave his girlfriend Nina Clock a radio for Christmas. Unable to afford the present outright, he arranged to pay for it at ten cents a day. By January 16, 1939, Skeezix had discovered that although it had not seemed like a hardship at the outset, the payment became a burdensome daily worry. At the end of January the payment had become the source of all his troubles, so Skeezix arranged to sell a half interest in his dilapidated car to cover the debt. His loss of the exclusive ownership of his car disrupted his courtship of Nina and undermined his friendship with Gooch, to whom he had sold the half interest. Both these stories suggested that consumption is prudent only when the means are readily available.

King's condemnation of time payment was ironic because the ex-pansion of installment credit was linked to the automobile industry that he celebrated. Martha Olney demonstrates a connection between the automobile industry and the expansion of purchases on time pay-ment. Beginning with the General Motors Acceptance Corporation

(GMAC), established in 1919, automobile manufacturers set up finance companies to smooth seasonal fluctuations in consumption and so hold down the cost of adjusting production. These companies financed the purchase of automobiles through time payment. They enjoyed so much success—in 1929 consumers owed five times as much for car purchases as they had in 1922—that entrepreneurs established finance companies to provide credit for other consumer goods. In 1920 there were fewer than 100 finance companies. By 1928 there were over 1,000. In the 1920s "most credit extended to households to facilitate purchases of durable goods was installment credit extended by . . . sales finance companies." Household debt increased at a rate of fourteen dollars per year in the 1920s as opposed to an annual increase of four dollars before the First World War.[19]

"Gasoline Alley" was not an analysis of America's economic development in the 1920s. Rather in it Frank King commented on the appropriate ways and means of incorporating commodities into middle-class lives. King depicted characters whose personalities shaped the products they consumed and the way they consumed them. But at the same time the centrality of commodities, particularly automobiles, to the strip's origin and format governed King's development of the characters' personalities. "Gasoline Alley" depicted middle-class lives in which the consumption of commodities constituted both the core of individual character and the basis for social relations among characters. The strip implied that one should only undertake consumption when one had the wealth to do so at hand. In King's view ownership of specific commodities should designate standards of wealth. His sole criticism of consumer culture was that it tended to promote ways of consumption that undermined the function of commodities as symbols of status.

King understood the link between the array of new commodities and the disappearance of the old countryside, which he described as progress, but he drew no conclusion about the contemporaneous availability of time payment. Mass production, particularly in the automobile industry, was responsible for the new commodities King alluded to, and time payment facilitated the mass consumption of these products. "Gasoline Alley" demonstrates his uncertainty about the formation and display of middle-class identity in the face of mass consumption. But the strip was not critical of the consumption of commodities.

A comic strip may seem an unlikely place to look for a critique of consumer culture. Nonetheless a contemporary of King's, Martin Branner, did develop a muted criticism in his strip "Winnie Winkle."

"WINNIE WINKLE": WORKING-CLASS ASPIRATION AND CONSUMPTION

"Winnie Winkle" commenced publication September 21, 1920. The daily and Sunday comic strip ran in the *New York Daily News* and the *Chicago Tribune,* and the Tribune-News Syndicate distributed it to other newspapers across the country. "Winnie Winkle" was the first of a genre of "working girl" comic strips. Until 1943 it carried the subtitle "The Breadwinner." The strip's creator, Martin Branner, set it in a large city, sometimes named Central City but most probably based on New York City, where Branner lived. The title character worked to support her lazy, stay-at-home father (Rip), her mother, and her adopted brother (Perry). Winnie was a stenographer who desired a middle-class life. In the early years of the strip Branner contrasted Winnie's aspirations to the behavior of Patricia (Patsy) Dugan, an office colleague who became Winnie's friend on October 6, 1920. Patsy's language, appearance, and outlook were clearly working class.

There are no accounts of Branner's inspiration for the strip, but it started less than a month after the enactment of the Nineteenth Amendment, which gave women the right to vote. Branner also created the strip against a backdrop of substantial changes in the status of women's work. The shortage of labor during America's involvement in the First World War led women to enter occupations previously closed to them. The expansion of the nation's businesses in the first two decades of the century, with the attendant centralization of control and management, created office jobs that women filled.[20] It is not clear that Branner favored or opposed women working and voting. The only sure thing "Winnie Winkle" can tell us about its creator is that he used the changing position of women as a source for his humor. His underlying theme was the place of women in society. He depicted American society as one in which the consumption of commodities was expanding, driven in part by a working class that sought to emulate the middle class. He associated this move to a consumer culture with a feminine desire for display.

Branner was not alone in regarding consumption as a feminine activity. In the 1920s a consensus existed among advertisers that women purchased between 70 and 85 percent of manufactured commodities. As Charles McGovern of the Smithsonian Institution has pointed out, advertisers depicted consumption as a social movement through which women could exercise their rights. Although couched in a language of political entitlement, the rights advertisers envisaged for women were often limited to product selection. For instance, "Are Women People?" a 1928 advertisement for the weekly magazine *Liberty,* presented an image of women made over by the consumption of commodities into people who read the same magazines as men. This advertisement posited that women became people, with personalities, through consumption. But whereas advertisers employed the vision of women as consumers to sell products, Branner incorporated the notion into a nascent criticism of consumer culture.[21]

The creator of "Winnie Winkle" developed his critique in three recurring story lines. First, he satirized Winnie's consumer-driven personality and behavior in stories about her search for social advancement and an appropriate mate. Second, he memorialized a fading vaudeville era and counterposed it to Hollywood's centralized production of entertainment. Finally, Branner criticized the commercialization of culture and depicted celebrity product endorsement as "sissy." In all these stories he exhibited a concern about the suitability of public display and the construction of images. "Winnie Winkle" commented on the appropriateness of incorporating commodities into working-class lives.

Branner's lampoons of Winnie's attempts to break into a higher class counterposed effete, richly commodified, middle-class lives with working-class lives. In his presentation the middle class derived pleasure from purchased commodities whereas working-class leisure was more organic in its use of available resources. Branner favored the twelve-panel Sunday version of the strip for these stories. The basic plot of these episodes had Winnie embarrassed by the low-class antics of either her work-shy father or more often her adopted brother, Perry.[22] For instance, on June 25, 1922, Winnie and Perry attended a society party aboard a private motor yacht. Perry, who went under protest, decided to join his friends who were swimming off a pier that the yacht passed. He stripped off his clothes and dove into the water. Perry's actions mortified Winnie, who tried to retrieve him only to compound her embarrassment by falling into the water herself. Branner derived a large part of the episode's humor from Winnie's humiliation. But the joke depended on contrasting the kids swimming off the pier and enjoying themselves with Perry, who was unhappily dressed in a formal suit.[23]

Perry hated the suits Winnie made him wear and took every opportunity to rid himself of them and engage in rough play with his friends. For instance, in the Sunday, May 14, 1922, episode, published before the strip went to a full page on Sunday, Perry exchanged his suit with another boy so that he could play baseball with the neighborhood gang. Perry frequently discarded the clothes in which Winnie dressed him to play, work, or simply avoid embarrassment.[24] Winnie generally punished Perry with a beating for his refusal to conform to her notion of appropriate dress and behavior, but occasionally her brother had the last laugh. In the May 21, 1922, episode Perry is spanked for doing "vulgar" dance steps with children at a society party. But at the end of the strip, to Winnie's puzzlement, Perry wins favor with the young society women by showing them the steps. The deliberate irony here is that Perry had picked up skills on the streets that gave him entrée to the social set Winnie hoped to enter.

Branner also presented Winnie's search for romantic love as an attempt to improve her class position and her ability to consume. He cast these stories as melodramas in which Winnie failed to find happiness because she had compromised her virtue in the selection of a suitor. For Winnie, love was only possible with a professional gentleman, such as a banker, doctor, or lawyer, who could provide for her needs. She rejected an inappropriate elderly, wealthy suitor but considered a stockbroker twenty years her senior until he was revealed as a potential bigamist. The forty-three-year-old stockbroker Kenneth Dare first appeared in the strip on October 9, 1922. On November 3, 1922, Branner revealed to the readers, but not to Winnie, that he was already married. Dare and Winnie made marriage plans before Dare's wife exposed him as a would-be bigamist on January 24, 1923.[25]

Branner used Mike Mulligan, Winnie's hick suitor, who first appeared in the strip on May 14, 1923, to highlight her tendency to associate wealth with happiness. Mulligan was an ill-dressed backcountry dweller. Short on manners, grooming, and intelligence, he was long on patience. For years he ignored Winnie's disinterest and pursued her relentlessly. Branner used Mulligan to lampoon fads. In December 1923 he had Mulligan go to college to play football. He picked up the language and mannerisms of the college set but was clumsy in their use. Although she was not interested in marrying Mulligan, Winnie enjoyed his attention and became somewhat jealous when she discovered his attraction to a college "widow." Eventually, when another man appeared on the scene, Winnie got tired of Mulligan's boorish behavior, and he disappeared from the strip for two years. When Mulligan next entered the strip in January 1926, he had acquired some social graces and a good deal of money. His newfound wealth appeared to come from his "interior decorator" business, but in fact he was a bootlegger. Branner apprised his readers of this fact a week after Mulligan reappeared. Attracted by his riches, Winnie agreed to marriage, only to be left at the altar, once again, when Mulligan was arrested.[26]

The Mike Mulligan stories followed much the same theme as the Kenneth Dare installment. Branner created the comedy of the college episode, and the melodrama of the bootlegger chapter, around the basic fact that Winnie wanted to get married but could not find the right partner. His use of the melodramatic formula set up a contest between Winnie's virtue and her consumer desire. Although Winnie desired a husband with the means to buy what she wanted, she disapproved of intemperance and bootleggers. The bootlegger episode also showed the failure of an attempt to legislate morality because most of the citizenry willingly colluded with Mulligan's activities. Branner's primary audience lived in the "wet" cities of New York and Chicago, and the story was probably written to their tastes. But his audience could have read the bootlegger episode, and Winnie's temperate attitude, as a demonstration of her hypocrisy given her relentless need to consume. In short, Winnie's virtue could not be squared with her need to consume.[27]

Branner liked to make fun of Winnie's consumer desire. The October 7, 1928, strip shows Winnie so distracted by shopping that she neglects a friend's baby she is minding and even mistakes a rubbish cart for its pram. The episode works on two levels. First, Branner employed the straightforward gag of Winnie mistaking a trash cart for a baby carriage. Then he drew on the underlying humor of Winnie's distraction. This component played off the notion of a woman's vanity and her need to consume to enhance her self-image. Branner reinforced his gendering of vanity and consumption by having only men laugh at Winnie.

Winnie's concern with her appearance fit the visual design of the strip. Every day Branner drew her wearing a new outfit. He resolved the dilemma of Winnie's ability to afford such fashion on her modest income in a 1921 series of strips. Responding to a reader's letter, Branner had Winnie followed by Gum-Shoe Gus, a detective, to ascertain the source of her extensive wardrobe. On October 28, 1921, Gus discovered that Winnie had a deal with a fashion shop to "model" their clothes in the strip. It was a clever story. Branner justified his depiction of Winnie in new outfits every day, indicated that readers were interested in the strip and that he paid attention to them, and made a self-referential claim that Winnie was an important enough comic strip celebrity that she modeled clothes on contract. After this story ran Branner occasionally drew Winnie modeling clothes rather than providing a gag or story continuity.[28] He also used Winnie's modeling status in a number of story lines from the 1920s to the 1950s. In the 1950s Winnie parlayed her modeling experience into a job, first as a dress designer and eventually as the chief executive of a large fashion house.[29] But "Winnie Winkle" was Branner's conceit from start to finish. If the structure of the strip demanded that Winnie be fashionably dressed, then Branner's ridicule of women's vanity was directed at his own image of women and his own success as a comic strip artist.

Although Branner criticized the economy of display embodied by consumer culture as feminine, he drew strips that reinforced the desirability of feminine women. For instance, in a series of strips in June 1924 Winnie toyed with the idea of getting a flapper haircut. On June 11 she decided to get her hair bobbed, "and be done with it." But while she waited her turn at the hairdresser's, Winnie observed two effeminate men discussing their "boyish" bob cuts. Disturbed by this gender transgression, Winnie left the salon expressing her intention to get a "longshoreman style" cut.

Another 1924 episode offers more evidence that Branner understood the effect of feminine display and used it to win and hold an audience for "Winnie Winkle." In the November 22 strip Winnie comments on the difficulty a "working girl" has in keeping a good "reputation these days," and proclaims, "Heavens knows I'm leading a clean life!!" (See Figure 25.) The gag turns on the definition of "clean." Winnie leads a "clean" life in the sense that the strip shows her taking a bath, but in taking a bath she exposes herself to the reader's gaze, which was surely not "clean" in terms of respectability. Branner entitled the strip "A Saturday Soliloquy," indicating that the episode should be read as a scene in a play in which an actor addresses the audience directly. Such scenes generally provide the audience and

25. Martin Branner, "Winnie Winkle," *Daily News* (November 22, 1924).
© Tribune Media Services, Inc. All Rights Reserved. Reprinted with permission.

character with a shared knowledge that excludes other players, in this case the intimacy of Winnie's bath. Branner not only created the scene for readers' titillation but labeled it as such.

The artist later recalled that he had had to be careful about the settings in which he showed Winnie dressing and undressing. So long as he depicted her behind a bolted door, the strip would pass syndicate censorship. As had Outcault and earlier comic strip artists, Branner set out to appeal to a heterosocial audience. He created love stories and depictions of fashion for the strip's female readers and jokes about her consumer desire and burlesque displays for the male readers. The only readership figures for "Winnie Winkle" show that slightly more males than females read it. In the November 22 strip Branner showed there was nothing unconscious about his use of feminine display to sell the comic strip as a commodity.[30]

Branner was not totally at odds with consumer culture. As well as having had a prurient interest in the display of the female body, he seems to have enjoyed radio. At the end of 1924 Winnie received a radio as a Christmas present. Branner used the occasion for a series of gags about the difficulty of tuning in stations and the hazards of wearing headphones. At first he treated radio as a fad to be lampooned, then passed over for another subject. On January 10, 1925, after exhausting his radio gags, Branner shifted to jokes about crossword puzzles. But radio was no fad. As had comic strips it became part of everyday life. An annotation on the January 2, 1925, strip contained in

Branner's file suggests that he got his first radio at this time.[31] An amateur enthusiast made it for him.

Branner returned to the radio as a subject of gags on a number of occasions. On November 17, 1926, he had Winnie fall in love with a radio announcer's voice. He spun this gag out for three weeks before Winnie discovered the announcer was ugly. By this stage the family radio had speakers. On September 16, 1928, much to his family's annoyance, Pa invented an early form of Muzak by piping the radio's sound through the house heating ducts. On September 13, 1931, a radio show made Pa believe there were burglars in the house. On June 11, 1933, the violence in a dime novel Pa read to Perry overshadowed the action of a radio serial. These strips were lighthearted jabs at the intrusion of modernity into private life. But the 1933 episode suggests that Branner thought radio simply a new medium of entertainment no worse than dime novels. Nonetheless, he retained a nostalgia for those dime novels.

Branner's nostalgia for a bygone era was most evident in his stories about vaudeville. He preferred vaudeville to movies and stated his case for the former a number of times in "Winnie Winkle." For instance, on March 8, 1925, he reproduced a Haverly's Minstrel Bill and commented that the show beat moving pictures. In September 1927 he had Winnie win a movie contract in a bathing beauty contest. She discovered the film company was simply a front for the moneymaking activities of the beauty pageants. But she stayed in Hollywood and eventually got a starring role in a movie through the intervention of a producer whose son's life she had saved. Winnie became engaged to the director of the movie, but he misdirected her performance because he was secretly involved with another actress. Eventually, the director cut Winnie's scenes from the movie, which proved to be a flop, robbed the producer, and left for Australia. Winnie hung on in Hollywood for another month before deciding to return home on March 7, 1928.

Because she had no money she had to work her way back across the country. One of Winnie's jobs on this trip was with a vaudeville revue. In contrast to Hollywood's back-stabbing atmosphere, Branner presented the vaudeville players as a tight-knit group. But his vision of vaudeville was not idyllic. After two weeks on the road the manager of the troupe disappeared with the takings. Branner then recalled vaudevillians' struggle against management by mentioning the White Rats, a 1910s attempt by performers to establish a union. His implied criticism was that management was to blame for the demise of vaudeville. Winnie eventually arrived home at the end of May 1928.[32]

But Branner was not done with vaudeville. He returned to the subject eleven years later, when Winnie attempted to earn a living as part of a dance act. Between April and August 1940 Winnie participated in an effort to revive vaudeville. But even though the troupe was self-managed, the revival failed, and Winnie, her partner, and agent headed for Hollywood. No matter how Branner tried to recapture the joys of vaudeville, he was forced to acknowledge its passing and replacement by Hollywood's movies. In the language of the comic strip Branner could only express resignation to this fact and present it as an inevitable development. But he did try to criticize other forms of consumer culture that, like Hollywood, employed the images of well-known figures to sell commodities.[33]

Branner used "Winnie Winkle" to ridicule celebrity endorsements and image-centered advertising. In April 1929, during one of Winnie's many stints working for the Bibb's Pin Company, Branner introduced Ad Lib, an advertising expert. To increase the sales of pins Ad Lib embarked on a campaign featuring Winnie as the Bibb's Pin Girl. Her image appeared on billboards and garnered much attention. But the attention was for Winnie, not for Bibb's pins. Letters poured in to the company offering Winnie substantial sums to endorse other products. Mr. Bibb ordered her posters covered up, which gave Branner the chance to rework some visual gags from the days of *Puck* and other late nineteenth-century illustrated humor journals.[34]

Branner's notion that advertising campaigns featuring spokespersons were ineffectual, because they focused attention on the person not the commodity, echoed the sentiments of the Hearst executive Hawley Turner.[35] But Branner took his critique a step further and suggested that celebrity endorsement was dishonest. On May 1, 1933, gazing out her office window, Winnie found herself attracted to the visage of the Doggy shirt collar model on a billboard. Wishing to meet the model, Jack Linyard, she persuaded Mr. Bibb to hire him for an advertising campaign. When Jack called on her at home on May 17, Winnie discovered that he did not use any of the products he advertised. Pa, who had overheard the conversation, commented, "That guy ain't on th' level!!" Winnie, too, was troubled by Jack's deception and broke off with him.

For Branner the dishonesty of celebrity endorsements was unmanly

26. Martin Branner, "Winnie Winkle," *Daily News* (June 14, 1935). © Tribune Media Services, Inc. All Rights Reserved. Reprinted with permission.

and a sign of a feminized, consumer culture. He made this opinion clear in an indictment in 1935. The story line at the time featured Marty Mulligan, Mike's cousin, a contender for the world heavyweight boxing championship. On June 14 Marty, who had won enough fights to make him a celebrity, signed five contracts and told Winnie, "Me fortune's made!" Rather than fight contracts, Marty had signed for a cigarette testimonial, a talcum powder ad, a vaudeville engagement, a silk pajama testimonial, and a nightclub job. His actions disgusted Winnie, and she said he was a "big sissy." (Paradoxically, the strip appeared directly above a celebrity endorsement for Welch's grape juice, see Figure 26.) The episode's critique seems to have been directed at cigarette testimonials. At the time the R. J. Reynolds tobacco company was running a series of comic-art-format advertisements for Camel cigarettes in the comic section of the *Daily News* and other newspapers across the country. These advertisements featured endorsements by leading sporting figures, such as the champion golfer Gene Sarazen.[36]

Branner had not licensed any of his characters to promote commodities, which added credence to his critique.[37] But it was ironic that this artist who drew a strip about a "working girl" found the most damning thing about consumer culture to be its unmanliness. If males who lent their images to advertisements were "sissy," and if consumption was a female activity, then what of Branner, whose career was based on creating images of women for national consumption as a comic strip? He may have thought of himself as a male commentator on the feminization of culture, but he encouraged and benefited from the promotion of this culture.[38]

Even when Branner directly criticized celebrity endorsements, he did nothing more than counterpose one celebrity image who was against them, Winnie Winkle, with another—say Gene Sarazen—who made endorsements. On the one hand, Branner's critique of celebrity endorsements reduced them to an inappropriate mechanism for promoting consumption because they were dishonest or unmanly. On the other hand, he probably regarded his favorable treatments of vaudeville and radio as appropriate because his stories flowed from honest contact with the forms. But there was little difference between advertisement and comic strip presentations of these commodities. The advertisements containing celebrity endorsements of products and comic strips such as "Winnie Winkle" both promoted a vision of life as a matter of style in the selection of commodities.

Branner's and King's commentaries on consumer culture were ordered by the status of their strips as commodities. For instance, as "Gasoline Alley" developed from a weekly gag panel to a daily comic strip, King had to adapt to the form of syndicated strips and develop a cast of characters. His original conception of the feature as a humorous observation on the effects of automobiles on middle-class lives determined these characters' personalities as consumers of automobiles and other commodities. In King's stories the characters were figureheads for a commentary on the appropriate ways and means of consuming. Branner's humor in "Winnie Winkle" relied on Winnie's consumer desire. But he created her desire to sell the comic strip. "Winnie Winkle" replicated the images of the consumer culture Branner criticized. King and Branner created their comic strips for a mass commercial medium. "Gasoline Alley" and "Winnie Winkle" were commodities that advertised the values and practices of consumer culture in the form of entertainment. Comic strip artists such as King and Branner promoted a vision of American life that centered on obtaining and consuming commodities. They envisioned consumer lifestyles.

6 THE COMIC BOOK

Comics as an Independent Commodity, 1939–1945

In the 1930s entrepreneurs associated with the printing industry created a new medium for comic art, the comic book. Originally confined to reprinting newspaper comic strips, the fledgling comic book publishers discovered that original material featuring costumed superheroes would increase their sales. Harry Donenfeld, the publisher of Detective Comics, Incorporated (DC), was the first to recognize the appeal of superheroes in 1938, when his *Action Comics,* which featured Superman, outsold DC's other titles. Donenfeld expanded publication of superhero character comic books. The other publishers soon followed suit, and by June 1941 over a hundred comic book titles sold at a combined rate of 10 million copies a month.[1]

The comic book business expanded just as comic strips had attracted a national audience at the turn of the century. Both comic strips and superhero comic books featured characters with distinctive appearances. Both media projected intimacy, giving readers the sensation of looking at and listening in on a private world. But comic books added a new dimension to the commodification of the art form. Whereas comic strips depended on newspapers to reach their market, comic books were packaged as discrete products. The production and consumption of comic art independent of newspaper distribution transformed its market.

Comic book publishers assumed they had a younger audience than those who purchased newspapers, and the initial content and marketing of comic books demonstrated this belief. Comic book creators were also young. Many of the artists and writers of comic books were in their teens or early twenties, a situation compounded when the United States entered the Second World War and many of the older creators joined the services.

THE INVENTION OF THE COMIC BOOK

Comic books owe their existence to the success of comic-art-style advertising in the early 1930s. Beginning in 1897 with the Yellow Kid, publishers marketed collections of comic strips, bound in cardboard, through toy stores and bookshops. Prices ranged from twenty-five to sixty cents, depending on the books' size and quality of paper and binding. In 1929 the Dell Publishing Company issued *The Funnies*, a tabloid-format comic magazine containing original comic strip material, but this publication ceased after a year and a half. These ventures did not produce the distinct comic book form.[2]

Not until the 1930s did companies publish works that had the properties of comic books. In 1933 Harry Wildenberg, an employee of the Eastern Color Printing Company, which printed Sunday comic sections for East Coast newspapers, convinced Gulf Oil to publish a tabloid-size comic to give away at its gas stations. After some experimentation Wildenberg developed a reduced format that allowed two pages of comics to fit on a standard tabloid sheet of paper. With the help of another Eastern employee, Maxwell (M. C.) Gaines, Wildenberg persuaded Procter & Gamble to commission *Funnies on Parade*, a thirty-six-page book of comic strip reprints, measuring seven and a half by ten and a half inches with a paper cover, to be given away as an advertising premium. This was the first comic publication with the physical attributes of a comic book. Eastern also produced comic book premiums for Kinney Shoe Stores, Milk-O-Malt, Wanamaker stores, Wheatena, and Canada Dry. All Eastern's comic book premiums reprinted popular newspaper comic strips.[3]

Wildenberg and Gaines's packaging of comic strips as advertising premiums followed the widespread use of comic art in advertisements in the 1930s. Manufacturers using these premiums wanted to attract the interest of children, who they hoped would induce their parents to buy the advertised product. For instance, the *Chicago Tribune* comic supplement for Sunday October 1, 1933, contained an advertisement for a free comic book from Wheatena. The ad read:

> Free! *Famous Funnies!* A book of popular comics. Boys and Girls— here's a book you'll all like. 32 pages including Mutt and Jeff, Hairbreadth Harry, Joe Palooka, Reg'lar Fellers and a lot more. . . . You can get a copy of this book free. Just fill out the coupon and mail it to us with the top cut from a package of Wheatena. If you haven't a Wheatena package in your home, ask mother to get you one from her grocer the first thing tomorrow morning!

Eastern produced *Famous Funnies,* which contained no advertising, as a free premium for various products. They printed between 100,000 and 250,000 copies for each product. The story goes that, struck by the demand for the comic books, M. C. Gaines believed they could be sold direct to the public through newsstands. In late 1933 he placed several dozen copies of *Famous Funnies,* with ten cents price stickers, on newsstands. When the newsstands sold all their copies in two days, Gaines convinced his employers that comic books had commercial promise. The story is probably apocryphal, though, given that contemporary sources, including Gaines himself, made no mention of it happening.[4]

Lacking experience as a magazine publisher and distributor, Eastern approached Dell with the idea for a salable comic book. Dell commissioned Eastern to produce 35,000 copies of a sixty-four-page book priced at ten cents a copy. This comic book, also entitled *Famous Funnies,* sold through chain stores. But Dell decided not to proceed with the book after potential advertisers objected to both the poor-quality paper and the use of reprint material. In early 1934 the Eastern Color Printing Company decided to publish a comic book itself and arranged for the distribution of 250,000 copies through the newsstands controlled by the American News Company. The first issue of the new book, the third comic book to bear the title *Famous Funnies,* containing sixty-four pages and priced at ten cents, appeared on newsstands in May 1934 with a cover date of July. Eastern lost $4,000 on the first issue, but by the twelfth issue the comic book netted $30,000. Eastern reversed its early losses by selling advertising space. The first issue contained no advertisements, but by the ninth issue the comic contained full-page ads for Buck Rogers 25th Century casters, Daisy repeater rifles, and Iver Johnson bicycles. As had Eastern's previous efforts the third version of *Famous Funnies* consisted entirely of reprints.[5]

Other companies associated with the comic strip business soon joined Eastern as comic book publishers. King Features and United Features, two of the largest comic strip syndicates, began to publish comic book reprints of their material in April 1936. Another major syndicate, McClure, prepared comic strip reprint material for Dell's *Popular Comics*, which began in February 1936. But a newcomer to the comic field, Maj. Malcolm Wheeler Nicholson, issued comic books consisting of original material, an innovation that led to the development of superhero characters. He published his first title, *New Fun Comics*, in late 1934. Nicholson, a military adventurer and pulp fiction writer before his brief career as a comic book publisher, was eased out of his company in 1936. The new publisher, Harry Donenfeld, produced comic books that focused on individual subjects. The first of these, *Detective Comics*, appeared in January 1937. *Detective Comics* became the flagship title of Donenfeld's company, which would be known simply as DC. The detectives of the title did little detecting and mostly engaged in fisticuffs and gunplay. Coulton Waugh, a comic art historian and a contemporary comic strip artist, noted that *Detective Comics* "looked and felt different from the others." Waugh regarded *Detective Comics* as a "bold and sensational" step away from the format of newspaper strips.[6]

SUPERMAN AS TRADEMARK

The first issue of *Detective Comics* contained two stories, Slam Bradley and Spy, by the Cleveland writer-artist team of Jerry Siegel and Joe Shuster. Siegel and Shuster had earlier sold a story to Nicholson's *New Fun Comics*, which appeared in the October 1935 issue under the pseudonyms Leger and Reuths. As teenagers in the late 1920s and early 1930s, both Siegel and Shuster had immersed themselves in science fiction, pulp magazines, and movies. In 1934, at age twenty, the pair had already devised their most famous character, Superman, but had been unable to sell him to a comic strip syndicate or a comic book publisher. In 1938 Harry Donenfeld decided to publish another single-theme comic book concentrating on fast-paced action stories. He purchased the Superman material and all subsidiary rights from Siegel and

Shuster. The first issue of DC's new comic, *Action Comics*, dated June 1938, featured Superman on the cover and as the lead story.[7]

According to Donenfeld, the first three issues of *Action Comics* did not have outstanding sales, but the fourth issue saw a significant increase. Its publisher conducted a newsstand survey and found that children asked for the comic book "with Superman in it." Donenfeld told a reporter in 1941 that he made sure subsequent issues of *Action Comics* displayed Superman prominently on the cover. Thereafter sales rose at a dramatic rate; by 1941 *Action Comics* sold 900,000 a month, a figure close to 10 percent of the monthly sales for all comic books. Superman became a ubiquitous comic art figure. In January 1939 the McClure syndicate began distribution of a Superman comic strip to 230 newspapers. In the summer of 1939, DC started a quarterly comic book composed solely of Superman stories. When the company converted it to a bimonthly book in September 1940, *Superman* had a circulation of 1,250,000 and grossed $950,000 for the year.[8]

When Jerry Siegel and Joe Shuster invented Superman, they created both a character and a type, the comic book superhero, around which comic book publishers could sell a product and expand their nascent market. Superman's success inspired a plethora of costumed superhero characters. The most familiar and lasting of these characters were DC's Batman and Wonder Woman, and Timely/Marvel Comics' Sub-Mariner, the Human Torch, and Captain America. But these were just a few of several hundred costumed adventurers who first appeared in the pages of comic books in the late 1930s and early 1940s. According to Coulton Waugh, the number of comic book titles published in this period peaked at 160 in 1940, then fell to 100 by the summer of 1942. But sales increased slightly from 10.0 million a month in 1940 to 12.5 million a month in 1942. These sales produced $15 million of revenue annually, of which 75 percent came from children's purchases. By the mid-1940s more than 90 percent of children aged six to eleven across the country read an average of fifteen comic books a month. Between ages twelve and eighteen, readership fell to 80 percent and the average number read fell to twelve a month.[9]

Between 1933 and the early 1940s, entrepreneurs transformed comic books from an advertising medium into a commodity and created a new market of mostly young readers. Comic-art-style advertising had already blurred the distinction between such art as entertainment and as advertising. Comic art had always been a commodity,

albeit one sold through another medium. But comic books transformed the market for it. The comic strip, an entertainment feature
within the larger newspaper, became an advertising tool for a variety
of commodities. With comic books the art form became an entertainment commodity in its own right.

Superhero characters, such as Superman, became synonymous with
the comic book form. Recognizing the commercial value of their characters, publishers moved to protect their property. For instance, Donenfeld's Detective Comics, Inc., sued Bruns Publications for copyright
infringement when the latter published a comic book featuring Wonder Man, a superhero whom DC successfully argued derived from
Superman. To give Superman further protection, DC registered his image, name, and the title logo of the comic book as trademarks. Trademark registration gave Superman a legal identity as a business symbol,
an asset or property, above and beyond that of a fictional character.
This status guaranteed DC's ownership and control of Superman for
all time since trademark protection, unlike copyright, can be renewed
perpetually. To ensure its trademark, DC labeled all of its comic books
"a Superman DC publication," even though most did not contain a
Superman story.[10]

Assured of its property rights in Superman, DC embarked on an extensive marketing campaign. The company licensed a Superman radio
series, which commenced broadcast in early 1940 and was soon heard
three nights a week across the country. In 1940 DC produced a special
World's Fair Comic featuring Superman, and 36,000 children attended
the fair on Superman Day. A Macy's Christmas Superman exhibit
drew an audience of 100,000. In 1941 Paramount Pictures released
the first of twelve Superman animated short features produced under
license from DC by the Fleischer studio. In that year DC also licensed
thirty-three Superman products, including a doll, a toy ray gun, two
wind-up mechanical toys, and a wristwatch.[11]

Detective Comics was not the first organization to promote a comic
art character as a business symbol. But DC's control of Superman and
the use of trademark rather than copyright law to protect its property
interest differed significantly from other efforts at marketing comic art
characters. Whereas Richard Outcault retained control of his creation
Buster Brown, and licensed companies' use of the character, Jerry
Siegel and Joe Shuster, the creators of Superman, lost all their rights to
DC. Outcault's legal rights in Buster Brown derived in part from his

personal rights as the character's creator. Detective Comics' ownership of Superman rested on their registration of the character as a business symbol and the successful denial of Siegel's and Shuster's authorial rights.[12] In the hands of a corporation, Superman was more important as a business asset than as a fictional character. Once DC recognized Superman's status as a commodity, they defined and sold him as a product in all his incarnations. By 1941 Superman was not so much a character who helped sell comic books as a product that comic books sold.

Superman's transition from a "character," however commercial, to a product occurred not just in his legal status but in his story lines. In his first two years Superman was both a simpleminded liberal reformer and an isolationist. In the first issue of *Action Comics* alone, he saved a woman mistakenly condemned for murder, confronted a wife beater, and discovered a plot by a U.S. senator to embroil the country in a European conflict. In the comic's second issue Superman prevented this outcome by giving the arms manufacturer behind the plot a firsthand taste of war. Exposed to gunfire and trench life, the manufacturer reformed. Superman also brought the opposing generals together so that they might realize their differences were artificial. Another story, in *Action Comics'* third issue, had Superman confront the owners of a dangerous mine. In his guise of Clark Kent, a reporter for "a powerful newspaper," he threatened to reveal the unsafe conditions. When this strategy failed to move the owner, Superman exposed him to the dangerous conditions in the mine, after which he quickly recognized his folly and vowed to improve the mine's safety.

Occasionally Superman resorted to more drastic measures to ensure change. In one story he destroyed a slum so that "the authorities" would be forced to replace it with the "splendid housing conditions" offered by "huge apartment projects." In another story he destroyed an automobile plant because its shoddy products and the owner's greed caused the loss of human lives.[13] The early Superman stories were a version of New Deal politics for juveniles. Jerry Siegel acknowledged that Hollywood's social consciousness films of the 1930s and Franklin Roosevelt's fireside chats inspired the reform content of his early stories.[14] But Superman's social activism dissipated as his owners and creators grew aware of his potential as a commodity.

The contrast between two stories, one from November 1938 and the other from January 1941, demonstrates the ascendancy of Superman's status as a commodity over any other feature of the character. In the first story, which appeared in the sixth issue of *Action Comics*, a businessman, Nick Williams, claimed to be Superman's manager and sold commercial rights to Superman's name. Products endorsed included a breakfast cereal, gasoline, automobiles, bathing suits, physical development exercises, movie rights, and a comic strip. But Williams, an unscrupulous promoter out to make a fast buck, did not represent Superman. The story presented the promoter as a criminal who not only stole Superman's name for profit but threatened to kill Lois Lane. Siegel and Shuster used Nick Williams to criticize Harry Donenfeld's appropriation and commercialization of their character. The pair had signed away all rights to Superman and in 1938 were contracted employees of Donenfeld, who paid them ten dollars for every comic book page. At the time they wrote the Nick Williams story, Siegel and Shuster were negotiating with Donenfeld for the right to do a comic strip version of the character for the McClure syndicate. The story may have suggested licensing possibilities to DC, but that was probably not Siegel and Shuster's intention.[15]

By 1941 Siegel and Shuster were more interested in Superman's commercial possibilities. They had reached a lucrative agreement with Donenfeld; in return for working exclusively for DC, they received twenty dollars a page and 5 percent of all other Superman royalties.[16] In a story in the January 1941 issue of *Action Comics*, Superman invented a krypto-ray gun that developed pictures in the camera and projected them on a wall. The story was little more than an advertisement for a new toy ray gun manufactured by Daisy. Daisy advertised the Superman "Krypto-Ray Gun" in the September 1940 issue of *Playthings*, the trade journal of the toy industry. The ad promised a special campaign by Daisy that would help retailers "cash in." The January 1941 issue of *Action Comics* appeared on the newsstands in November 1940, in time to create a demand for the toy.[17] Siegel and Shuster set aside any claims to Superman's integrity as a literary character in favor of his commercial worth.

THE SUPERHERO AS WHOLESOME SYMBOL

Superman sold more than ray guns; in the early 1940s he sold the virtues of comic books themselves. In 1941 DC offered Superman as a symbol of the quality and wholesomeness of their comic books. The company's actions followed a campaign against comic books launched by Sterling North, the literary editor of the *Chicago Daily News*. North argued that comic books were violent, crude, and an assault on the sensibilities of children. He accused parents of an indifference to their children's reading matter and denounced comic book publishers as "completely immoral." North's attack did not result in a widespread public campaign against comic books. The New York State legislature enacted Section 22-a of the Code of Criminal Procedure, which allowed municipalities "to seek an injunction against the sale or distribution of comic books which are obscene, lewd, lascivious, filthy, indecent or disgusting," but no prosecutions were brought under the law.[18]

Nonetheless DC, whose offices were in New York City, took steps to protect their business. To establish the virtuousness of their products, DC hired an advisory editorial board of child psychologists, educators, and welfare workers. Around this time DC also enacted standards for Superman stories that prohibited—among other things—the destruction of private property other than that belonging to a villain. By mid-1941 villains were no longer auto plant owners but mad scientists or common criminals. Members of DC's editorial advisory board included Robert Thorndike of Columbia University Teachers College; Ruth Eastwood Perl, a psychologist; the former heavyweight boxing champion and Catholic Youth Organization director Gene Tunney; C. Bowie Millican of the English Department at Columbia University; and Josette Frank of the Child Study Association. The company also employed Whitney Ellsworth as a copy editor to correct Jerry Siegel's grammar and syntax. DC proclaimed that they had always had a rigid policy of selecting material that upheld the "standards of wholesome entertainment." The company explained that with the increased number of comic book titles on the market, it was important "to discriminate between them," and that the Superman/DC symbol served as a guide "to better magazines."[19]

The same issue of *Action Comics* that introduced the editorial advisory board contained the first "Supermen of America" page, which ran in the bimonthly *Superman* comic book as well. The feature offered readers advice from Superman on the conduct of their lives. The first column, on "self reliance," set the tone for Superman's new role as the defender of traditional American values. The column evoked the authority of God, Country, Freedom, Liberty, Father, and Mother to proclaim the necessity for children to be self-reliant. Superman told readers, "It is your duty to yourself, your God, your country and your parents to care for yourself in body and mind. You must accept your share of responsibility thereby lessening the weight of responsibility from the shoulders of others. At home, in school on the playground— be Self-Reliant."[20]

The advisory board and the "Supermen of America" column positioned DC as a trustworthy publisher that sought to inculcate a sense of morality among youth. The company probably created the two features more to convince parents of the wholesome nature of Superman/DC comics than for the stated purpose of ensuring their moral quality. DC even commercialized the morality page. The first "Supermen of America" page contained an advertisement for the new Superman Club. Over 250,000 children joined the club at a cost of ten cents, for which they each received a pin and a Superman decoder, which suggests that the column succeeded in teaching children to be self-reliant consumers, or at least convinced parents of the harmlessness of DC's products.[21] At the same time DC, and Siegel and Shuster, adjusted Superman's story lines in a way that, if it did not make them moral, probably made them more acceptable to parents.

Detective Comics used the Second World War to make Superman not simply a defender of virtue and wholesomeness but synonymous with American democracy. In 1941 Siegel and Shuster, who had attacked armaments manufacturers as the cause of war in Superman's first two episodes, created a series of stories in which Superman confronted fifth columnists and saboteurs working for an unnamed European power bent on destroying America's munitions plants. These stories established DC's commercial trademark, Superman, as a defender of American democracy. For instance, in the May 1941 issue of *Action Comics*, Superman battled an enemy invasion that had been facilitated by fifth columnist campaigning against rearmament. The story's opening panel declared, "The fate of the United States hangs in the balance as Superman . . . ventures forth to engage the foe in a gigantic battle with the future of democracy at stake!" DC also gave *Action Comics'* covers a militaristic hue. The April, June, August, September, and December 1941 issues all showed Superman combating Germanic soldiers or saboteurs. All six 1941 *Superman* comic books contained war-related stories about saboteurs, terrorists, and fifth columnists.

Siegel and Shuster's stories were neither prophetic nor distinct. The United States had begun war preparations soon after Germany

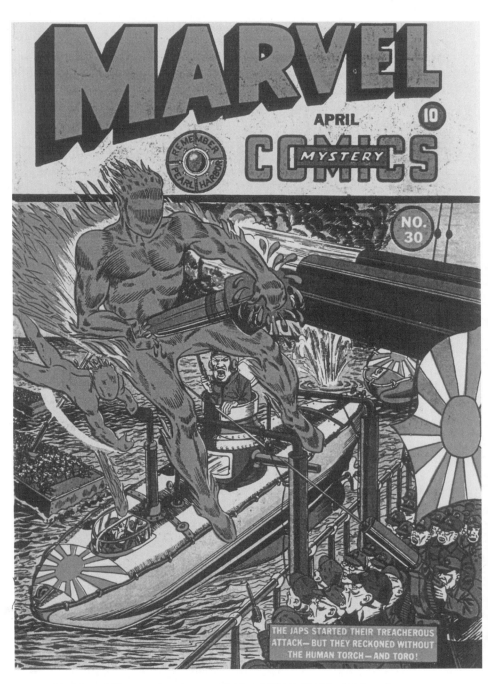

27. *Marvel Mystery Comics,* no. 30 (April 1942). TM & © Marvel
Characters, Inc. All rights reserved.

invaded Poland in 1939, and many comic books addressed the threat of war between the United States and the Axis powers.[22] As far as comic book publishers were concerned, the prospect of America's entry into the Second World War may have been fortuitous, giving them a dramatic and exciting context in which to set their stories. Many publishers tried to forestall criticism of comic books by having their most violent characters battle fascists. For instance, Timely Comics' superhero characters, the Sub-Mariner, the Human Torch, and Captain America, fought Axis foes before and after the United States entered the war (see Figure 27).[23] But as I will show, throughout the war DC's characters embodied American values by staying at home and expressing confidence in the fighting ability of the American people. Whereas Timely's characters marched off to war and slew America's opponents, DC's two major superheroes, Superman and Batman, stayed in the United States and fought domestic opponents of democracy. Moreover, DC did not simply use the war to sell comics, it used comics to sell the war.

COMIC BOOKS AND WORLD WAR II

Between 1941 and 1944 sales of comic books doubled from 10 million to 20 million copies a month despite paper shortages.[24] Much of this increase can be attributed to the reading habits of servicemen. In 1944, 41 percent of men between the ages of eighteen and thirty read comic books regularly, which researchers defined as more than six comic books a month. In military training camps, 44 percent of men read comic books regularly and 13 percent read them occasionally. Female readership of comic books, which from ages six to seventeen was only 4 to 6 percent less than male readership, dropped to 28 percent for women between eighteen and thirty. At age thirty-one and over the difference between male and female readership returned to 4 percent. In that age-group 16 percent of men and 12 percent of women read comic books. The disparate rates of male and female readership between ages eighteen and thirty suggests that military service, predominantly a male activity, led to increased comic book readership.[25]

John Jamieson's semiofficial account of the Army's Second World War Library Service attributes a general increase of readership among soldiers to boredom. The Army operated a library service in order to maintain morale. As Jamieson put it the alternatives were apathy, discontent, drunkenness, and a soaring rate of venereal disease. As part of its attempt to provide soldiers with a regular supply of reading material, the Library Service organized a set of magazine subscriptions for companies posted overseas. In 1943, when this system proved cumbersome, the service began the centralized distribution of an overseas magazine set. The *Superman* comic book was one of the eighteen titles in this set and the only comic book. Through 1943 and early 1944 the Army distributed at least 100,000 copies of this comic book every other month, or about 10 percent of the comic's sales. The Army dropped *Superman* from the magazine set in 1944 because it was readily available at post exchanges. Comic books outsold the combined circulation of *Reader's Digest, Life,* and *The Saturday Evening Post* by a ratio of ten to one at these exchanges.[26]

Comic books were one of the most regular contacts overseas servicemen had with America. In 1944, as a result of the Soldier Voting Law, the War Department determined the magazines for which soldiers had shown a preference through paid subscriptions and readership.[27] Comic books accounted for over a quarter of the 189 soldier preference magazines. A major in the Southwest Pacific combat zone observed the precious status of comic books among the men on troop transport ships. U.S.O. hostesses noticed that comic books were the first items to leave their tables. A photograph in *National Geographic* of a soldier with a pile of comic books showed that servicemen accumulated large numbers of the books, and officers reported that they passed among men until they fell apart.[28] In Australia, where a great number of American troops took rest and recreation, and where American comics were banned because of currency exchange restrictions, a local company published *Gripping Yank Comics* in the hope of cashing in on the servicemen's demand for American comic books. The deception that this was an American comic book was enhanced by the "price in Australia" label. This comic book was successful during the war but ceased publication in 1945, when the Americans went home.[29]

Comic books owed their popularity among soldiers to a number of obvious features. They were cheap, easy to read, and light to carry. But two other factors probably contributed to their ubiquitous presence. First, the extraordinarily high prewar readership of comic books by young males may have given them an iconic status during the war. In owning and reading comic books, soldiers likely possessed a small part of what they fought for. Such an explanation parallels the war correspondent John Hersey's report that the Marines on Guadalcanal fought the war for "a piece of blueberry pie," "scotch whisky," "dames," "books," "music," and "movies." It also echoes the sentiments of an American soldier who wrote home that he fought to maintain the right to drink Coca-Cola. Robert Westbrook has recently demonstrated that pinups served as iconic representations of soldiers' private obligations to the war effort through their evocation of a generalized American womanhood in need of protection. Comic books may also have echoed pinups as reminders of home and like them given the individual soldier a reason to fight.[30] Second, comic book story lines accounted for their standing among soldiers. Many comic books contained witless tales in which American forces easily defeated their foes. But the most popular comic book characters, Superman and Batman, appeared in stories set exclusively on the home front. These two characters both supported the war effort and protected American society from its domestic opponents. As well as reminding soldiers of home, the content of these comic books probably helped reinforce the purpose of the war in their minds.

Comic books from DC were the most popular of the war era.[31] Part of this success was due to the company's identification of Superman and Batman with the war effort, which established them as defenders of an American way of life. In the December 1941 issue of *Action Comics,* the "Supermen of America" page said readers could express their confidence in the U.S. government "and the Principles of Freedom and Justice and Democracy" by purchasing U.S. Savings Bonds or Stamps for Defense. The message from Superman stressed that, although young people could not hope to purchase bonds, defense stamps could be had "for as little as twenty five cents." The column also urged readers to "do a little salesmanship job on the older folks."

This bond promotion was part of a campaign by Henry Morgenthau, secretary of the Treasury, "to use bonds to sell the war, rather than vice versa." In a radio address during the spring of 1941, Morgenthau explained that there were quicker and easier ways for the government to raise the money than through bond issues. But the Treasury had decided "to give every one of you a chance to have a financial stake in American democracy—an opportunity to contribute to the defense of that democracy."[32] Once the United States entered the war,

Morgenthau continued the bond program to give civilians a sense of participation in the war effort.

Throughout the war DC supported the Treasury's bond campaign. The company donated space in the comic books for advertisements directed at children and used war bonds themes for comic book covers. For instance, in the summer of 1942 DC comics carried a message from Morgenthau to the "boys and girls of America" reminding them that every stamp they bought would help their male kin defend the country. In 1943, after the Treasury Department's market research discovered that anti-Japanese messages sold bonds, the cover of *Action Comics* featured Superman promoting the slogan "Slap a Jap with War Bonds and Stamps." A *Batman* cover showed a smiling Batman firing a machine gun with a plea to "Keep Those Bullets Flying! Keep on Buying War Bonds & Stamps!"[33]

Most wartime issues of DC's comic books carried an advertisement for war bonds and stamps. These promotions of war bonds made Superman and Batman salesmen for the war effort and suggested that a democratic society was something citizens could buy their way into. Furthermore by 1944 a large number of adolescent comic book readers had money to spend. A census survey of April 1944 revealed that one in five schoolboys ages fourteen to fifteen had jobs, as did two in five sixteen- to seventeen-year-olds. By the latter age 35 percent had left school and were working full-time. Girls were not as likely to be employed, but of sixteen- to eighteen-year-olds a third had jobs.[34]

Detective Comics, Incorporated's promotion of war bonds was part of an intensive national campaign to sell the war that encompassed a variety of businesses and practices. Many businesses promoted war bond purchases. Entertainment industry figures lent their celebrity to bond drives. The singer Kate Smith sold $40 million of bonds in a sixteen-hour radio session on September 21, 1943. The Hollywood starlet Loretta Young sold bonds at a Kiwanis meeting, and the pinup girl Betty Grable auctioned off her stockings.[35] Moreover the bond campaigns fit with the convergent thinking of the advertising industry, government, and consumer advocates on the notion of citizens as consumers.

Beginning in 1939, with George Sokolsky's *American Way*, the advertising industry consciously depicted consumer choice as a constituent element in and guarantee of political democracy. Advertisers had associated advertising and consumption with American values throughout the 1930s, but Sokolsky's book raised the conception to an ideology of "the American Way." During the war the industry's War Advertising Council acted as a clearinghouse for both the government's and private industry's wartime propaganda. Much of this advertising addressed citizens as consumers, urging them to cut back on their consumption of goods and cooperate with government measures to increase war production. The consumer advocate Caroline Ware saw responsible consumption as a "contribution to the war effort."[36]

Even before the United States entered the war, advertisements propagated Sokolsky's notion of a citizen-consumer democracy. A November 29, 1939, *Good Housekeeping* advertisement in the *Chicago Tribune* linked democracy to the availability of a wide variety of commodities. Under the heading "No Permit . . . No Stockings," the ad counterposed an anonymous dictator state, which limited women's purchase of stockings to six pairs a year each, against the United States, where a consumer could choose from 745 makes of hosiery and buy as many pairs as she could afford. *Good Housekeeping*'s version of democracy required more than simple consumer choices. Those choices needed to be guided by the testing and approval of products conducted by the magazine's laboratories. Democracy entailed the consumption of appropriate commodities, to which the sure guide was the *Good Housekeeping* Seal of Approval.

During the Second World War, this conception of appropriate consumption was used by many advertisers, including those selling war bonds. For instance, a number of department store advertisements for war bonds linked their purchase to an appropriate and responsible style of consumption. A May Co. advertisement for war bonds in the May 4, 1943, edition of the *Los Angeles Times* suggested that American soldiers were dying for want of ammunition. The voice of a dead soldier stated:

> I was ready to die for freedom, but you've robbed me of a soldier's death . . . some of you didn't believe I was important enough to live . . . if you had, I would have had bullets. I died because some of you didn't have enough faith in my living. I died because you, John Smith, had to buy a new house. I wanted a new house too, but your freedom came first. Those pickets in your new white fence cost me my life.

Elsewhere in the same edition of the *Times,* May Co. advertised lingerie and other women's apparel. These two advertisements posited that consumption had to be tempered by a commitment to those defending the right to consume. The dead soldier, and May Co., objected to John Smith's purchase of a new house, which was inappropriate consumption. But May Co. wanted its customers to buy both bonds and clothes, an acceptable mix of purchases.[37]

An advertisement for Foreman & Clark, another Los Angeles retail store, acknowledged, "Sure we like to make money. But we have greater love for the American way of life." To prove their commitment the store, its employees, and all 5 million retail store workers would buy and sell war bonds to defeat "hitlerism and tojoism." A January 1945 advertisement for yet another Los Angeles department store, Bullock's, defined the American way as "the unregimented right of every American to earn a living for himself and his family according to his desires and capabilities . . . unhampered by paternalistic and enterprise-stalling regulations. It is not synonymous with Capital. Neither does it mean Labor. The American Way is a unity of effort Capital and Labor . . . for the common good." Bullock's judged the American way superior to any other economic system of production and distribution because it provided "the highest standard of living in the world."[38]

Other wartime advertisements stressed their products' contribution to the war effort. For instance, the ads for Rainer ale suggested that it was proper for Americans to consume ale because the British allies deemed beer essential to their national morale, and the American brewing industry contributed $386,000,000 in federal taxes, equal to the cost of eight aircraft carriers or a thousand bombers. Other advertisers held out the promise of a richly commodified postwar era but warned Americans to temper their optimism and win the war so as to win the peace. A March 1943 Consolidated Vultee Aircraft Corporation advertisement foresaw a postwar global economy driven by a new air-age geography. The ad promised that in this new geography, distances would be measured by elapsed flying time rather than miles. It suggested that "the peace we win must be built on a clear understanding of this new global geography and how it can work *for* us." America had to be "supreme in the air—to win the war today, to win peace tomorrow."[39]

A September 13, 1943, advertisement in the *Los Angeles Times* for *Popular Science* warned, "Keep your shirt on, America"; too many saw Victory as "too close, too easy." *Popular Science* advised Americans that they could count on "better stuff, of better materials" but not to "count on them too soon." A life insurance industry advertisement published in the *Times* on September 9, 1943, listed seven practical steps to build a "*personal* post war world." The first step was to buy war bonds, the second to pay taxes, the third to buy life insurance. The overall message was to spend less and save more. The ad suggested that "good American families" understood that even though war production put more money in their pockets, "self-denial" was important in "the battle for a future not only secure, but full of the good things of life."[40]

There was a striking similarity between the rhetoric of these advertisements and the content of stories featuring DC's two most popular characters, Superman and Batman. General works on American society between 1941 and 1945 and internal histories of the comic book industry note that comic book superheroes and publishers contributed to the war effort. But these accounts only touch on the sale of war bonds and the superpatriotism of some superheroes, such as Timely's Captain America; they do not consider the content of Superman and Batman stories.[41] Superman and Batman stories often stood in marked contrast to the covers of DC's comic books. In addition to their war bonds covers, DC published a large number of battle action covers and patriotic scenes. For instance, between May 1942 and April 1943, eight of the twelve *Action Comics* covers dealt with the war. On the cover of the May 1942 issue, Superman fought a Japanese plane; on the November cover he opposed a German submarine. Superman also appeared with the U.S. flag on the cover of two issues of *Superman*.[42] DC's covers gave the superheroes a military tone, but this characterization was largely symbolic and set off by the stories inside, which were about civilian life. Throughout the war DC published only one story in which Superman battled enemy armed forces, and even this occurred on American soil.[43] Except for an explanatory note in *Superman*, no. 25 (November–December 1943), DC avoided the issue of Superman's service. But in mid-February 1942 the comic strip version of Superman had Clark Kent fail his physical by accidentally using his X-ray vision to read the eye chart in the next office. Shortly after, on March 11, Superman told the U.S. Congress that "the American armed forces are powerful enough to smash their treacherous foes without the aid of Superman." DC kept Superman out of the war because there was no way to explain why someone with his powers could not put an end to it.

Batman also stayed out of uniform, although he offered no excuse for his failure to join the armed services. Unlike Superman, and most other costumed heroes, Batman had no super powers. Batman was the secret identity of the playboy industrialist Bruce Wayne, who as a child had witnessed the murder of both his parents. Wayne then devoted his life to fighting crime and trained his body and mind for the task. If there was anything super about Batman, it was his psychotic drive to destroy criminals. Batman stories implied that he, as did Superman, believed the American people, empowered by democracy, needed no help from him on the battlefront to defeat fascism. Both characters dealt with fascist spies and saboteurs, and both *Batman* and *Superman* comic books ran stories about military training and on the need for greater public cooperation with the government's war effort. These stories stressed that "America's secret weapon [lay in] the courage of the common soldier" and that the war amounted to "Your Battle, Your Future, Your America!!!"[44]

But DC published fewer than 15 of these stories among the over 500 Superman and Batman stories that appeared during the war. Most of these stories featured villains and criminals and had little military content. The powers and established characters of Superman and Batman probably limited DC's options for involving the two heroes in the war effort. But these limitations proved fortuitous as the company aligned the characters with home front campaigns for responsible consumption—an alignment that led to Superman's identification with the American way.[45]

The majority of war-era Superman and Batman stories depicted a universe in which American soldiers fought to establish world peace while the two superheroes helped to maintain a domestic order that supported the country's military endeavors. Most stories showed an American society relatively free from war-related strife and shortages but plagued by mad scientists, supervillains, and common criminals. Although the comic books encouraged the purchase of war bonds and supported paper, rubber, and metal salvage drives, writers and artists continued to present the United States as a consumer society with a bright future.

Consumption was not an explicit theme. Rather it formed the social backdrop in which stories were set. DC's writers and artists used Superman and Batman in stories about seemly manners of consumption in a war economy. Sometimes the company published comic book covers that affirmed consumption as a way of life. For instance, the No-vember–December 1942 cover of *Superman* showed him carrying a car in which a family had all the accoutrements of a picnic. The comic appeared at the time of national concern over the shortage of rubber, and the cover showed tireless wheels. Amid the war-related covers of most of DC's comic books in 1942–43, this illustration attests to the validity and continuity of the family's way of life, even under war con-ditions. The cover was a celebration of ordinary American life enjoyed by the children and older folk pictured in the car and defended by men of service age, absent from the illustration. Life went on despite the absence of tires, sons, and fathers. The concurrent absence of service-men and tires suggested that the two would return together.[46]

Unlike war themes, which DC limited to covers and "Supermen of America" pages, writers created parables of consumption for Super-man and Batman tales. Most Batman stories counterposed criminal consumer desire with virtuous acquisition of commodities through work. Batman dealt with a series of foes obsessed with acquiring gems and other high-priced gewgaws. Many Batman stories began with full-page surrealistic representations of these commodities, which sug-gested that it was an unreal desire for extravagant wealth that moti-vated criminals.[47] Batman, who was in fact a millionaire, eschewed such wealth except insofar as it enabled him to combat crime. More important, he instilled the values of hard work and responsible con-sumption in his ward, Dick Grayson, who as Robin fought criminals alongside Batman. In a 1944 story Bruce Wayne puzzled over Dick's frequent absences from the house, only to discover that he had taken a job as a telegram boy to raise money for a birthday present because he had spent all his allowance on war bonds.[48]

Superman combated a somewhat more powerful group of criminals and mad scientists than Batman did. But in general the plots of stories featuring the characters were much the same. In a May 1942 story Superman confronted a group of secondhand car dealers who, in search of quick profits and under the influence of a mysterious figure known as the Top, sold faulty vehicles. Confronted by mounting accidents and bad publicity, most of the dealers sought to reorganize their busi-nesses and run them in legitimately. They were able to do so when Superman broke up the Top's criminal organization. The story associ-ated criminal activities with illicit business practices. It also linked le-gitimate business practices, in this case the fair trade of commodities in the market, with patriotism as the dealers, "freed from the Top's evil influence, . . . donated their imperfect cars" to the government's scrap metal drive for national defense.[49]

One Superman tale, "The Million-Dollar Marathon," stands out from other comic book stories as a commentary on appropriate and responsible consumption under wartime conditions. The story centered on Roger Treadwell's attempt to spend a million dollars in twenty-four hours so that he might inherit a larger sum. This theme figured in a number of mass entertainment forms. Several film versions of *Brewster's Millions,* four of which preceded the Superman story, used this plot device, and Cliff Sterrett used a similar theme for an extended story line that began in his comic strip "Polly and Her Pals" on November 20, 1927. All these stories centered on the struggle of the principal character to maintain his virtue, or unassuming manner, under the pressure of tremendous wealth and unrestricted consumption. But the Superman story stands out, for, unlike Brewster's and Polly's Pa's, Treadwell's virtue never falters, largely because he enlists the aid of Superman to accomplish his task.[50]

Treadwell, a research physician at a children's hospital, planned to give his inheritance to the hospital but faced "the most perplexing problem he [had] ever encountered" in determining how to dispose of the initial million dollars, which he had to spend in single purchases of a thousand dollars each. His only idea was to buy a thousand dollars' worth of war bonds. With Lois Lane's help, he summoned Superman, who informed Treadwell, "It's a lot of money and you mustn't waste it . . . even though you can't give it away you'll have to spend it where it will do good." Superman then proceeded to buy laboratory supplies, save a mortgage that was about to be foreclosed, underwrite small businesses, and bid on art treasures at a sale to aid servicemen's families. In his most ambitious project Superman bought the material to construct a ship for an expedition in search of rare plants that would provide drugs to cure sick children. He even persuaded the government bureaucrat in charge of wartime resource allocation of the ship's importance to the war goal of caring for children, America's "best safeguard for the future." With Superman's aid Treadwell met the requirements of his inheritance, and all monies went to the children's hospital.[51]

"The Million-Dollar Marathon" recast familiar tales about the dangers of unrestricted consumption as a parable of responsible wartime expenditure. But it was hardly a criticism of consumption as such. Approximating the numerous versions of *Brewster's Millions* and "Polly and Her Pals," the Superman story figured consumption as a test of virtue while inviting readers to enjoy vicariously its pleasures. The story's prologue informed readers that they would be "excited . . . over this amazing story of a man who wanted . . . to get rid of that magnificent sum, all within twenty-four hours! And if you think it's easy to spend and keep on spending, $41,666 an hour, nearly $695 a minute, you'll get a new slant on high finances as you watch Superman."

Other Superman tales also depicted a highly commodified society. For instance, in a 1943 story Lois Lane obtains a mink coat and goes on a shopping spree for accessories in six department stores, all of which are abundantly stocked. In 1944 DC prepared a special Superman comic book as a Christmas promotion for Bailey's department stores in Cleveland. The message of this twenty-page book was that American servicemen fought the war to ensure the right to celebrate Christmas. The accompanying advertising copy made it clear that Americans observed Christmas by purchasing and distributing large numbers of gifts, preferably from a Bailey's store. Shortly before the war's end a *Superman* cover depicted a domestic scene complete with refrigerator, anticipating a postwar America with a plentiful supply of consumer goods.[52]

Comic books were advertisements that tied the promise of a society abundant in consumer goods to the defense of the nation.[53] But they were also commodities themselves. Between 1941 and 1945 American servicemen purchased more of these commodities than any other reading material. The Second World War helped make comic books and the most popular superheroes, such as Superman, American institutions. Sales of comic books expanded to 60 million copies a month in 1947. The Superman/DC line of comic books was the most popular, selling an average of 8,500,000 copies a month in that year.[54] DC expanded their marketing of Superman as a product. For instance, in the late 1940s the company licensed Superman movie serials and a television show that promoted him as a hero who fought for "Truth, Justice, and the American Way." DC also protected their market by suing the publishers of another comic book superhero, Captain Marvel, for copyright infringement. The success of this case removed Superman's major competitor and ensured DC dominance of the comic book field throughout the 1950s.[55]

28. *With Victory* (Washington, D.C.: Congress of Industrial Organizations, 1944). © AFL-CIO.

Comic book publishers, particularly DC, bound the war effort, democracy, consumer culture, and their superheroes together in the comic book and sold the total package as a commodity. Comic books illustrate the close connection in American society of democratic ideals and consumer culture. Superheroes' promotion of the war effort by upholding American values, such as the sanctity of private property and the pleasure of shopping, and the consumption of those heroes through comic books, demonstrate how corporate America has defined democracy in terms of the consumption of commodities. So successful were Superman and comic art in promoting the American way that even relatively militant unions produced comic book stories about democracy and consumption. In 1944 the Congress of Industrial Organizations (CIO) published a million copies of a comic-book-format pamphlet, *With Victory*, that looked forward to a richly commodified postwar America provided workers organized and voted to ensure the government took appropriate action (see Figure 28). According to this comic, every soldier at the front dreamed of "a good job, a good wife, a good car, and some good kids." Reading comic books was one way soldiers sustained that dream throughout the war.

EPILOGUE

The Persistence of Comic Art as Commodity

From 1896 until the 1950s, the market for comic art expanded with little encumbrance. But in the 1950s a brief disruption occurred in its steadily increasing place in American culture. Fredric Wertham's *Seduction of the Innocent,* published in 1954, highlighted the violence of the crime and horror comic books that had sprung up after the Second World War and drew a simple causal link between comic book readership and juvenile delinquency. Ignoring the distinctions among comic books, he attacked superhero and funny animal comic books with the same ferocity as horror and crime books. Wertham's work galvanized criticism of comic books, forced publishers to establish a code of self-censorship, and energized Estes Kefauver's Senate Subcommittee to Investigate Juvenile Delinquency. Among comic book enthusiasts Wertham's efforts to ban comic books, and the publishers' establishment of a code limiting violence, are held to have destroyed a "Golden Age."[1]

The production and sale of comic books declined after Wertham's attack, and many comic book publishers went out of business. But the industry survived and began to recover as early as 1956, when DC relaunched one of their lesser superhero characters, the Flash.[2] In 1961 Stan Lee of Marvel Comics added a new twist to the superhero character. Lee's heroes were neurotic individuals who sought therapeutic redemption through superhero do-gooding. Marvel's comic books found a large audience, and the industry boomed.[3]

If comic books suffered a temporary setback in the 1950s, comic strips retained their place in American culture, and syndicates introduced new features. One of the most successful comic strips of all times, Charles Schulz's "Peanuts," featuring Charlie Brown and Snoopy, began on October 2, 1950. "Peanuts" is one of the most extensively licensed strips; products include dolls, watches, sheets, a Top 40 pop song, a Broadway play, television specials, greeting cards, toy catalogs, reprint books, posters, and an ad campaign for Metropolitan Life insurance. The strip also featured in a 1990 exhibition on childhood in the 1950s at the Smithsonian Institution's National Museum of American History.

Superhero characters also withstood Wertham's onslaught on comic books. Even amidst the outcry against comic books in the mid-1950s, Superman appeared in yet another licensed venture, a television series, as did another comic book superhero, Captain Midnight. Although comic book aficionados believe television aggravated the decline of comic books in the 1950s, television proved to be an important factor in the persistence of comic art as a commodity. In the 1960s artists such as Roy Lichtenstein and Andy Warhol created pop art by recycling comic book and advertising images. Although formulated as an elite critique of mass culture in the camp tradition of a knowing, smirking beholder, pop art posed as the discovery of an egalitarian aesthetic in the objects of everyday life.[4]

In 1966 the television network ABC sought to cash in on the pop art phenomenon by creating the campy *Batman* series. Producer William Dozier reasoned that if the show played up the comic book origins of Batman to present a hyperreal conflict between good and evil in garish colors, adults would find it funny. At the same time he believed children would watch the show for its comic book superheroes. The show ran for three years, allowing DC to license numerous Batman products.

For DC licensing profits exceeded revenue from comic books in the late 1960s. This licensing success caught the attention of executives at the entertainment conglomerate Warner Bros., which subsequently bought DC for the licensing rights of its superhero characters. In 1978 Warners released the first of four big budget Superman movies. The first movie grossed $245 million at the box office, and Warners licensed a range of ancillary products. Profit margins for the film and spin-off products were not reported, but they certainly exceeded profits from Superman's comic book incarnation, which at best grossed

$500,000 in 1979. The movies invigorated the character of Superman, reinforcing his mythological dimension, which DC and Warners continue to cultivate.[5]

In 1983 the president of DC comics described Superman as the "first god of a new mythology: definitely American, not borrowed, wholly our own." Although Superman may not be the first god used to turn a profit, he is, as Neil Harris has pointed out, the first to be privately owned. In 1988, on the occasion of Superman's fiftieth anniversary, *Time* magazine featured the character on its front cover. In the accompanying article, his hagiographer Otto Friedrich praised Superman for embodying "that nebulous thing known as American character." Appropriately, Friedrich compared Superman with another product, Classic Coke, to explain his position in the market. Americans, he said, regard Superman as "the real thing" because they have consumed so many of his products.[6]

Warners followed *Superman* with the 1989 release *Batman*, promoting the movie as a celebration of Batman's fiftieth anniversary. The film grossed $250 million at theaters and was the year's highest earning box office feature. In 1989–90 licensed Batman merchandise enjoyed retail sales of over $500 million. Warners generated even more profits from the Batman movie through a sound track album and an album of music featured in the film by Prince. Warner Books published a paperback novel version of the movie, and DC brought out a series of Batman graphic novels, comic-art-format, paperbound books printed on glossy paper. The company then rush-released the movie on video to catch the lucrative Christmas market. Three years after the Batman movie's release, estimates put the total revenue from its licensed products at $1 billion.[7]

Warners continues to merchandise the comic book superheroes it owns. In 1990 the company spent a previously unheard of $6 million on a two-hour premiere for a television series featuring the Flash, hoping to recoup their investment through product licensing.[8] Although this venture failed Warners' commitment to comic book superheroes remains firm. The company released a second Batman movie in the summer of 1992, a third in 1995, and a fourth in 1997.

Beginning in 1993 Superman appeared in yet another incarnation on television in *Lois & Clark (The New Adventures of Superman)*. Although it received only modest ratings in America, the show consistently ranked in the top ten in Australia. Nineties demographics ensure that the current Superman is a sensitive new age guy who consults his parents about troubling issues. He hangs out in T-shirt and boxer shorts in his apartment and seems to need sleep just as we mere mortals do. Dean Cain, who plays Superman, is somewhat the modern Renaissance man. A graduate of Princeton, he was a star athlete on the college football team and dated his fellow student Brooke Shields. Moreover Cain is part Japanese, which gives him multicultural credibility. No slapping "Japs" for this Superman.

Warners is not alone in marketing comic art figures. Other heavily promoted figures have included the Teenage Mutant Ninja Turtles, a set of characters who began life in 1984 as a satirical jibe at mainstream comic book heroes in a comic book published by their creators, Kevin Eastman and Peter Laird, at a cost of $1,200. By 1990 they had sold $650 million of merchandise. By the mid-1990s the Turtles had spawned, and been superseded by, the Mighty Morphin Power Rangers, a live-action television series complete with the usual product tie-ins, before they too faded and were replaced by the VR Rangers.[9]

There are comic art commodities for all tastes and expenses. At the end of 1991 Sotheby's held their first auction of rare comic art collectibles. Comic books sold for up to $38,000. By 1996 the price of *Action Comics*, no. 1, was $125,000. In the early 1990s the demand for a piece of the comic industry was so strong that Marvel Entertainment Group floated its stock and reached a high of thirty-four dollars a share in 1993 before crashing back to earth when the company accumulated a billion dollars of debt. Ironically Marvel's problems were caused by rival company DC. The 1989 Batman movie heated up the market for comic books and comic-book-related merchandise. The two companies released a swag of new titles and tie-in products. Both promoted comics as collectibles, and many people bought comics as an investment. In 1992 DC decided to "kill" Superman in a marketing ploy, setting off a wave of speculation about the collectibility of the "death" issue. Buyers seemed little deterred by the availability of thousands of copies of the "collectible." When Superman made his inevitable return, the bubble burst and the industry's billion-dollar-a-year turnover was cut in half. Marvel's immediate troubles stem from soft sales of comic books and from trading cards. But in the long term Marvel's weakness, compared with DC, has been their inability to invigorate their characters through Hollywood blockbuster movies. Marvel has not realized the full commodity potential of their characters through other media.[10]

Meanwhile comic strip syndicates after a slow start have adapted to the possibilities offered by the Internet and Web sites. Syndicates such as King Features, United Features, and Tribune Media Services have all set up Web home pages that offer links to electronic versions of their comic strips. What makes these Web sites profitable is the potential to sell comic strip merchandise to those visiting the sites. Independent artists have also set up Web sites, complete with product tie-ins, each trying to find a character that resonates with the buying public.

Comic strip and comic book characters have surpassed the media of their creation. As commodities they are available through a wide range of artifacts. With the advent of the comic book, the art form—as distinct from the celebrity trademark character—was no longer dependent on its place in another medium. The transmission of images across the Internet means the form is no longer dependent on paper and ink for its existence. But collapsing the fictive entertainment function of characters appearing in comic strips and books into the instances of their commodification and equating the two would be a mistake. Characters developed solely as figures to be marketed, such as the Strawberry Shortcake dolls and the He-Man characters featured on Saturday morning television in the 1980s, have so far had short life spans compared with those such as the Peanuts gang, originally given form by Charles Schulz as a comic strip. Charlie Brown and company are among the most widely licensed comic strip characters, but this merchandising flowed from the characters' popularity established in newspaper comic strips, not from their development as part of a corporate marketing strategy.[11]

One hundred years after the development of comic strips and comic strip characters as part of the marketing strategy of Pulitzer and Hearst, it is somewhat ironic that the origin of a character in this form seems to give it an authenticity lacking in characters developed in other media. But this authenticity is not some inherent characteristic; rather it stems from a long familiarity with the form and the way it has become a defining element of the culture. Our cultural practices have naturalized comic strips, so they are, for adults, less obviously part of a commercial world than Saturday morning television cartoon characters. Moreover characters developed specifically for Saturday morning television cartoon series are specifically targeted at young audiences and lack the heterosocial character of comic strip characters. In the hands of Pulitzer and Hearst, mass media appealed to the broadest spectrum of people, first in cities such as New York, and then across the country in a unified national market. The market segmentation strategy of a mass medium such as Saturday morning television requires a large potential audience delivered across national and international boundaries, and an ability to track that audience through survey techniques developed by Gallup and others. But the same may be said of *The Simpsons,* an adult cartoon show that also appeals to children and whose creators have licensed a dazzling array of merchandise for all ages.

I may seem a Gloomy Gus, despairing of a world entangled in advertising, commodities, and comics, but this is not the case. These things are all products of our own endeavors and as such encapsulate our fears, hopes, and aspirations. The commodification of comic art does not necessarily rob it of a critical edge, witness *The Simpsons* and more obviously Art Spiegelman's Pulitzer Prize–winning comic book *Maus.*[12] Indeed *Maus,* a holocaust tale that represents Nazis as cats and Jews as mice, draws its power from our familiarity with the comic form, its conventions, and commodification. *Maus* plays to rather than subverts these conventions. It is the very ubiquity of comics that gives *Maus* its narrative power. Which is to say, without Mickey Mouse there would be no *Maus.*

APPENDIX
CIRCULATION AND
SYNDICATION DATA

Table 1
Circulation of Newspapers Examined, 1901–1913

Newspaper	City	1901	1903	1908	1913
Alabama					
Age Herald	Birmingham	7,174	8,000	26,613*	24,000*
Register	Mobile	5,000	5,000	9,000*	17,917*
Advertiser	Montgomery	10,975	14,625	20,553*	20,015
Arizona					
Arizona Republican	Phoenix	5,083	6,014	6,519	6,926
Daily Citizen	Tucson	1,475	1,950	3,952*	3,017
Arkansas					
Arkansas Democrat	Little Rock	4,500	6,528	9,402*	12,017
Arkansas Gazette	Little Rock	8,000	9,151	18,750	35,000
California					
Los Angeles Examiner	Los Angeles	—	55,000*	70,000*	140,506*
Los Angeles Herald	Los Angeles	24,501	31,051*	30,000*	113,257
Los Angeles Times	Los Angeles	39,224	51,097	76,741*	97,440*
Union	Sacramento	8,100	7,850	11,993*	12,817*
San Francisco Chronicle	San Francisco	91,000	93,569*	70,000*	100,000*
San Francisco Examiner	San Francisco	109,452	144,260*	167,500*	243,075*
Colorado					
Gazette	Colorado Springs	7,277	8,220	14,350*	5,032
Evening Post	Denver	31,801	43,009*	83,407*	100,620*
Rocky Mountain News	Denver	35,675	66,200*	85,818*	56,162*
Connecticut					
Courant	Hartford	10,000	10,350	13,500	16,798
Times	Hartford	15,949	16,172	19,592	24,054
Register	New Haven	11,594	13,612	15,523	16,059
Delaware					
Evening Journal	Wilmington	5,740	6,024	10,213	15,479
Every Evening	Wilmington	9,450	10,811	10,000	10,926
District of Columbia					
Evening Star	Washington	33,468	34,234	37,395*	53,651*
Washington Herald	Washington	—	—	28,826	30,509*
Washington Post	Washington	50,000	41,288	40,000*	54,000*
Washington Times	Washington	19,648	28,000	42,837	39,224
Florida					
Florida Times Union	Jacksonville	5,000	5,000	14,731*	25,684*
Georgia					
Atlanta Constitution	Atlanta	24,500	24,500*	42,928*	45,000*
Georgian	Atlanta	—	—	29,313	79,800*
Journal	Atlanta	32,190	34,653*	55,927*	56,377*

Continued on next page

Table 1 *continued*

Newspaper	City	1901	1903	1908	1913
Chronicle	Augusta	6,200	8,533*	6,500*	9,212*
Morning News	Savannah	10,000	10,000	8,000	18,403
Idaho					
Daily Statesman	Boise	2,689	3,401	5,804*	12,640*
Illinois					
American-Examiner	Chicago	300,000	480,000*	567,298*	511,820*
Daily News	Chicago	279,489	294,147	326,976	410,000
Daily Tribune	Chicago	125,000	175,000*	319,781*	558,398*
Inter Ocean	Chicago	62,831	79,632*	108,500*	110,000*
Record Herald	Chicago	110,000	201,078	195,228*	236,825*
State Journal	Springfield	4,250	4,505	6,424*	10,678*
State Register	Springfield	5,000	3,500	11,176*	13,429*
Indiana					
Journal	Indianapolis	12,612	12,439*	—	—
News	Indianapolis	51,000	68,269	82,543	107,729
Sentinel	Indianapolis	21,450	47,243*	—	—
Star	Indianapolis	—	—	66,545	92,307*
Iowa					
Register	Des Moines	9,702	32,500	26,266*	50,821*
Times Journal	Dubuque	10,943	16,516	13,480*	14,000
Journal	Sioux City	15,166	19,312	10,000	20,000*
Kansas					
Daily Globe	Atchison	4,000	5,200	6,267	6,683
Gazette	Emporia	1,500	1,600	2,836	3,300
Times	Leavenworth	8,900	12,000	13,295	7,641
Daily Capital	Topeka	13,427	15,628*	26,462*	33,042*
State Journal	Topeka	13,473	13,342	17,173*	20,598*
Kentucky					
Courier Journal	Louisville	34,000	34,000*	44,750*	51,241*
Louisiana					
Daily Picayune	New Orleans	32,000	32,000	40,000	35,000*
Times Democrat	New Orleans	37,500	37,500	30,000	34,252*
Maine					
Kennebec Journal	Augusta	4,016	5,076	8,721	11,171
Daily News	Bangor	8,322	8,420	11,491	13,380
Evening Journal	Lewiston	6,752	6,643	8,139	10,600
Eastern Argus	Portland	5,259	5,183	5,248	6,790
Maryland					
American	Baltimore	54,605	58,803*	91,182*	109,290*
Sun	Baltimore	56,980	66,980	84,138	86,381*
Massachusetts					
American	Boston	—	—	300,000*	315,712*

Continued on next page

Table 1 *continued*

Newspaper	City	1901	1903	1908	1913
Daily Advertiser	Boston	24,620	23,170	32,672	5,448
Daily Globe	Boston	258,700	283,753*	320,634*	289,068*
Evening Transcript	Boston	24,240	24,569	29,186	29,052
Herald	Boston	100,000	100,000	175,000*	93,000
Morning Journal	Boston	53,105	65,000	110,556*	50,000
Post	Boston	122,196	169,520*	231,557*	303,926*
Berkshire Eagle	Pittsfield	4,572	5,375	8,288	12,781
Daily Republican	Springfield	13,646	14,606	17,265	15,973
Michigan					
Free Press	Detroit	51,315	51,260	58,269*	125,000*
News	Detroit	41,471	53,456*	68,043*	124,190*
Herald	Grand Rapids	11,097	12,775	12,500*	12,500*
Minnesota					
News Tribune	Duluth	9,500	11,643	19,624*	24,006*
Journal	Minneapolis	47,454	57,285*	72,483*	92,263*
Morning Tribune	Minneapolis	45,420	60,457*	79,470*	165,118*
Pioneer Press	St. Paul	30,353	31,281	34,934*	61,743*
Mississippi					
Democrat	Natchez	1,200	1,500	2,250*	4,150
Herald	Vicksburg	4,400	—	—	2,000
Missouri					
Star	Kansas Cty	100,000	111,222	140,887	198,209
Globe Democrat	St. Louis	110,288	155,000*	160,000*	173,197*
Post-Dispatch	St. Louis	157,038	204,209*	262,161*	333,207*
Republic	St. Louis	88,836	115,539*	125,581*	92,946*
Montana					
Standard	Anaconda	14,184	14,704*	14,075*	15,000*
Independent	Helena	6,298	6,298*	6,300	5,880
Nebraska					
State Journal	Lincoln	16,000	16,000	12,500	16,205
World Herald	Omaha	29,700	29,069*	39,264*	46,711*
Nevada					
State Journal	Reno	1,200	1,200	5,600	5,634
New Hampshire					
Evening Monitor	Concord	2,511	2,511	2,500	2,557
Union	Manchester	12,893	15,310	16,000	24,811
New Jersey					
Advertiser	Newark	21,015	—	—	—
Evening News	Newark	46,042	51,799	67,764	74,444
Star	Newark	—	—	—	44,949
True American	Trenton	5,285	5,405	5,000	—

Continued on next page

Table 1 *continued*

Newspaper	City	1901	1903	1908	1913
New Mexico					
Citizen	Albuquerque	1,800	1,800	1,800	—
Journal	Albuquerque	1,800	2,003	4,000	7,608*
New Mexican	Santa Fe	1,030	1,350	1,100	1,730
New York					
Evening Journal	Albany	17,242	17,521	16,486	17,266
Daily Eagle	Brooklyn	50,000	65,000	80,000*	—
Morning Express	Buffalo	61,640	56,816	50,000	50,598
Democrat & Chronicle	Rochester	21,234	24,470	39,792*	57,823
Union Advertiser	Rochester	19,197	18,578	25,356	39,051
New York City					
New York Herald		245,000	245,000*	200,000*	200,000*
New York Journal-American		600,000	800,000*	700,000*	690,889*
New York News		125,000	95,000	—	—
New York Press		100,000	100,000*	100,000*	110,869
New York Times		—	100,000	150,000	318,274
New York Tribune		75,000	75,000	87,000	50,446
New York World		450,000	450,000*	465,685*	460,000*
North Carolina					
Gazette News	Asheville	—	1,800	4,500*	4,578*
Observer	Charlotte	4,500	5,500	11,250	16,923*
News & Chronicle	Raleigh	6,400	8,086	12,274	18,000
Morning Star	Wilmington	2,650	2,650	3,200	4,474
North Dakota					
Tribune	Bismarck	850	850	1,500	4,468
Forum	Fargo	3,061	4,069	7,382	9,684
Herald	Grand Forks	3,995	5,031	8,154	12,000
Ohio					
Commercial Tribune	Cincinnati	59,494	62,305	59,813*	28,919*
Enquirer	Cincinnati	183,000	183,000*	175,000*	200,000*
Plain Dealer	Cleveland	45,000	59,275*	87,500*	164,712*
Press	Cleveland	100,385	127,231	156,359	178,579
State Journal	Columbus	18,291	21,156*	31,000*	30,170*
Oklahoma					
State Capital	Guthrie	12,104	19,868	21,055	—
Daily Phoenix	Muskogee	1,600	1,600	4,677	13,109
Oklahoman	Oklahoma City	1,250	1,250	25,863*	43,647*
Oregon					
Daily Journal	Portland	—	8,143*	29,118*	52,443*
Oregonian	Portland	29,000	33,950	43,000*	71,122*
Statesman	Salem	3,000	2,500	3,000	2,871

Continued on next page

Table 1 *continued*

Newspaper	City	1901	1903	1908	1913
Pennsylvania					
Patriot	Harrisburg	7,800	7,150	10,859	19,808
Evening Bulletin	Philadelphia	127,106	142,597	241,929	351,577
Inquirer	Philadelphia	167,883	156,368*	197,935*	275,903*
Sunday Item	Philadelphia	184,796	205,146	—	—
North American	Philadelphia	139,883	125,000*	140,000*	171,660*
Press	Philadelphia	125,000	92,952	132,334*	160,000*
Public Ledger	Philadelphia	65,000	90,000	100,000	105,000
Record	Philadelphia	157,518	169,532	142,082*	142,174
Dispatch	Pittsburgh	72,860	72,860*	73,888*	70,000*
Post	Pittsburgh	55,092	54,737*	70,000*	77,347*
Rhode Island					
Evening Times	Pawtucket	15,000	16,193	18,073	21,459
Evening Bulletin	Providence	32,500	36,476	45,306	49,415
Journal	Providence	15,000	18,351	25,400	34,861
South Carolina					
News & Courier	Charleston	7,500	7,500	10,500	11,250
State	Columbia	4,963	6,346	14,142	19,033*
South Dakota					
Argus Leader	Sioux Falls	3,822	8,369	8,282	10,088
Tennessee					
Daily Times	Chattanooga	20,000	21,534	20,000	19,500
Journal & Tribune	Knoxville	11,255	9,236*	15,594*	16,300*
Commercial Appeal	Memphis	29,475	37,213*	60,285*	94,778*
American	Nashville	14,221	19,052*	24,812*	—
Banner	Nashville	16,371	18,400	36,109	50,780
Texas					
Morning News	Dallas	33,897	57,976	67,480*	49,046*
Post	Houston	19,560	22,150*	28,500*	33,625*
Express	San Antonio	—	—	21,000	30,000
Utah					
Deseret News	Salt Lake City	4,578	5,545	8,478	17,781
Salt Lake Tribune	Salt Lake City	14,150	14,150	16,411	35,919*
Vermont					
Free Press	Burlington	4,614	4,683	8,348	9,814
Daily Herald	Rutland	3,000	3,300	4,342	5,000
Virginia					
Gazette	Alexandria	1,200	1,200	1,000	1,600
Virginian Pilot	Norfolk	10,386	11,715	14,852*	32,358*
Times Dispatch	Richmond	10,500	10,500*	28,500*	33,000*

Continued on next page

Table 1 *continued*

Newspaper	City	1901	1903	1908	1913
Washington					
Daily Times	Seattle	24,334	35,882*	71,857*	81,786*
Post-Intelligencer	Seattle	14,000	30,000	39,500*	42,162*
Spokesman-Review	Spokane	11,274	15,988*	32,395*	51,256*
Daily Ledger	Tacoma	8,650	14,195	25,688	27,000*
West Virginia					
Register	Wheeling	14,800	14,800	13,100*	12,341*
Wisconsin					
State Journal	Madison	1,800	3,334	5,143	9,244
Journal	Milwaukee	24,982	34,504	54,503	72,399
Sentinel	Milwaukee	23,000	62,654*	42,414*	50,000*
Wyoming					
State Tribune	Cheyenne	1,200	2,400	4,987	4,783
Total		7,110,914	8,489,324	10,040,861	11,980,973

Circulation figures are for Sunday editions where given, otherwise for aggregate daily sales. Figures from N. W. *Ayer & Son's American Newspaper Annual* (Philadelphia: N. W. Ayer & Son, 1913 not available, 1915 used). Some information from *Dauchy Co.'s Newspaper Catalogue* (New York: Dauchy Co., 1909).

*Sunday comic strips.

Table 2

Growth in Population and Newspaper Circulation, 1903–1913

	1903	1908	1913
Total U.S. population*	75,994,575	91,972,266	91,972,266
Population of cities and towns with comic strips	11,794,977	17,636,388	19,268,082
Population of cities and towns with comic strips as percentage of total population	15.50%	19.18%	21.00%
Total circulation of newspapers examined	8,489,324	10,040,861	11,980,973
Total circulation of newspapers with Sunday editions	7,570,133	8,678,165	10,577,388
Total circulation of newspapers with Sunday comic strips	5,038,024	7,144,821	9,075,511
Total circulation of newspapers with Sunday comic strips as percentage of total population	6.60%	7.77%	9.86%
Circulation of all papers with comic strips as percentage of population of cities and towns with comic strips	42.70%	54.25%	54.30%
Total circulation of newspapers with daily comic strips	2,423,395	7,818,798	—

*Figures for 1908 and 1913 from the 1910 census.

Table 3
Syndication of Comic Strips, 1903–1913

	1903	1908	1913
Number of newspapers using syndicated comic strips	45	81	115
Percentage of population in cities and towns with comic strips	15.00%	19.18%	21.00%
Percentage of Sunday comic strip market covered*			
Hearst	70.00%	66.00%	74.47%
World Color Co.	22.00	44.10	28.22
McClure	43.00	57.70	42.10
New York Herald	48.00	51.80	32.88
New York World	38.25	38.75	52.80
Percentage of daily comic strip market covered*			
Hearst	—	—	66.40%
McClure	—	—	18.00
New York World	—	—	48.65

*Defined by populations of cities with newspapers.

Table 4
Distribution of "Buster Brown," 1903–1908

	1903	1908
Population of cities and towns with newspapers containing "Buster Brown"	5,813,173	8,071,469 (1900 Census) 11,432,359 (1910 Census)
Population of cities and towns with newspapers containing "Buster Brown" as percentage of total population	7.6%	10.62% (1900 Census) 12.40% (1910 Census)
Circulation of newspapers containing "Buster Brown"	566,590	3,133,064

NOTES

INTRODUCTION

1. Peter Carlson, "It's an Ad Ad Ad Ad World," *Washington Post Magazine* (November 3, 1991), p. 16.

2. Ibid., pp. 15, 17, 19. The figures for licensing represent international sales of licensed products. In 1989 comic art characters represented 18.5 percent ($12 billion) of that business. See N. R. Kleinfield, "Cashing in on a Hot New Brand Name," *New York Times* (April 29, 1990), sec. 3, pp. 1, 6. Tom Engelhardt, "The Shortcake Strategy," in Todd Gitlin, ed., *Watching Television* (New York: Pantheon, 1986), p. 71, mentions in passing that licensing of characters began in 1904 with Buster Brown.

3. Fredric Wertham, *Seduction of the Innocent* (New York: Holt, Rinehart and Winston, 1954), pp. 33, 64. For a discussion of the impact of Wertham's book, see James Gilbert, *A Cycle of Outrage: America's Reaction to the Juvenile Delinquent in the 1950's* (New York: Oxford University Press, 1986). Wertham, *The World of Fanzines: A Special Form of Communication* (Carbondale: Southern Illinois University Press, 1973), p. 35. In this latter work Wertham avoids reference to *Seduction of the Innocent,* which is listed in Robert M. Overstreet's annual *Comic Book Price Guide* (New York: House of Collectables) and in original condition can fetch up to $300.

4. Wertham, *Seduction of the Innocent,* pp. 14–15. John K. Ryan, "Are the Comics Moral?" *Forum,* 95 (May 1936), p. 304. It is interesting that Ryan also suggested that psychologists should study the "effects of the worst type of comic strip upon immature minds."

5. For changes in the organization of work and its effects, see Roy Rosenzweig, *Eight Hours for What We Will: Workers and Leisure in an Industrial City, 1870–1920* (New York: Cambridge University Press, 1983); David Montgomery, *The Fall of the House of Labor* (New York: Cambridge University Press, 1987); Herbert Gutman, *Work, Culture and Society in Industrializing America: Essays in American Working-Class and Social History* (New York: Vintage Books, 1976). See also Harry Braverman, *Labor and Monopoly Capital: The Degradation of Work in the Twentieth Century* (New York: Monthly Review Press, 1974); and E. P. Thompson, "Time, Work-Discipline, and Industrial Capitalism," *Past and Present,* 38 (1967), pp. 56–97.

Works tracing the emergence of a culture of consumption to the last two decades of the nineteenth century include Richard Wrightman Fox and T. J. Jackson Lears, eds., *The Culture of Consumption: Critical Essays in American History, 1880–1980* (New York: Pantheon, 1983); and Daniel Horowitz, *The Morality of Spending: Attitudes toward the Consumer Society in America, 1875–1940* (Baltimore: Johns Hopkins University Press, 1985). See also Richard S. Tedlow, *New and Improved: The Story of Mass Marketing in America* (New York: Basic Books, 1990), for a more celebratory account of the business practices associated with the emergence of mass consumption.

Works examining the new leisure economy include Lewis A. Erenberg, *Steppin' Out: New York Nightlife and the Transformation of American Culture, 1890–1930* (Chicago: University of Chicago Press, 1981); John F. Kasson, *Amusing the Million: Coney Island at the Turn of the Century* (New York: Hill & Wang, 1978); Lawrence W. Levine, *Highbrow/Lowbrow: The Emergence of Cultural Hierarchy in America* (Cambridge, Mass.: Harvard University Press, 1988); and Kathy Peiss, *Cheap Amusements: Working Women and Leisure in Turn of the Century New York* (Philadelphia: Temple University Press, 1986). Both Neil McKendrick, John Brewer, and J. H. Plumb, *The Birth of a Consumer Society: The Commercialization of Eighteenth Century England* (Bloomington: Indiana University Press, 1982), and Simon Schama, *The Embarrassment of Riches: An Interpretation of Dutch Culture in the Golden Age* (New York: Alfred A. Knopf, 1987), discuss earlier patterns of consumption. Works that stress the importance of the 1920s in shaping a fully realized modernist culture include Roland Marchand, *Advertising the American Dream: Making Way for Modernity: 1920–1940* (Berkeley: University of California Press, 1985); Alice Goldfarb Marquis, *Hopes and Ashes: The Birth of Modern Times* (New York: Free Press, 1986); and Jeffrey L. Meikle, *Twentieth Century Limited: Industrial Design in America, 1925–1939* (Philadelphia: Temple University Press, 1979).

For overviews of consumer history, see Jean-Christophe Agnew, "Coming Up for Air: Consumer Culture in Historical Perspective," *Intellectual History*

Newsletter, 12 (1990), pp. 3–21; and Charles McGovern, "The Emergence of Consumer History" (paper presented at the annual meeting of the Organization of American Historians, 1988).

6. See Tedlow, *New and Improved;* and Susan Strasser, *Satisfaction Guaranteed: The Making of the American Mass Market* (New York: Pantheon, 1989). Jackson Lears's *Fables of Abundance: A Cultural History of Advertising in America* (New York: Basic Books, 1994) is a far- reaching account of advertising's place in American culture. Among other things Lears shows connections between twentieth-century advertising and earlier notions of religious redemption.

7. Kirk Varnedoe quoted in "The Modern Prepares for the Twenty-first Century," *New York Times* (March 6, 1988), sec. 2, cited in Levine, *Highbrow/Lowbrow,* p. 247.

8. Kirk Varnedoe and Adam Gopnik, *High & Low: Modern Art and Popular Culture* (New York: Museum of Modern Art, 1990), pp. 153, 154.

9. Daniel Joseph Singal, "Toward a Definition of American Modernism," *American Quarterly,* 39 (Spring 1987), p.16; Steven Watts, "Walt Disney: Art and Politics in the American Century," *Journal of American History,* 82 (June 1995), p. 87; T. J. Jackson Lears, "Uneasy Courtship: Modern Art and Modern Advertising," *American Quarterly,* 39 (Spring 1987), p. 134; and Daniel Bell, "Modernism Mummified," ibid., p. 125.

10. Fox and Lears, *Culture of Consumption,* pp. xiii, xv.

11. Norman Bryson, "Semiology and Visual Interpretation," in Norman Bryson, Michael Ann Holly, and Keith Moxey, eds., *Visual Theory: Painting and Interpretation* (Cambridge: Polity Press, 1991), pp. 69–70. Bell, "Modernism Mummified," p. 125.

12. See for instance Lary May, *Screening Out the Past: The Birth of Mass Culture and the Motion Picture Industry* (New York: Oxford University Press, 1980), for the former, and Lears, *Fables of Abundance,* for the latter.

13. Standard works include Maurice Horn, ed., *The World Encyclopedia of Comics* (New York: Chelsea House, 1976); Alan Aldridge and George Perry, *The Penguin Book of Comics* (Harmondsworth: Penguin, 1967); Stephen Becker, *Comic Art in America* (New York: Simon & Schuster, 1959); Bill Blackbeard and Martin Williams, *The Smithsonian Collection of Newspaper Comics* (Washington, D.C.: Smithsonian Institution, 1977); Martin Sheridan, *Comics and Their Creators* (Boston: Ralph T. Hale, 1942); and Coulton Waugh, *The Comics* (1947; reprint, Jackson: University Press of Mississippi, 1990). See also Russel Nye, *The Unembarrassed Muse: The Popular Arts in America* (New York: Dial Press, 1970), chap. 9. Horn, *World Encyclopedia,* pp. 10–11.

14. For work typical of the sociological approach, see "The Researchers Report" section of David Manning White and Robert H. Abel, eds., *The Funnies: An American Idiom* (New York: Free Press, 1963). Two recent

works that maintain comic strips are uniquely American are M. Thomas Inge, *Comics as Culture* (Jackson, Miss.: University Press of Mississippi, 1990); and Richard Marschall, *America's Great Comic Strip Artists* (New York: Abbeville Press, 1989). Marschall, however, dismisses much of the myth surrounding "The Yellow Kid" and goes further than anyone else in acknowledging European and American illustrated humor magazine influence on comic strips. In her recent work Judith O'Sullivan, without explanation, dates the origin of comic strips as 1892. She too regards comic strips as uniquely American. *The Great American Comic Strip: One Hundred Years of Cartoon Art* (Boston: Bulfinch Press, 1990), p. 9.

15. Horn, *World Encyclopedia*, p. 9. For an extended presentation of the European origins of comic strips, see David Kunzle, *History of the Comic Strip*, vol. 1: *The Early Comic Strip* (Berkeley: University of California Press, 1973); and *History of the Comic Strip*, vol. 2: *The Nineteenth Century* (Berkeley: University of California Press, 1990). Scott McCloud's *Understanding Comics* (New York: Harper Perennial, 1993) provides a clear and remarkably nuanced demonstration of comic art's "linguistic" structural form.

16. See Peter Bailey, "Ally Sloper's Half Holiday: Comic Art in the 1880's," *History Workshop*, no. 16 (Autumn 1983), pp. 4–31; Ian Gordon, "From *The Bulletin* to *The Lost Patrol*: Comic Art in Australia, 1890–1950," in *Bonzer: Comic Books Down Under* (Melbourne: CIS, 1998); Gordon, "The Symbol of a Nation: Ginger Meggs and Australian National Identity," *Journal of Australian Studies*, no. 34 (September 1992), pp. 1–14; and Gordon, "Stop Laughing This Is Serious: The Comic Art Form and Australian Identity, 1880–1960" (B.A. honours thesis, University of Sydney, Department of History, 1986), for accounts of the development of comic art in England and Australia.

17. Inge, *Comics as Culture*, p. xi; O'Sullivan, *Great American Comic Strip*, p. 9.

18. "Boston *Herald*'s Abandonment of Comic Supplement," *Nation*, 87 (November 5, 1908), p. 426. Waugh, *Comics*, p. 57. For the 1950s debate on mass culture, see Bernard Rosenberg and David Manning White, eds., *Mass Culture: The Popular Arts in America* (Glencoe, Ill.: Free Press, 1957). Commentaries on the debate include James Gilbert's *Cycle of Outrage* and Andrew Ross, *No Respect: Intellectuals and Popular Culture* (New York: Routledge, 1989), chap. 2.

19. As for the Bayeux tapestry, Egyptian hieroglyphics, and prehistoric cave drawings, it is sufficient to note that to speak meaningfully of any relationship these have with the comic art form would require histories of the development of language and visual representation. Although the comic art form embodies language, representation, and narrative, it does not follow that all instances of these forms relate to comics except insofar as they are all products of human society.

20. Roland Barthes describes myths as "a system of communication, a message, a signification, a form defined not by the object of its message but the way in which it utters this message." "Myth Today," in his *Mythologies* (London: Paladin, 1972), p. 109.

21. See McCloud's *Understanding Comics* for a discussion of the formal techniques of comics, including the narrative implications of the space betweeen panels. See also Martin Barker, *Comics: Ideology, Power, and the Critics* (Manchester: Manchester University Press, 1989), on readers' ability to distance themselves from comic strip characters.

22. Alfred McClung Lee, *The Daily Newspaper in America* (New York: Macmillan, 1937), p. 580. A daily newspaper published six or seven days a week. The Library of Congress holds only a fraction of these papers. It has 339 papers for 1900 and 272 for 1903. I excluded nondaily papers and those from Hawaii and Alaska from my survey. I also excluded papers in languages other than English and African American papers because I wished to focus on constructions of Americanness that did not specifically acknowledge race and ethnicity.

1. FROM CARICATURE TO COMIC STRIPS

1. From a study of account books John Modell estimates that in 1889 in the northeastern states 89.5 percent of local-born American and 87 percent of Irish-born, working-class families "had significant expenditures for newspapers and books." Modell, "Patterns of Consumption, Acculturation and Family Income in Late Nineteenth Century America," in Tamara K. Hareven and Maris A. Vinovskis, eds., *Family and Population in Nineteenth-Century America* (Boston: Little, Brown, 1978), p. 214. See also Lee Soltow and Edward Stevens, *The Rise of Literacy and the Common School in the United States* (Chicago: University of Chicago Press, 1981), whose strict literacy test indicates "that 89% of northern artisans and 76% of northern farmers and laborers were literate in the period between 1830 and 1895." Cited in Michael Denning, *Mechanic Accents: Dime Novels and Working-Class Culture in America* (New York: Verso, 1987), p. 31.

2. William Murrell, *A History of American Graphic Humor*, vol. 2: *1865–1938* (New York: Macmillan, 1938), p. 82. Gillam's cartoon appeared in *Puck* (April 16, 1884). McDougall's cartoon was not the first to appear in an American newspaper. There was an editorial cartoon in the *New York Evening Post* in 1814. The *New York Evening Telegram* published a cartoon on March 9, 1872, and in 1879 a number of cartoons by C. G. Bush, who later worked for the *World*'s comic supplement. Murrell, *History*, p. 129.

3. *New York World* (December 6, 1895), p. 1.

4. At the same time *Puck, Life,* and *Judge* often printed cartoons from European journals. Generally these were limited to one or two per issue, and they were primarily used to fill up blank space on the pages reserved for advertisements.

5. In 1881 the respective circulations of the English and German editions of *Puck* were 85,000 and 19,500. Keppler published the German edition until the end of the 1890s. *Judge* was established in 1881, when a group of disgruntled artists left *Puck.* Whereas the political tone of *Puck* was independent Democratic, *Judge* was Republican, especially after 1884, when the Republican Party gained control of the magazine. *Life,* established in 1884, was less political than the other two magazines, although it too was independent Democratic in tone. In the 1890s *Life*'s double-page center spreads were almost exclusively devoted to Charles Dana Gibson's social cartoons featuring the "American" or "Gibson Girl." For more details see the entries for each magazine in David E. E. Sloan, ed., *American Humor Magazines and Comic Periodicals* (New York: Greenwood Press, 1987). Other illustrated humor journals included the in-house magazines of a watch manufacturer and a gentlemen's clothing store. See *The Waterbury* and *Smith, Gray & Company's Illustrated Monthly.* Both are in the Warshaw Collection of Business Americana, Archives Center, National Museum of American History, Smithsonian Institution, Collection 60 (hereafter NMAH 60), Watches, box 4, and Men's Clothing, box 1, respectively.

6. Lawrence W. Levine, *Highbrow/Lowbrow: The Emergence of Cultural Hierarchy in America* (Cambridge, Mass.: Harvard University Press, 1988); Roy Rosenzweig, *Eight Hours for What We Will: Workers and Leisure in an Industrial City, 1870–1920* (New York: Cambridge University Press, 1983); John F. Kasson, *Amusing the Million: Coney Island at the Turn of the Century* (New York: Hill & Wang, 1978). See also Lewis A. Erenberg, *Steppin' Out: New York Nightlife and the Transformation of American Culture, 1890–1930* (Chicago: University of Chicago Press, 1981); and Kathy Peiss, *Cheap Amusements: Working Women and Leisure in Turn of the Century New York* (Philadelphia: Temple University Press, 1986). For a good overview of the changes in the organization of work and its effect, see Harry Braverman, *Labor and Monopoly Capital: The Degradation of Work in the Twentieth Century* (New York: Monthly Review Press, 1974).

7. Denning, *Mechanical Accents,* p. 59; Francis G. Couvares, *The Remaking of Pittsburgh: Class and Culture in an Industrializing City, 1877–1919* (Albany: State University of New York Press, 1984), p. 97.

8. John Bodnar, *The Transplanted: A History of Immigrants in Urban America* (Bloomington: Indiana University Press, 1985), pp. xvi, 118, 205; Robert W. Snyder, *The Voice of the City: Vaudeville and Popular Culture in New York* (New York: Oxford University Press, 1989), p. 43.

9. *New York Herald Tribune* (June 12, 1934), p. 21, cited in Snyder, *Voice of the City,* p. 117.

10. "Editorial," *Judge,* 3 (April 7, 1883), p. 2. The combined circulations of *Puck, Judge,* and *Life* in the 1890s were approximately 240,000. See entries for each magazine in Sloan, *American Humor Magazines.*

11. Albert Dodd Blashfield, "A Thanksgiving Study," *Life,* 14 (November 21, 1899), p. 287; Blashfield, "The Involution of the Messenger Boy," *Life,* 18 (December 17, 1891), p. 360; Hy Mayer, "The Evolution of the English Sovereign," *Life,* 24 (December 13, 1894), p. 382; "All Balled Up," *Puck,* 29 (April 8, 1891), p. 102.

12. "What Will Become of the Men Who Stay Out Late," *Judge,* 29 (July 13, 1895), p. 21; "A Study in Expression of the Motorman on Any Electric Car," *Judge,* 23 (September 24, 1892), p. 199; Jerome H. Smith, "A Study of Facial Expression at the 'Phone,'" *Judge,* 23 (August 20, 1892), p. 120; Albert Dodd Blashfield, "Gentlemen Who Eat at Lunch Counters Should Be Careful," *Life,* 20 (October 20, 1892), p. 218; W. McNaly, "A Lovers' Quarrel," *Judge,* 22 (April 2, 1892), p. 223; Frederick Burr Opper, "Puck's Easy Lessons in Caricature, for Little Learners," *Puck,* 34 (July 25, 1894), p. 358; Louis Dalrymple, "The Transformation of a Paying Teller," *Puck,* 28 (November 26, 1890), p. 213.

13. *Who Was Who in American Art* (Madison, Conn.: Sound View Press, 1985), p. 295; Roy L. McCardell, "Opper, Outcault and Company: The Comic Supplement and the Men Who Make It," *Everybody's Magazine,* 12 (June 1905), p. 769; and Maurice Horn, ed., *The World Encyclopedia of Comics* (New York: Chelsea House, 1976), p. 323. The division between editorial cartoons and comic strip work was by no means fixed. Major editorial cartoonists such as Walt McDougall and Frederick Opper enjoyed extensive careers as comic strip artists. Winsor McCay, known today primarily for his "Little Nemo" comic strip and his early animated films, spent his last two decades working as an editorial cartoonist. Nonetheless the two forms of comic art are largely regarded as separate spheres of endeavor. The point here is that Howarth was one of the first to restrict himself to one type of comic art.

14. See Walter Arndt, *The Genius of Wilhelm Busch* (Berkeley: University of California Press, 1982), for a reprint of *Max und Moritz.*

15. Franklin Morris Howarth, "The Unexpected," *Life,* 17 (April 23, 1891), p. 253. See Chapter 4 for a discussion of advertisers' research on comic strips. Richard Marschall claims that many of the techniques discussed here, such as "motion lines, sweat beads, clouds of dust, explosion lines, and footprints indicating motion," were "introduced or institutionalized" by a later comic strip artist, Rudolph Dirks. *America's Great Comic Strip Artists* (New York: Abbeville Press, 1989), p. 45. Such a claim reinforces the notion

that comic strips are uniquely American. Marschall, who wrote his master of arts thesis on early American illustrated magazines, should know better. Töpffer invented motion lines, and they were well and truly institutionalized in the work of American comic artists in the 1890s. See Rodolphe Töpffer, *Monsieur Pencil* (1840), reproduced in David Kunzle, *History of the Comic Strip*, vol. 2: *The Nineteenth Century* (Berkeley: University of California Press, 1990), pp. 60–61. In addition to borrowing from Busch, Howarth, along with numerous other artists, adopted Töpffer's use of lines to depict motion. Explosion lines are simply an outgrowth of motion lines, and they too can be found on a regular basis in work of the 1890s. Clouds of dust, which indicate very quick motion, are also a development of motion lines, and Howarth used a technique along these lines as early as 1888. Howarth, "The Country Bumpkin," *Life*, 11 (January 5, 1888), p. 11. The point comes back to what Marschall means by "institutionalized." For him the institution is comic strips, and because he believes these developed only after 1896, and were uniquely American, it follows for him that Dirks's use of various techniques institutionalized them. But if one regards American comic strips as simply a specific development within a particular art form, then Dirks's use of these techniques can be regarded as derivative.

16. Franklin Morris Howarth, "Children's Portraits No Longer a Specialty," *Puck*, 32 (April 12, 1893), back cover; Howarth, "Woman's Inhumanity to Woman," *Puck*, 33 (June 7, 1893), back cover; Howarth, "Love Will Find the Way," *Puck*, 30 (February 17, 1892), back cover; Howarth, "A Too- Accommodating Shutter," *Puck*, 32 (December 7, 1892), back cover; Howarth, "A Tale of the Orient," *Life*, 13 (April 11, 1889), pp. 216–17; Howarth, "An Elopement in High Life, and Why It Failed," *Life*, 12 (October 11, 1888), p. 206; Howarth, "Her Mother's First Visit," *Puck*, 32 (January 4, 1893), back cover; and Howarth, "Asking Alicia's Pa's Consent," *Puck*, 31 (March 23, 1892), back cover.

17. For examples see Frank Bellew, Sr., "The Haughty Dame and Her New Pet," *Life*, 11 (February 23, 1888), p. 106; Bellew Sr., "Discouraging Art," *Life*, 11 (January 19, 1888), p. 40; Frank "Chip" Bellew, Jr., "How a Naughty Boy Was Caught," *Life*, 13 (January 24, 1889), p. 47; Bellew Jr., *Life*, 26 (July 4, 1895), p. 12; and Bellew Jr., "The Bad Boys and the Hornets' Nest," *Judge*, 29 (November 2, 1895), p. 302. Frank Bellew the elder was one of the first American cartoonists to sign his work, a mark of his standing as an artisan. Unlike other cartoonists, such as Nast, Bellew not only drew his cartoons but engraved them. The right to sign work that appeared in illustrated humor magazines and newspaper comic supplements became an important issue for artists because it offered them some copyright protection.

18. Howarth was not the only artist to draw full-page comic strips in panels for *Puck*, *Life*, and *Judge*. A number of others, most notably Sydney B. Griffin, George B. Luks, the Australian-born Frank Nankivell, and Gustav

Verbeck (Verbeek), also worked this genre. Many of their strips were in color. But Howarth was the trendsetter and, in the 1890s, master proponent of this type of illustration. See Syd B. Griffin, "The Boarding-House Problem," *Puck,* 29 (August 12, 1891), back cover; George B. Luks, "Coppered," *Puck,* 39 (May 6, 1896), p. 22; and Frank Nankivell, "Mr. Johnson Invites Miss Jackson to the Circus—Almost," *Puck,* 39 (August 5, 1896), back cover.

19. Franklin Morris Howarth, "The Wicked Grandsons," *Life,* 18 (October 1, 1891), p. 180; Howarth, "Uncle Samuel's Whiskers," *Puck,* 31 (May 11, 1892), back cover; Howarth, "A Misplaced Cue," *Puck,* 33 (May 10, 1893), p. 183; Howarth, "The Funny Boys, the Terrorized Canine, and the Man Who Changed His Mind," *Puck,* 40 (August 19, 1896), p. 3; Howarth, "The Fate of Two Mischievous Boys," *Puck,* 40 (January 13, 1897), p. 4; Michael Angelo Woolf, "The Spanish Craze in Mulligan Lane," *Life,* 17 (March 12, 1891), p. 160; Woolf, "Gymnastics in Brophy's Alley," *Life,* 19 (April 14, 1892), p. 235.

20. Richard Felton Outcault, "Origin of a New Species, or The Evolution of the Crocodile Explained," *New York World* (November 18, 1894); Outcault, "From the Eiffel Tower," *Life,* 15 (April 17, 1890), p. 232.

21. Murrell, *History,* p. 136; and Martin Sheridan, *Comics and Their Creators* (Boston: Ralph T. Hale, 1942), p. 17. Marschall notes that Charles Saalburgh, later Outcault's editor at the *World,* created a feature entitled "Ting-Ling Kids" for the *Chicago Inter-Ocean* in 1893. It appeared every week and ran in color, but it too was not a comic strip. *America's Great Comic Strip Artists,* p. 24. Pulitzer's biographer George Jurgens also cites Outcault's November 18, 1894, illustration as the first comic strip, although he refers to it incorrectly as "Shantytown." *Joseph Pulitzer and the New York World* (Princeton, N.J.: Princeton University Press, 1966), p. 115. See also Moses Koenigsberg, *King News: An Autobiography* (Philadelphia: F. A. Stokes, 1941), pp. 366–67, for an account of the development of halftone etching and color web presses.

22. "Three Popular Women," *New York Times* (October 27, 1891), p. 4, cited in Snyder, *Voice of the City,* p. 25; McCardell, "Opper, Outcault and Company," p. 768.

23. William Henry Shelton, "The Comic Paper in America," *Critic,* 39 (September 1901), p. 228.

24. Michael Angelo Woolf, *Life,* 19 (April 14, 1892), p. 229; Richard Felton Outcault, "Up to Date," *Truth* (April 15, 1893), p. 88.

25. The small figure holding hands with a girl to the left of "Up to Date" and to the right of "Feudal Pride in Hogan's Alley" may have been an early version of the Yellow Kid. What makes his appearance in "Fourth Ward Brownies" decisive is his nightshirt with ink-smudged handprints on it. This was a feature of the Yellow Kid in his early *World* appearances.

26. A typical account of the Yellow Kid's origins is given by Bill Blackbeard in Horn's *World Encyclopedia of Comics* (pp. 711–12). But the dates
of Outcault's tenure at the *World* are wrong. These have been corrected in
the recent *The Yellow Kid: A Centennial Celebration of the Kid Who Started
the Comics* (Northampton, Mass.: Kitchen Sink Press, 1995), for which
Blackbeard provided the introduction.

Until recently it was generally accepted that the nightshirt was colored
yellow as a test of the ability of yellow ink to bond to newsprint. Richard
Marschall argues that this could not have been so because yellow had been
used earlier. *America's Great Comic Strip Artists,* p. 22. But it is possible that
yellow would not take on new presses operated at higher speeds and so new
stabilizing agents had to be tested. Blackbeard gives a detailed account of the
*World'*s use of color in his introduction to *The Yellow Kid: A Centennial
Celebration* (pp. 30–34), which makes clear that the testing yellow ink theory is incorrect. Blackbeard suggested to me that yellow was used because it
was the best background for the text printed on the Kid's shirt. Conversation
with the author, August 13, 1991. Although this seems a good explanation,
yellow was used three months before text was added to the Kid's nightshirt.

Why a certain color was used may seem a small point, of interest only to
comic strip aficionados, but the Yellow Kid gave his name to the yellow
press, and inaccurate statements about his origin crop up in social histories
of the era. For a typically wrongheaded account of Outcault's career and the
origins of the Yellow Kid, see Joyce Milton, *The Yellow Kids: Foreign
Correspondents in the Heyday of Yellow Journalism* (New York: Harper &
Row, 1989). Blackbeard agrees with Milton that Hearst's promotion of a
bike race employing cyclists dressed in yellow led to the term *yellow press.*
The historian Mark D. Winchester has demonstrated that the term *yellow
journalism* came into use during the Spanish- American War in 1898 to
describe the war hysteria whipped up by Hearst and Pulitzer. "Hully Gee, It's
a War!!! The Yellow Kid and the Coining of 'Yellow Journalism,'" *Inks,* 2
(November 1995), pp. 22–37. The Yellow Kid was transformed into a symbol of yellow journalism during this campaign rather than giving his name
to it. The distinction is subtle but crucial.

27. Outcault quoted in La Touche Hancock, "American Caricature and
Comic Art," *Bookman,* 16 (October 1902), p. 130.

28. R. F. Outcault to A. R. Spofford, Librarian of Congress, September 7,
1896, Division of Prints and Photographs, Library of Congress. The letter
and illustration were first reprinted in Judith O'Sullivan, *The Great
American Comic Strip: One Hundred Years of Cartoon Art* (Boston: Bulfinch
Press, 1990), p. 149.

29. W. B. Howell, Assistant Secretary, Treasury Department, to W. Y.
Connor, *New York Journal,* April 15, 1897, reprinted in *Decisions of the*

United States Courts involving Copyright and Literary Property, 1789–1909,
bulletin 15 (Washington, D.C.: Library of Congress, 1980), pp. 3187–88.

30. The Warshaw Collection of Business Americana, Archives Center,
National Museum of American History, Smithsonian Institution, Collection
60, contains a number of advertisements for Yellow Kid products, including
the two chewing gums in box 1, folder 1, of Chewing Gum. See also two collectors' newsletters, *The Yellow Kid Notes* and *The R. F. Outcault Reader,*
for details on Yellow Kid products.

31. The American Humorist Supplement to the *New York Journal*
(October 18, 1896), front-page headline.

32. The term *flat* referred to an apartment. It retains this usage in parts of
the United States and other English-speaking countries. "McFadden's Flats"
appeared in every issue of the *Journal*'s supplement from October 1896 to
the end of May 1897. The October 25 issue featured both a "McFadden's
Flats" illustration and a semi–comic strip, "The Yellow Kid and His New
Phonograph." This was the first time the Yellow Kid appeared as a named
character in a humor supplement. It was also the first time he appeared in a
series of illustrations that approximated a comic strip. Thereafter the Yellow
Kid often appeared in his own comic strip as well as in "McFadden's Flats."
He also started to show up in other forms. On Friday, October 30, 1896,
J. Campbell Cory used the kid as a metaphor in an editorial cartoon in the
daily *Journal.* On November 8 the *Journal*'s Sunday humor supplement
included sheet music for "The Yellow Kid: The Latest and Greatest." At the
same time Outcault experimented with laying out Yellow Kid stories in panels, and on January 24, 1897, a Yellow Kid illustration appeared with all the
accoutrements of a comic strip. But this was a rare occurrence. Outcault
preferred the large splash illustration of "Hogan's Alley" and "McFadden's
Flats" to the panel sequence format.

33. Why Outcault left Hearst is not certain. It is not satisfactory to say, as
Blackbeard's entry for "The Yellow Kid" in Horn's *World Encyclopedia of
Comics* does, that Outcault and his wife were sensitive to the views of the
"better people" who criticized Hearst's yellow journalism and the vulgarity
of "The Yellow Kid" (p. 712) because Outcault returned to the employ of
Pulitzer, who was just as much a yellow journalist as Hearst, and he continued to create rowdy features such as "Casey's Corner" and "Kelly Kids" for
the *World* between 1898 and 1900. If anything the new features were more
worrisome to "better people" than "The Yellow Kid" had been. "Casey's
Corner" was dominated by the New Bully, a caricatured African American
who wielded a cutthroat razor (see Chapter 3). Outcault's last Yellow Kid
appeared in the *Journal* on January 23, 1898. The New Bully appeared in
the *World* on February 13, 1898.

34. All these artists were listed as contributors to the *Journal*'s comic

supplement on May 2, 1897. Another early contributor, Carl Anderson (1865–1948), drew a feature entitled "Journal Kinescope" beginning on January 3, 1897; it depicted comic art in panels drawn as movie film frames. Kinescope was the name of Hearst's film company. In 1934, at the age of sixty-nine, Anderson enjoyed major success with his comic strip "Henry."

35. The standard histories of comic strips state that the comics editor for the *Journal*, Rudolph Block, suggested to Dirks that he adapt Busch's *Max und Moritz*. See for instance Marschall, *America's Great Comic Strip Artists*, p. 42. This may be true, but the publication of Greening's "Tinkle Brothers," and earlier work by Howarth and others in the illustrated humor journals, demonstrates a general awareness of Busch's work and a desire to emulate its success. The point here is that, more than likely, "The Katzenjammer Kids" was not simply the result of an interaction between a single editor and artist but representative of a conscious, deliberate decision, by many comic artists, to imitate Busch.

American comic strips then were built on European foundations. The German term *katzenjammer* means "cats howling" and is used as slang for a hangover. On February 9, 1896, Walt McDougall published a full-page cartoon in the *World*'s humor supplement that depicted Teddy Roosevelt, then police commissioner of New York City, as the proprietor of "Teddy's Katzenjammer Kindergarten." This cartoon was apparently a response to Roosevelt's proposal advocating the education of children to avoid intemperate vices. Given the tight-knit world of New York comic artists, it is possible that Block derived the title for Dirks's strip from this cartoon. See also Elsa Ann Nystrom, "A Rejection of Order: The Development of the Newspaper Comic Strip in America, 1830–1920" (Ph.D. diss., Loyola University of Chicago, 1989), p. 133, n. 47.

36. On October 9, 1898, the *Journal* published the first of many "Katzenjammer Kids" strips signed by Rudolph's brother Gus. On October 30, 1898, a "Katzenjammer Kids" strip by Gus Mager was published. Both Gus Dirks (1879–1902) and Mager (1878–1956) had careers as comic artists apart from their occasional work on "The Katzenjammer Kids." Before his suicide death Gus Dirks drew "Latest News from Bugville" for Hearst. This strip had an innovative layout and used narrative text blocks within the panels, which later became a hallmark of comic books. There is some dispute as to when Gus Dirks died. Marschall, *America's Great Comic Strip Artists*, p. 53, cites 1903, but *Who Was Who in American Art*, p. 166, cites June 10, 1902. Mager drew the strip "Sherlocko the Monk."

37. Koenigsberg, *King News*, p. 378.

38. In "'Personality' and the Making of Twentieth-Century Culture" (p. 280), Warren Susman pointed out that every manual on development of personality he consulted "stressed the importance of the human voice" in presenting one's personality. The essay is in his *Culture as History: The*

Transformation of American Society in the Twentieth Century (New York: Pantheon, 1984), pp. 271–85. It may simplify matters to consider *character* and *personality* in David Riesman's terms as inner- and other- directed personality types respectively. See his *Lonely Crowd* (New Haven: Yale University Press, 1950).

39. Because Outcault did not think of the Yellow Kid as an individual, he may not have thought it particularly important for his "character" to have a "voice." See Hancock, "American Caricature," p. 130.

40. Word balloons were used in American political cartoons especially in the 1830s and 1840s. After 1850 the technique fell out of favor but was used once in a while in illustrated humor journals. See for instance F. M. Howarth's "Smart Boy and His Grand-Papa," *Life*, 13 (March 21, 1889), pp. 170–71, and Michael Angelo Woolf's "Supreme Moment," *Life*, 20 (October 20, 1892), p. 224. The technique can be traced back to early European broadsheets, but it was not until Opper employed them in his comic strips that word balloons flourished as an integral part of comic art.

41. By this time Rudolph Dirks had begun to use word balloons in "The Katzenjammer Kids," but as Richard Marschall notes they were mostly afterthoughts and contributed little to Dirks's depictions of the kids' antics. Marschall, *America's Great Comic Strip Artists*, p. 41.

2. COMIC STRIPS, NATIONAL CULTURE, AND MARKETING

1. The name of Hearst's morning and Sunday New York newspaper varied. Before March 1903 it was titled in chronological order *New York Journal, New York Journal and Advertiser, New York Journal and American,* and *New York American and Journal*. From March 2, 1903, to 1937 it was titled *New York American*. After a number of merges and suspensions this publication finally ceased on May 5, 1967. Ironically by that time it was merged with the two other papers that pioneered comic strips, the *World* and the *New York Herald*. I will refer to it as the *Journal* up to March 1902 and thereafter as the *American*. From September 1896 to 1937 Hearst also published the *New York Evening Journal*. The figures for newspapers carrying comic strips are based on my survey of Library of Congress newspapers on microfilm, see my introduction, n. 22.

2. The Sunday *World*'s circulation increased from 266,000 in 1893 to 450,000 in 1896. See *World* (December 6, 1895). Frank Luther Mott, *American Journalism: A History of Newspapers in the United States through 250 Years, 1690–1940* (New York: Macmillan, 1941), p. 648.

3. Mott, *American Journalism*, p. 646.

4. For details on syndication and chain ownership of newspapers, see Sidney Kobre, *The Yellow Press and Gilded Age Journalism* (Tallahassee:

Florida State University, 1964); Moses Koenigsberg, *King News: An Auto-biography* (Philadelphia: F. A. Stokes, 1941), pp. 363–405; Richard Marschall, "A History of Newspaper Syndication," in Maurice Horn, ed., *The World Encyclopedia of Comics* (New York: Chelsea House, 1976), pp. 721–27; Mott, *American Journalism,* pp. 645–50; and Elsa Ann Nystrom, "A Rejection of Order: The Development of the Newspaper Comic Strip in America, 1830–1920" (Ph.D. diss., Loyola University of Chicago, 1989), chap. 6.

5. The Library of Congress does not hold Hearst's Chicago, Boston, or Los Angeles papers. See tables in the appendix for details on newspapers that carried comic strips in 1903.

6. I derived the population figure by adding the 1900 census populations of all incorporated places that my survey showed had newspapers that published comic strips. As noted in the introduction, my figures are on the conservative side because they reflect a bias in favor of larger cities and also do not take into account significant populations in surrounding regions for cities such as New York, Chicago, Boston, Minneapolis, and San Francisco. Census figures from *World Almanac* (New York: Press Publishing, 1908), pp. 635–37.

7. Circulation figures from *Memphis Commercial Appeal* (July 27, 1902) and *Topeka Daily Capital* (November 11, 1903, and February 16, 1904). In the absence of any other notable change in the two newspapers, it seems that comic strips were primarily responsible for these increases.

8. Daniel Boorstin, *The Americans: The Democratic Experience* (New York: Random House, 1973), p. 132. Wide circulations were not limited to newspapers with comic strips. The *Rochester Democrat & Chronicle* of November 9, 1913, reported that of its 57,210 circulation, 14,610 was outside the city. The paper had carried strips in 1908 but apparently dropped them in response to a national "decency" campaign. See Nystrom, "Rejection of Order," chap. 5, for a discussion of this campaign.

9. The *Indianapolis Journal* and the *Indianapolis Sentinel,* which carried comic strips, merged with the *Star* in 1904 and 1906 respectively. The *Star* did not carry comic strips in 1908. The *Helena Independent* dropped comic strips.

10. "A Crime against American Children," *Ladies' Home Journal,* 26 (January 1909), p. 5; Ralph Bergengren, "The Humor of the Colored Supplements," *Atlantic Monthly,* 98 (August 1906), p. 270; and "Sounding the Doom of the 'Comics,'" *Current Literature,* 45 (December 1908), p. 632. See also "The Comic Supplement," *Outlook,* 97 (April 15, 1911), p. 802; "A Growl for the Unpicturesque," *Atlantic Monthly,* 98 (July 1906), p. 141; and Amos Stote, "Figures in the New Humour," *Bookman,* 31 (May 1910), pp. 286–93.

11. Annie Russell Marble, "The Reign of the Spectacular," *Dial,* 35 (November 1, 1903), pp. 297–99. Later in life Marble may have changed her mind about the educative value of the "spectacular"; she produced nine pageants between 1915 and 1931. See her entry in *National Cyclopaedia of American Biography* (Ann Arbor, Mich.: University Microfilms, 1967), vol. 27, p. 59.

12. Boorstin, *Democratic Experience,* p. 133. Benjamin Rader, "The Quest for Subcommunities and the Rise of American Sport," *American Quarterly,* 29 (Fall 1977), pp. 335–69.

13. Boorstin, *Democratic Experience,* p. 145.

14. For the importance of Rural Free Delivery to the book trade, see Richard B. Kielbowicz, "Mere Merchandise or Vessels of Culture?: Books in the Mail, 1792–1942," *Papers of the Bibliographical Society of America,* 82 (1988), pp. 187–90. See also his "Postal Subsidies for the Press and the Business of Mass Culture, 1880–1920," *Business History Review,* 64 (Autumn 1990), pp. 451–88.

15. Artists developed the naughty kid theme mostly in urban settings, although occasionally they used rural themes. Mark Twain's Tom Sawyer and Huckleberry Finn demonstrate that the Victorian icon of the innocent child always had strong competition from mischievous nonurban types.

16. A prototype appeared in the *New York World* on January 24, 1897. In a cartoon entitled "In the Heat of the Conflict," Outcault depicted a young boy with long hair dressed in fancy clothes. He was accompanied by a dog similar to Buster's Tige. The caption beneath the illustration named the boy as Tommy.

17. Warren Susman, "'Personality' and the Making of Twentieth-Century Culture," in his *Culture as History: The Transformation of American Society in the Twentieth Century* (New York: Pantheon, 1984), pp. 271 –85. See also Nystrom, "Rejection of Order," p. 108. Susman did not acknowledge it, but his concepts seem to have been influenced in part by Daniel Boorstin's in *The Image: A Guide to Pseudo-Events in America* (1962; reprint, New York: Atheneum, 1987).

18. See Susman, "'Personality,'" p. 273; and Philip Rieff, *The Triumph of the Therapeutic: Uses of Faith after Freud* (New York: Harper & Row, 1966), pp. 2–3.

19. William R. Taylor, "The Launching of Commercial Culture: New York City, 1860–1939," in John Hull Mollenkopf, ed., *Power, Culture, and Place: Essays on New York City* (New York: Russell Sage Foundation, 1988), p. 122. Nystrom, "Rejection of Order," p. 120. Nystrom is on firmer ground when she suggests that the broad appeal of comic strips lay in the variety of readings that could be brought to them (pp. 110, 120–21). She argues that there are two types of comic strips, topical and elemental: "Topical comic

strips appeal to the particular needs of society at a given time" (p. 109); elemental strips have "themes that touch the longstanding basic values and traditional beliefs held by the majority of Americans" (pp. 110–11). In addition
elemental strips have "prismatic personalities." This latter concept Nystrom
borrowed from William Taylor, who had defined "a socially prismatic personality" as one found in a character that would "have comic significance to
those approaching it from different social perspectives." Taylor, "Toward the
Launching of a Commercial Culture: New York City, 1860–1939" (paper
presented at a meeting of the Social Science Research Council, March 16–19,
1984), pp. 51 –52, cited in Nystrom, "Rejection of Order," p. 109.

20. In 1903 "Buster Brown" appeared in four newspapers: the *New York
Herald,* the *Chicago Tribune,* the *St. Louis Post-Dispatch,* and the *Los
Angeles Herald.* But as I show Outcault was interested in expanding the
strip's circulation across the nation. According to Richard Marschall,
America's Great Comic Strip Artists (New York: Abbeville Press, 1989),
p. 38, Outcault lived in the then semirural Flushing, Long Island.

21. Louis M. Glackens (1866–1933) worked primarily for *Puck* until
1914. He then worked as an animator.

22. Maud Summers, *Editor & Publisher,* 19 (September 1908), p. 3, cited
in Nystrom, "Rejection of Order," p. 172; and "The Comic Nuisance,"
Outlook, 91 (March 6, 1909), p. 528. Buster Brown was also praised by
Norman Hapgood, editor of *Collier's Weekly,* at a New York meeting of the
League for the Improvement of the Children's Comic Supplement; see "Make
Comics Educational," *Survey,* 26 (April l5, 1911), p. 103.

23. "Buster Brown and the Bull," *New York Herald* (May 14, 1905).

24. Outcault's ambiguity may explain John Swartz's difficulty in quantifying values expressed in "Buster Brown." See his "Anatomy of the Comic Strip
and the Value World of Kids" (Ph.D. diss., Ohio State University, 1978).

25. The basis of the decision in favor of the *Herald* was that it had copy-
righted the title of the comic strip "Buster Brown" by publishing the strip.
See *New York Herald Co. v. Star Co.,* 146 Federal Reporter 204; and
Outcault et al. v. New York Herald, 146 Federal Reporter 205 and 146
Federal Reporter 1023, for the Circuit Court of Appeals decision upholding
the lower court verdict. In *Outcault et al. v. Lamar,* 119 New York
Supplement 930, the New York Supreme Court Appellate Division found
that Outcault had retained all other rights to Buster Brown in an agreement
with the *Herald* of October 1, 1902. See *Outcault et al. v. Bonheur,* 104
New York Supplement 1099, for details of Outcault's earnings from the
stage show. Around this time Buster declared, "Yes you can find *justice* in the
dictionary, not in the court house." *New York American* (October 4, 1908).

26. A readership of 2.5 people per copy of a newspaper would give the
papers carrying "Buster Brown" a coverage of 10.30 percent of the population according to the 1900 census and 8.50 percent by the 1910 census. In

1908 the five largest cities in America—New York, Chicago, Philadelphia, St. Louis, and Boston—made up 55.90 percent of the potential audience for comic strips. Hearst's version of "Buster Brown" was published in New York, Chicago, and Boston, which together accounted for 43.00 percent of the total comic strip audience. Smaller centers accounted for the rest of the potential audience that received Hearst's "Buster Brown." The *Herald*'s version added three locations: St. Louis, which represented 3.90 percent of the potential audience, and Des Moines and Wheeling, which between them represented 0.50 percent of that audience. Buster's audience then was mostly in large urban centers but with a significant percentage in rural regional centers. "Buster Brown" was carried by newspapers in cities and towns with a total population of 11,432,359. Of this 1,573,571, or 13.76 percent, resided outside the five major cities.

27. "They All Do It" [Knox hat advertisement], *Life*, 25 (January 3, 1895), p. 17; "As a Matter of Course" [Knox hat advertisement], *Life*, 25 (April 4, 1895), p. 225; Pears' soap advertisement, *Puck*, 25 (May 15, 1889), p. 204; Vin Mariani advertisement, *Life*, 23 (May 24, 1894), p. 344; "An Artist's Trials," *Life*, 15 (March 6, 1890), p. 141; "The Value of Advertising" [*Life* advertisement], *Life*, 17 (April 30, 1891), p. 283; Frederick Burr Opper, "Happy Hooligan," *Cincinnati Enquirer* (December 6, 1903). The "Happy Hooligan" strip may have been a spoof; I cannot find any reference to a "Happy Hooligan" cast-iron toy of this sort in standard works on toys and collectibles. If Opper's strip was a spoof it was in the tradition of earlier gags about Kodak's slogan "Just Press the Button, We Do the Rest," which appeared in illustrated journals. See for instance "Another Version," *Life*, 18 (December 10, 1891), p. 357.

28. See Susan Strasser, *Satisfaction Guaranteed: The Making of the American Mass Market* (New York: Pantheon, 1989), pp. 182–83; and Stephen R. Fox, *The Mirror Makers: A History of American Advertising and Its Creators* (New York: William Morrow, 1984), pp. 46–47.

29. Robert Lesser, *A Celebration of Comic Art and Memorabilia* (New York: Hawthorn Books, 1975), p. 120.

30. Author's telephone conversation with Frances Charman (a former employee of Buster Brown Textiles Incorporated), November 11, 1991. Unfortunately the company disposed of most of its early records in the 1950s.

31. The 1902 advertisement mentions four plants. The Brown Shoe Co. catalog 31, circa 1907, contains an illustration of the company's eight plants. Both items held in the Warshaw Collection of Business Americana, Archives Center, National Museum of American History, Smithsonian Institution, Collection 60 (hereafter NMAH 60), Shoes, box 9. J. H. Sawyer, "Buster Brown Advertises Shoes," *Judicious Advertising*, 8 (March 1910), pp. 27–30, 89. Until the late 1970s Frances Charman arranged similar shows in department stores for Buster Brown Textiles. Telephone conversation, July 9, 1991.

32. *Printers' Ink,* 64 (July 8, 1908), p. 16, cited in Daniel Pope, *The Making of Modern Advertising* (New York: Basic Books, 1983), p. 69; and Michael Schudson, *Advertising: The Uneasy Persuasion: Its Dubious Impact on American Society* (New York: Basic Books, 1984), p. 160. For a discussion of trademarks and brand names, see also Strasser, *Satisfaction Guaranteed;* and Richard S. Tedlow, *New and Improved: The Story of Mass Marketing in America* (New York: Basic Books, 1990).

33. The Lion Store advertisement, *Daily Oklahoman* (December 13, 1908), p. 7; Oklahoma Steam Baking Co. advertisement, *Daily Oklahoman* (December 6, 1908), p. 7; Jim Thompson, *Bad Boy* (1953; reprint, New York: Mysterious Press, 1988), p. 3. Buster Brown must have left a strong impression on Thompson for him to remember this item of clothing after fifty years and a life resembling his novels. Reading comic strips itself required an act of consumption, the purchase of a newspaper. The population of Oklahoma City went from 10,037 to 64,025 between 1900 and 1910.

34. "Ah Well, Boys Will Be Boys," *New York American* (April 19, 1914). It is almost redundant to note the range of Buster Brown suits, shoes, and stockings.

35. The Seattle advertisement is reprinted in Richard F. Outcault, *Buster Brown,* Hyperion Library of Classic American Comic Strips (Westport, Conn.: Hyperion, 1977). Nystrom cites the same resolution in an advertisement in the *Los Angeles Times* (March 19, 1911). "Rejection of Order," p. 128, n. 28.

36. "A Visit to Papa's Office," *New York American* (April 22, 1906).

37. *Providence Journal* (December 7, 1913). Outcault also included outright plugs for Buster Brown products in the comic strip. One episode contained a sign in the background advising, "Try a Buster Brown Mixture For Colds." "Buster Brown at the Soda Water Fountain," *New York Herald* (May 31, 1903). The May 6, 1906, strip, "How to Tame a Lion," in the *New York American* had a man in a lion suit saying to Buster, "Hello Old Chap. Don't you remember—I used to play Tige in your show," a reference to the Buster Brown stage show.

38. The original graphics for the copyrighted advertisements are now held by the Library of Congress Prints and Photographs Division, but unfortunately they have not been organized since being transferred from the Copyright Office and are not available for consultation. These two sides to Buster's character probably account for the different interpretations of the strip by Maud Summers and the *Outlook* editorial writer.

39. Hal Barron, "With All the Fragrant Powders of the Merchant: Mail-Order Buying in the Rural North, 1870–1920" (unpublished paper in author's possession).

40. Marian Anderson, selection from *My Lord, What a Morning,* in Jill Ker Conway, ed., *Written by Herself: Autobiographies of American Women:*

An Anthology (New York: Vintage Books, 1992), p. 81; Bush cited in "Buster Brown and Tige," *Kiplinger Magazine* (June 1959), p. 28; Michael Barton, posting H-AMSTDY, May 13, 1996.

41. See Jane M. Gaines, *Contested Culture: The Image, the Voice, and the Law* (Chapel Hill: University of North Carolina Press, 1991), for an account of intellectual property law and culture.

3. COMIC ART AND THE COMMODIFICATION OF AFRICAN AMERICAN TYPOGRAPHIES

1. Joseph Boskin, *Sambo: The Rise and Demise of an American Jester* (New York: Oxford University Press, 1986), chap. 1; Walter Lippmann, *Public Opinion* (1922; reprint, New York: Free Press, 1965), p. 65. Boskin sidesteps the representation of African American women, arguing that Sambo was a means of social control and that to "effect power over males was to control women and children." The long tradition of depicting African American women as mammies suggests that this characterization was a bit hasty. See also Jan Nederveen Pieterse, *White on Black: Images of Africa and Blacks in Western Popular Culture* (New Haven: Yale University Press, 1992).

2. A key work in the scholarship of the construction of white identity is David Roediger, *The Wages of Whiteness: Race and the Making of the American Working Class* (New York: Verso, 1991). David Stowe discusses this and other books in his review essay "Uncolored People: The Rise of Whiteness Studies," *Lingua Franca* 6 (September–October 1996), pp. 69–77. See also Peter Jackson and Jan Penrose, eds., *Constructions of Race, Place and Nation* (London: UCL Press, 1993).

3. The first of Outcault's Possumville cartoons appeared in *Judge* on March 24, 1900, the last on February 16, 1901. See "Hamlet Ghost Scene" and "How the New Parson Aroused the Congregation," *Judge,* 38 (March 24, 1900, and April 4, 1900, respectively) for the general tone.

4. See Norman Bryson, "Semiology and Visual Interpretation," in Norman Bryson, Michael Ann Holly, and Keith Moxey, eds., *Visual Theory: Painting and Interpretation* (Cambridge: Polity Press, 1991), for the concept of visual representation as language, particularly pp. 69–70. Scott McCloud's *Understanding Comics* (New York: Harper Perennial, 1994) is the definitive work on the codes and conventions of comic art. The standard account of minstrelsy is Robert C. Toll, *Blacking Up: The Minstrel Show in Nineteenth Century America* (New York: Oxford University Press, 1974).

5. "Poor Lil Mose," *New York Herald* (December 2, 1900).

6. Boskin, *Sambo*, p. 6.

7. Maurice Horn, ed., *The World Encyclopedia of Comics* (New York: Chelsea House, 1976), pp. 479–80, entry by Richard Marschall.

8. For illustrations of the Katzenjammer Kids, see Rudolph Dirks, *The Katzenjammer Kids: Early Strips in Full Color* (New York: Dover, 1974); and Richard Marschall, *America's Great Comic Strip Artists* (New York: Abbeville Press, 1989).

9. T. J. Jackson Lears, *Fables of Abundance: A Cultural History of Advertising in America* (New York: Basic Books, 1994), p. 309. The link between Sambo's Phoebie and the Buffalo & Lackawanna Railroad's trademark character was made clear in the April 25, 1909, episode of the strip, when Sambo recited that he was "on mah way to Buffalo to see mah goil Miss Phoebie Snow."

10. Other examples may exist, but I have not seen them. My study of comic strips between these dates was extensive but by no means exhaustive. The reduction of African Americans to caricature for the sake of comic representation occurred even in the black press but with nowhere near the ferocity or frequency as in mass-circulated media. See for instance "Sunnyboy Sam" by Wilbert Holloway in the *Pittsburgh Courier* (April 4, 1929).

11. See Richard Waterhouse, "The Internationalisation of American Popular Culture in the Nineteenth Century: The Case of the Minstrel Show," *Australasian Journal of American Studies*, 4 (July 1985), pp. 1–11.

12. See John Canemaker, *Felix: The Twisted Tale of the World's Most Famous Cat* (New York: Pantheon, 1991), for an account of Pat Sullivan.

13. Ibid., p. 38.

14. Ibid., pp. 80–81.

15. Jay Cantor, *Krazy Kat: A Novel in Five Panels* (New York: Alfred A. Knopf, 1988); Gilbert Seldes, *The Seven Lively Arts* (New York: Harper Brothers, 1924); e. e. cummings, "Introduction," in George Herriman, *Krazy Kat* (New York: Grosset & Dunlap, 1977), pp. 10–16. Quotations from Seldes' chapter "The Krazy Kat That Walks by Himself" reprinted in Patrick McDonnell, Karen O'Connell, and Georgia Riley de Havenon, *Krazy Kat: The Comic Art of George Herriman* (New York: Harry N. Abrams, 1986), pp. 15, 22; Kirk Varnedoe and Adam Gopnik, *High & Low: Modern Art and Popular Culture* (New York: Museum of Modern Art, 1990), pp. 168, 172.

16. Early strips from the bottom of "The Family Upstairs" are reprinted in Herriman, *Krazy Kat*, pp. 23 and 27; Bill Blackbeard, "The Kat's Kreation," in George Herriman, *Krazy & Ignatz: The Komplete Kat Komics*, vol. 1: *1916* (Forestville, Calif.: Eclipse Books, 1988), p. 9.

17. Reprinted in Herriman, *Krazy & Ignatz*, vol. 1, p. 47. Dates for "Krazy Kat" strips vary because they sometimes appeared in different papers in different weeks. The variation seems to have been only a week.

18. On July 14, 1918, Krazy visited "Madame Kamouflage's Beauty Parlour" and emerged a blond, whereon Ignatz fell in love. The cat and crazy reference is from the June 17, 1917, episode. Both episodes reprinted in

Herriman, *Krazy & Ignatz*, the former in volume 3: *1918*, p. 33, the latter in volume 2: *1917*, p. 29.

19. McDonnell et al., *Krazy Kat*, p. 30.

20. Ibid., p. 40. See also La Touche Hancock, "American Caricature and Comic Art," *Bookman*, 16 (November 1902), pp. 263–74.

21. See David Kunzle, "World Upside Down: The Iconography of a European Broadsheet Type," in Barbara A. Babcock, ed., *The Reversible World: Symbolic Inversion in Art and Society* (Ithaca: Cornell University Press, 1978); Kunzle, *History of the Comic Strip*, vol. 2: *The Nineteenth Century* (Berkeley: University of California Press, 1990). The world-turned-upside-down tradition was related to *charivari;* see Natalie Zemon Davis, *Society and Culture in Early Modern France* (Palo Alto: Stanford University Press, 1975), pp.137, 139, 131, and 143; E. P. Thompson, *Whigs and Hunters: The Origins of the Black Act* (New York: Pantheon, 1975), pp. 71, 228, and 256; and Lynn Hunt, *Politics, Culture and Class in the French Revolution* (Berkeley: University of California Press, 1984), chaps. 2 and 3. For the transmission of African traditions to America, see John W. Nunley, *Caribbean Festival Arts: Each and Every Bit of Difference* (St. Louis: St. Louis Art Museum, 1988); and Frank E. Manning, ed., *The Celebration of Society: Perspectives on Contemporary Cultural Performance* (Bowling Green, Ohio: Bowling Green University Popular Press, 1983). William Piersen's *Black Legacy* (Amherst: University of Massachusetts Press, 1993), gives an account of "Negro Election Day," in which blacks and whites participated in role reversals. See Sinclair Lewis, *Main Street* (1920; reprint, New York: Harcourt Brace, 1946), p. 121, for a fictive twentieth-century instance of *charivari.*

22. Cited in McDonnell et al., *Krazy Kat*, p. 54.

4. COMIC STRIPS AS CULTURE

1. See Stephen R. Fox, *The Mirror Makers: A History of American Advertising and Its Creators* (New York: William Morrow, 1984), chap. 4; and Roland Marchand, *Advertising the American Dream: Making Way for Modernity, 1920–1940* (Berkeley: University of California Press, 1985), chap. 4, for general accounts of the use of comic art by advertisers in the 1930s.

2. Michael Schudson, *Discovering the News: A Social History of American Newspapers* (New York: Basic Books, 1978).

3. "Buster Brown" was the most commonly reprinted comic strip, but other strips, including "The Katzenjammer Kids" and "Happy Hooligan," were also reprinted. See *Playthings*, 7 (June 6, 1908), pp. 31, 126–28.

4. Bernard Mergen, "Children's Play in American Autobiographies, 1820–1914," in Kathryn Grover, ed., *Hard at Play* (Amherst: University of Massachusetts Press, 1992).

5. "Editorial," *Playthings,* 18 (January 1920), p. 227.

6. Dorothy S. Coleman, Elizabeth A. Coleman, and Evelyn J. Coleman, *The Collector's Encyclopedia of Dolls,* vol. 2 (New York: Crown Publishers, 1986), p. 730.

7. *Playthings,* special issue New York Toy Fair, 24 (1926), n.p. See David Longest, *Character Toys and Collectibles* (Paducah, Ky.: Collector Books, 1984), p. 10, and Longest, *Character Toys and Collectibles: Second Series* (Paducah, Ky.: Collector Books, 1987), p. 21, for examples of "Barney Google" and "Bringing Up Father" dolls. Also see these sources for examples of German and Japanese comic-strip-based dolls, toys, and games.

8. The Motion Picture, Broadcasting, and Recorded Sound Division of the Library of Congress has several early live-action comic strip shorts, including *Foxy Grandpa Shows the Boys a Trick,* from 1902, and *The Katzenjammer Kids and the School Marm,* from 1903. The division also holds a number of early animated shorts based on comic strip characters. See Kemp R. Niver, *Early Motion Pictures: The Paper Print Collection in the Library of Congress* (Washington, D.C.: Library of Congress, 1985), for details of early movies featuring comic strip characters. John Canemaker, *Winsor McCay: His Life and Art* (New York: Abbeville Press, 1987), p. 132. For a photograph of the Katzenjammer amusement park, see negative LC-D4-18215 in the Prints and Photographs Division of the Library of Congress. Mark Winchester graciously supplied information on Gus Hill based on his "Cartoon Theatricals from 1896 to 1927: Gus Hill's Cartoon Road Shows for the American Road Theatre" (Ph.D. diss., Ohio State University, 1995). Bill Blackbeard, "A Kat of Many Kolors," in George Herriman, *Krazy & Ignatz: The Komplete Kat Komics,* vol. 7: *1922* (Forestville, Calif.: Eclipse Books, 1991), p. 1.

9. George Gallup, "Guesswork Eliminated in New Method for Determining Reader Interest," *Editor & Publisher,* 62 (February 8, 1930), pp. 1, 55; and Gallup, "What Do Newspaper Readers Read?" *Advertising & Selling* (March 31, 1932), pp. 22–23. Gallup defined "best" as the story or feature that attracted the most readers. The content of his second article was almost identical to that of the first, although the second contained additional graphs. Gallup, "Guesswork Eliminated," p. 55. See also "Minutes of Staff Meeting," June 16, 1931, p. 6, J. Walter Thompson Archives, Special Collections Library, Duke University (hereafter JWT Archives). Gallup divided the population into four occupational groups, salaried, skilled, day laborers, and farmers, and surveyed both male and female members of each group. Three of the newspapers surveyed were published in cities with popu-

lations over 500,000, two with populations over 100,000, and one with fewer than 100,000 people.

10. Harvey C. Lehman and Paul Witty, "The Compensatory Function of the Sunday Funny Paper," *Journal of Applied Psychology* 11 (June 1927), pp. 204, 208. Lehman and Witty attributed the popularity of the comic strips to the uninhibited activities of their characters and suggested that a child "who looks at the Sunday 'funnies' is enabled to identify himself" with its characters (p. 210). They did not bother to explain why or how this supposed identification took place. Martin Barker criticizes the concept of identification as reductive in chapter 5 of his *Comics: Ideology, Power, and the Critics* (Manchester: Manchester University Press, 1989).

11. Marchand, *Advertising the American Dream,* p. 110, n. 78.

12. A report at a staff meeting of the J. Walter Thompson agency on March 3, 1931, noted the Hearst decision. One Thompson employee proposed testing the medium with coupons, but the agency did not place comic strip advertisements before the Grape-Nuts ad, which a Hearst executive, Hawley Turner, sold direct to the manufacturer, General Foods. Gallup's work was not mentioned at the March 1931 meeting. "Minutes of Staff Meeting," March 3, 1931, p. 8, and "Minutes of Staff Meeting," October 11, 1932, pp. 1–2, JWT Archives. See also W. E. Berchtold, "Men of Comics," *New Outlook,* 165 (April 1935), p. 36. For the early use of coupons, see Susan Strasser, *Satisfaction Guaranteed: The Making of the American Mass Market* (New York: Pantheon, 1989), pp. 146–47.

13. General Foods published the advertisements for Grape-Nuts in the Hearst newspapers' comic supplement on June 7, June 21, July 5, August 30, September 27, and November 1, 1931. See "Minutes of Staff Meeting," March 12, 1932, pp. 2–3, JWT Archives. The first Postum ad appeared January 17, 1932, and the first Jell-O ad, January 24, 1932. In 1932 the comic supplement appeared in Hearst's seventeen Sunday newspapers, which had a combined circulation of 5,581,137. "The Greatest Common Denominator among All Publications," *Printers' Ink* (July 14, 1932), p. 24. See also Frank Luther Mott, *American Journalism: A History of Newspapers in the United States through 250 Years, 1690–1940* (New York: Macmillan, 1941), p. 646. The same comic supplement, with the same advertisements, appeared in each paper.

14. Gallup's authority was used on a number of occasions to bolster claims for comic strip advertising in particular newspapers or magazines; see for instance the *Liberty* advertisement in *Printers' Ink* (May 12, 1932), pp. 46–47, and the Hearst advertisement "The Greatest Sales Conference in History Opens," *Printers' Ink* (July 19, 1934), pp. 33–44.

15. "The Fortune Quarterly Survey: VIII," *Fortune* (April 1937), p. 112.

16. Ibid., p. 190. *Fortune* also noted that a majority of adults among "all

economic levels except the Negroes" read the strips. Sixty percent of salaried executives and 64.9 percent of salaried workers had a favorite. *Fortune* offered no explanation of why comic strip readership was lower in the South.

17. Advertising Research Foundation, *The Continuing Study of Newspaper Reading,* no. 138: *Study Summary* (New York: Advertising Research Foundation, 1950), pp. 15, 13. In this survey the four occupational categories were business and professional, salaried, skilled, and unskilled. The survey also provided gender breakdowns for the reading of individual strips.

18. I have seen three early advertisements that used comic strip techniques. A July 6, 1902, ad for Cascaret Candy Cathartic in the *Atlanta Constitution* used sweat beads long before this technique appeared anywhere else. A more important early use of comic-strip-style advertising was two ads by Ray Barnes that appeared in the *Grand Rapids Herald* in October 1913. The first, on October 1, entitled "Teaching Grand Rapids 'Kids' to Save Money," told a story in panels and word balloons that promoted school-based savings accounts for the Grand Rapids Savings Bank. "The Evolution of Electric Current," on October 5, employed panels and rhyming verse to explain and promote the use of electric current. But these advertisements were probably oddities; I came across no others like them in my survey of newspapers from 1903 to 1913.

19. Advertisements for Michelin Tires, Kohler Plumbing Fixtures, Hammermill Bond Paper, and Denver Gas & Electric Light Co. also used comic art in the 1920s. See *Saturday Evening Post* (October 9, 1926), pp. 120 and 215; (October 23, 1926), pp. 77 and 135; and *Electrical Merchandising,* 27 (January 1922), pp. 69–70.

20. Charles A. Voight (1887–1947) began the daily comic strip "Petey Dink" in the *Boston Traveler* in 1908. Maurice Horn, ed., *The World Encyclopedia of Comics* (New York: Chelsea House, 1976), p. 687. An alternative title of this strip was "Mrs. Worry," which seems prescient given Voight's advertisements for Rinso. See *New York American* (April 10, 1932) for examples of both advertisements.

21. "Minutes of Staff Meeting," October 11, 1932, pp. 17–19, JWT Archives.

22. "Greatest Common Denominator." Beginning September 20, 1931, the Hearst comic supplement bore the title, motto, and logo of *Puck,* the preeminent American illustrated humor journal of the late nineteenth century. This may have been part of a marketing strategy to ensure the Hearst supplement's leading status, which was under challenge from the *Chicago Tribune–New York Daily News* syndicate's supplement.

23. "Competitive Comics," *Tide* (June 8, 1932), p. 14; and "Funny Paper Advts.," *Fortune* (April 1933), pp. 98, 101.

24. "The Greatest Sales Conference in History Opens," *Printers' Ink* (July 19, 1934), pp. 33–44; "Is It Smart to Be Snooty Even to a Cat?" *Printers' Ink* (July 27, 1933), pp. 52–53; "He Wouldn't Use 'Comics' Until,"

Tribune (February 16, 1938), p. 9; "What the Comic Weekly for a Quality Product?" *Tribune* (April 13, 1938), p. 13.

25. "Greatest Common Denominator," p. 25. See Marchand, *Advertising the American Dream,* pp. 88–94 and 108–10, for a discussion of advertising on early radio.

26. See *New York American* (May 17, 1936).

27. See "Minutes of Staff Meeting," October 11, 1932, pp. 24–25, JWT Archives.

28. See "Minutes of Staff Meeting," March 3, 1931, p. 8, JWT Archives.

29. Comic strip characters were not entirely absent from Hearst's comic supplement advertisements. "Little Billy the Buster," the Parker Pen advertisement of November 6, 1932, evoked Buster Brown in its title and its use of a resolution-like block of word-ballooned text. An Ovaltine advertisement of November 13, 1932, concluded by offering a Little Orphan Annie mug and included an illustration of Annie. But "Little Orphan Annie" was not a Hearst strip, so the distinction between talent and product was maintained. It would be interesting to know if there was any discussion in the Hearst ranks about the appearance of a competitor's comic strip character in their newspapers.

30. See Duco Polish advertisement, *Saturday Evening Post* (September 10, 1932), p. 43; Wheaties advertisement, ibid. (August 26, 1933), pp. 62–63; Bayer Aspirin advertisement, ibid. (September 16, 1933), p. 37; Chase and Sanborn Coffee advertisement, ibid. (September 16, 1933), p. 59; Colgate Rapid Shave Cream advertisement, ibid. (September 30, 1933), p. 77; Taylor Instruments advertisement, ibid. (September 30, 1933), p. 74; Taylor Instruments advertisement, *Ladies' Home Journal* (September 1933), p. 88; Colgate Ribbon Dental Cream advertisement, ibid. (September 1933), p. 49. Arthur H. Little, "If the Egg-Talk Sounded Tall, Consider Talk of Men!" *Printers' Ink* (September 7, 1933), p. 61. *Advertising & Selling* also ran a short comment on the proliferation of word balloons. (September 14, 1933), p. 16.

31. "Minutes of Staff Meeting," March 12, 1932, pp. 8–9, JWT Archives. Jesse Thompson, "What a Decade of Depression Has Done to Advertising Copy," *Advertising & Selling* (August 1939), p. 74 (emphasis in original).

32. N. W. Ayer Advertising Agency Records, Archives Center, National Museum of American History, Smithsonian Institution, Collection 59 (hereafter NMAH 59). "Minutes of Staff Meeting," March 12, 1932, p. 8, JWT Archives.

33. Hy-Pro advertisements, NMAH 59, oversize box 426.

34. See for instance, "The Katzenjammer Kids," "Happy Hooligan," "Buster Brown," "Winnie Winkle," and more recently "Hägar the Horrible."

35. Atlantic advertisements, NMAH 59, bks. 580, 581.

36. Ibid., bk. 582.

37. Atlantic was based on the eastern seaboard, and most of its advertisements were published in newspapers and magazines whose distribution was limited to this area or a part of it.

38. Atlantic advertisements, NMAH 59, bks. 582, 584, 586.

39. Ibid.

40. Ibid., oversize box 50.

41. Ibid., oversize box 51.

42. Ibid., oversize box 52.

43. See for instance the "Birthright" advertisement extolling American individualism in ibid.

5. ENVISIONING CONSUMER CULTURE

1. Julian M. Drachman, "A Prospectus for an American Mythology," *English Journal,* 19 (December 1930), pp. 781–88.

2. The establishment of daily comic strips dates from the publication of Bud Fisher's "Mutt and Jeff" in the *San Francisco Chronicle* in November 1907. Originally titled "A. Mutt," this strip was about a compulsive gambler. It featured a daily gag and an ongoing story line. *Washington Post* (February 23, 1991), p. A21.

3. See Ernest Brennecke, "The Real Mission of the Funny Paper," *Century Magazine* (March 1924), pp. 665–75, for a contemporary account of the middle-class nature of comic strips. William Henry Young, "Images of Order: American Comic Strips during the Depression, 1929–1938" (Ph.D. diss., Emory University, 1969).

4. The auto supplement in the *Tribune* (January 26, 1919), pt. 7, p. 1, noted that in 1918 there were between 125,000 and 130,000 cars registered in Cook County, Illinois, which means that car ownership extended to 15 to 20 percent of Chicago's populace. The location of "Gasoline Alley" was tied to Chicago because the strip began as a commentary on the motoring habits of the city's residents. It was set in a middle-class locale, probably a suburb on the outskirts of Chicago, but the exact location was never stated because once the strip developed it had to appeal to a syndicated audience across the country.

5. James J. Flink, *The Automobile Age* (Cambridge, Mass.: MIT Press, 1988), p. 188; Martha L. Olney, *Buy Now, Pay Later: Advertising, Credit, and Consumer Durables in the 1920s* (Chapel Hill: University of North Carolina Press, 1991), p. 11.

6. George C. Diehl, "Next a National Highway System," *Tribune* (November 24, 1918), pt. 5, p. 6. See *Tribune* (January 26, 1919), pt. 7, for a typical automobile show supplement.

7. See *New York Herald* advertisement in *Chicago Tribune* (January 30, 1923), p. 28. Standard Oil Company advertisement, ibid. (August 26, 1919), p. 11; Continental Motors Corporation advertisement, ibid. (November 12, 1920), p. 21; Interstate Garage Corporation advertisement, ibid. (June 20, 1921), p. 24; (July 20, 1921), p. 30; (January 7, 1923), pt. 2, p. 7; (January 28, 1923), pt. 3, p. 6.

8. Frank King, "Gasoline Alley," *Chicago Tribune* (November 24, 1918), pt. 5, p. 1. "Cold Weather and Engine Efficiency," ibid. (November 24, 1918), pt. 5, p. 6.

9. King used both a single-panel format and the more familiar multipanel format until mid-1920, when he switched exclusively to the strip format. The Sunday episode continued as a single panel until October 24, 1920, when the strip was moved to a full page in the color comic section. The *Tribune* syndicated "Gasoline Alley," and the strip ran in newspapers across the nation, including the *New York Daily News,* the *Los Angeles Times,* and the *Washington Post.*

10. Frank King, "Gasoline Alley," *Chicago Tribune* (January 19, 1921). King frequently adapted a language associated with cars to other areas of life. On March 3, 1921, Walt shopped for a baby carriage as he would shop for a car. On March 10, 1921, he bathed Skeezix, referring to him as if he were a car. On January 17, 1923, Doc testified at Walt's adoption hearing for Skeezix. According to Doc, Walt took better care of Skeezix than he did of his own car.

11. Marshall Field & Company advertisement, *Chicago Tribune* (December 25, 1920), p. 12; *Chicago Tribune* advertisement, ibid. (December 29, 1921), p. 9; McCall's magazines advertisement, ibid. (July 20, 1921), p. 16. Political metaphors were frequently used in advertising. In the language of advertising many products were elected by consumers. See, for instance, A & P advertisement, ibid. (November 9, 1932), p. 13, and *Detroit News* advertisement, ibid. (November 9, 1932), p. 23. See also Charles McGovern, "The Political Language of American Advertising, 1890–1940" (paper presented at the annual meeting of the American Studies Association, Baltimore, Md., 1991).

12. Car ownership was widespread by the mid-1920s. For instance, in 1923 approximately two out of every three families in Muncie, Indiana, owned cars. Sixty of the 123 working-class families surveyed owned cars. Robert and Helen Merrell Lynd, *Middletown: A Study in Modern American Culture* (New York: Harcourt Brace and Jovanovich, 1929), pp. 253–55. Walt Wallet took the job as sales manager on January 6, 1928, for the Wicker Furniture Company. The proprietor, Mr. Wicker, was a "Gasoline Alley" regular. King indicated Walt's ambiguous financial position during the Depression. On January 27, 1935, Walt calculated it would take him seven

years to pay off the mortgage on his house. On April 30, 1936, Walt considered foreclosing on a farm mortgage he held.

13. Sinclair Lewis, *Babbitt* (1922; reprint, New York: Signet, 1980), p. 63. A Westcott advertisement in the *Tribune* on January 28, 1923, offered a "closed car at an open car price," which suggests that advertisers were aware of the importance of the status associated with a closed car. Protection from inclement weather was a comparatively minor concern.

14. "Gasoline Alley" also depicted flowers as an appropriate gift from a man to a woman at times of domestic strife, or as a symbol of love. See for instance March 26, 1926; May 17, 1929; February 15 and May 26, 1939; and February 12, 1940.

15. *Chicago Tribune* (August 29, 1919).

16. Other notable examples of Avery's tightness include saving unburnt coals from his fireplace (January 6, 1923), rigging a radio aerial so as to save the cost of a movie ticket (January 30, 1925), and draining the tonic he has used as a water substitute in a car radiator so that he can resell the tonic (July 27, 1935). For representations of Walt's abundant consumption, see September 15, November 1 and 30, 1924; March 12, 1927; September 23, 1929; January 30 and March 15, 1931; September 11, 1935; and September 7 and December 7, 1941.

17. King aged the strip's younger characters, such as Skeezix, chronologically. This move set "Gasoline Alley" apart from other strips, whose characters' ages were frozen.

18. See David Grimsted, *Melodrama Unveiled: American Theater and Culture, 1800–1850* (Chicago: University of Chicago Press, 1968), especially chapter 9, for a discussion of the reward of virtue in melodrama.

19. Olney, *Buy Now, Pay Later,* pp. 134, 92, 109, 91.

20. See William E. Leuchtenburg, *The Perils of Prosperity, 1914–32* (Chicago: University of Chicago Press, 1958), chaps. 9 and 10. See also Harry Braverman, *Labor and Monopoly Capital: The Degradation of Work in the Twentieth Century* (New York: Monthly Review Press, 1974). Branner's creation of "Winnie Winkle" paralleled motion picture depictions of the new woman. See Mary P. Ryan, "The Projection of a New Womanhood: The Movie Moderns in the 1920s," in Jean E. Friedman and William G. Shade, eds., *Our American Sisters: Women in American Life and Thought* (Boston: Allyn & Bacon, 1976), pp. 366–84.

21. McGovern, "Political Language of American Advertising." McGovern lists nineteen advertising industry articles from the 1910s to 1930s that cite the figure 85 percent. See also Silas Bent, *Ballyhoo: The Voice of the Press* (New York: Boni & Liveright, 1927), pp. 235–36; and Roland Marchand, *Advertising the American Dream: Making Way for Modernity, 1920–1940* (Berkeley: University of California Press, 1985), p. 66. For other discussions of the perception of consumption as a feminine activity, see Neil Harris,

"The Drama of Consumer Desire," in his *Cultural Excursions: Marketing Appetites and Cultural Tastes in Modern America* (Chicago: University of Chicago Press, 1990), pp. 174–97; Rosalind Williams, *Dream Worlds: Mass Consumption in Late Nineteenth Century France* (Berkeley: University of California Press, 1982); and William R. Leach, "Transformation in a Culture of Consumption: Women and Department Stores, 1890–1925," *Journal of American History,* 71 (September 1984), pp. 319–42. "Are Women People?" *Liberty* advertisement, *Chicago Tribune* (February 27, 1928), p. 13.

22. Perry was the son of Rip's brother William, who left his estate to Rip on the condition that he take care of Perry. The estate soon disappeared, but Perry remained in the strip until 1954. Shortly after Perry's introduction the *Daily News,* and other papers carrying the syndicate's strips, published the first color, full-page "Winnie Winkle" Sunday episode on June 11, 1922. For the next thirty-two years the Sunday strip was devoted mostly to the adventures of Perry and his friends. Winnie and the family appeared but primarily as support characters. Likewise Perry would crop up occasionally in the daily strips. His clothing and general manner resembled Buster Brown's, and Branner probably created Perry in an attempt to fill the vacancy for a mischievous boy Sunday comic strip left by Outcault's and Buster's retirements in late 1921.

23. City kids swimming off a pier was an illustrative genre that united editorial cartoons, comic strip artists, photographers, and the Ashcan School of artists. These illustrations depict rough-hewn groups of kids engaged in spontaneous play. Artists idealized youthful spontaneity and counterposed it to a restrictive bourgeois order. See the illustration "The Way the Street Boys of New York Keep Cool during the Dog Days," *New York World* (August 18, 1895), p. 33, in which a cop at the extreme left hastens to put an end to the boys' fun. See also Rebecca Zurier, "Hey Kids: Children in the Comics and the Art of George Bellows," *Print Collectors' Newsletter* (November–December 1987), pp. 196–203; and Rebecca Zurier, Robert W. Snyder, and Virginia M. Mecklenburg, *Metropolitan Lives: The Ashcan Artists and Their New York* (New York: W. W. Norton, 1995), p. 120. Winnie was a frequent guest of the well-to-do, although Branner never explained how she came to be so familiar with them. I think he expected his readers to understand that many doors would open for such a pretty young woman.

24. See, for instance, the episodes of June 11, 1922, and April 20, 1924.

25. In the August 20, 1921, episode Winnie celebrates her eighteenth birthday. Although Winnie grew older over the next twenty-four years, she appears to have been only in her early thirties, at most, by 1945. Winnie's early suitors included Simon Konshus, a shy, young clerk (November 10, 1920); Mr. Ganzy, an elderly, wealthy industrialist acquaintance of her father (October 29, 1920); Mr. Kale, a banker (May 9, 1921); the twins Harry and Larry Tyler, wealthy young men about town (February 27, 1922); Kenneth

Dare, a stockbroker (October 9, 1922); Mike Mulligan, a hick (May 14, 1925); Harry Sherwood, a doctor (March 30, 1925); and Robert Degen, a lawyer (March 30, 1925). Winnie rejected Konshus and Mulligan as unsuitable because they did not aspire to, or could not, improve their class standing. Of the other suitors Ganzy was too old, and the rest suffered character flaws, which Winnie eventually discovered.

26. See January 25, 1924, for Mulligan's attempts to ape collegiate manners. The college yarn could be read as a critique of the hype surrounding college athletics and the collegiate fad of the 1920s, which manufacturers and advertisers sold as a style. See Paula S. Fass, *The Damned and the Beautiful: American Youth in the 1920's* (New York: Oxford University Press, 1977), on the collegiate fad. Mulligan reappeared in the strip on January 13, 1926. Pa discovered his secret on January 22. Winnie was left at the altar on April 5, 1926. She had previously been left at the altar by Dare and one of the Tyler twins. In some ways these two Mulligan stories were low-rent versions of F. Scott Fitzgerald's novels *This Side of Paradise* (1920) and *The Great Gatsby* (1925).

27. Branner's ambiguity about temperance may have been an attempt to straddle the different stands of the strip's rural and urban audiences. On the urban-rural division regarding prohibition, see Leuchtenburg, *Perils of Prosperity,* pp. 213–17; and Lawrence W. Levine, *Defender of the Faith, William Jennings Bryan: The Last Decade, 1915–1925* (1965; reprint, Cambridge, Mass.: Harvard University Press, 1987), pp. 206–13, and 255. Mike Mulligan eventually found happiness with Patsy Dugan. They were married June 7, 1927. The character was so popular though that Branner introduced his identical cousin, Marty Mulligan, on February 4, 1930.

28. See "Winnie Winkle," *Daily News* (April 15, 1922).

29. Winnie became a chief executive on January 8, 1955. Hollywood also employed fashion model stories to depict women as consumers. According to Mary Ryan, thirty-eight movies used this theme in the 1920s. "Projection of a New Womanhood," p. 373.

30. For Branner's recollections, see Martin Sheridan, *Comics and Their Creators* (Boston: Ralph T. Hale, 1942), p. 190. For readership figures, see Advertising Research Foundation, *The Continuing Study of Newspaper Reading,* Studies 1–142 (New York, 1939–50). Study 30 of the *Spokane Spokesman Review* on November 8, 1940, showed that 65 percent of both male and female newspaper readers looked at "Winnie Winkle." Study 38 of the *Atlanta Journal* on April 30, 1941, showed 54 percent of male readers and 40 percent of female newspaper readers looked at the strip. Study 116 of the *Hollywood Citizen-News* on January 28, 1948, showed 46 percent of male readers and 42 percent of female newspaper readers looked at the strip. These episodes of "Winnie Winkle" correspond to the bath and lingerie

scenes of the new woman movies Mary Ryan discusses. "Projection of a New Womanhood," p. 369.

31. Martin Branner's personal files of "Winnie Winkle" are held at the Archives Center, National Museum of American History, Smithsonian Institution, Collection 265.

32. See Robert W. Snyder, *The Voice of the City: Vaudeville and Popular Culture in New York* (New York: Oxford University Press, 1989), pp. 74–78, for the story of the White Rats. Branner used Winnie's trip to have her spend time in cities where the comic strip ran in local papers. The vaudeville story ran from April 10 to April 21, 1928. Branner cited the White Rats on April 21.

33. Winnie's dance partner was her husband, William Wright (Mr. Wright), whom she married on June 11, 1937. Branner and his wife were a vaudeville dance team before he became a successful comic strip artist. Hollywood film production studios used the star system to sell their products—movies. See Lary May, *Screening Out the Past: The Birth of Mass Culture and the Motion Picture Industry* (New York: Oxford University Press, 1980).

34. "Winnie Winkle," *Daily News* (May 20 and May 28, 1929). See "Winnie Winkle," *Daily News* (June 1, 1929), for Branner's reworking of "A Startling Metamorphosis," *Judge* (Christmas Issue 1891), p. 22, in which layered posters peel away to give messages different from the original intention.

35. See "Minutes of Staff Meeting," J. Walter Thompson Agency, June 16, 1931, p. 6, J. Walter Thompson Archives, Special Collections Library, Duke University.

36. Camel's advertisement, *Sunday News* (June 15, 1935), comic sec.

37. Cupples & Leon of New York published four volumes of "Winnie Winkle" reprints between 1930 and 1933. Until the late 1940s they were the only Winnie Winkle products available other than the comic strip. In 1948 Denny Dimwit, a character introduced to the Sunday page in November 1942, appeared as a doll. No information is available about whether it was licensed by Branner. See David Longest, *Character Toys and Collectibles: Second Series* (Paducah, Ky.: Collector Books, 1987), p. 36.

38. In 1934 Branner's annual salary was $50,000. Frank King earned $75,000 for "Gasoline Alley" that year. At the time the highest paid comic strip artist was Sidney Smith, who received $100,000 yearly. In 1935 Smith renegotiated his contract to receive $150,000. The mean income for a comic strip artist in 1934–35 was $15,000. By comparison, a U.S. senator made $15,000 and the U.S. president, $75,000. See "Funnies: Colored Comic Strips in the Best of Health at Forty," *Newsweek*, 4 (December 1, 1934), pp. 26–27; and W. E. Berchtold, "Men of Comics," *New Outlook*, 165 (April 1935), pp. 34–40; (May 1935), pp. 43–47.

6. THE COMIC BOOK

1. John Kobler, "Up, Up and Away! The Rise of Superman Inc.," *Saturday Evening Post*, 213 (June 21, 1941), p. 73; Ron Goulart, *Over Fifty Years of American Comic Books* (Chicago: Publications International, 1991), p. 99; Norbert Muhlen, "Comic Books and Other Horrors," *Commentary*, 7 (January 1949), p. 80.

2. For details of early comic strip collections, see Denis Gifford, *American Comic Strip Collections, 1884–1939* (Boston: G. K. Hall, 1990). Advertisements and reviews for these collections appeared in the toy trade journal *Playthings* throughout the early 1900s. See, for instance, June 1908, pp. 23, 31, and 126–27.

3. "The Comics and Their Audience," *Publishers' Weekly*, 141 (April 18, 1942), p. 1477; Gifford, *American Comic Strip Collections*, pp. 86–87; Coulton Waugh, *The Comics* (1947; reprint, Jackson: University Press of Mississippi, 1990), pp. 338–39; Goulart, *Over Fifty Years*, p. 18.

4. The sticker story is told in Waugh, *Comics*, p. 339. Goulart, *Over Fifty Years*, gives a truncated version that leaves the question open, pp. 49–50. The *Publishers' Weekly* article "The Comics and Their Audience" states simply that "Eastern Color decided to try out comic books for retail sale" (p. 1477). M. C. Gaines, "Narrative Illustration: The Story of Comics," *Print*, 3 (Summer 1942), pp. 25–38. Gaines writes: "*Famous Funnies* was used also as the title of the first book to be put on sale to the general public market, at first, through chain stores and later on newsstands" (p. 36).

5. Waugh, *Comics*, pp. 339–40; Goulart, *Over Fifty Years*, p. 20; Gifford, *American Comic Strip Collections*, p. 104. From the 1930s to the present most comic books have appeared on newsstands two to three months in advance of their cover dates.

6. "Comics and Their Audience," pp. 1477–78; Waugh, *Comics*, pp. 340–42. See Goulart, *Over Fifty Years*, chapters 2 and 3, for more details on the development of comic books.

7. Waugh, *Comics*, p. 343; Thomas Andrae, "Of Superman and Kids with Dreams: An Interview with the Creators of Superman, Jerry Siegel and Joe Shuster," *Nemo* (August 1983), pp. 6–19; Kobler, "Up, Up and Away!" p. 73.

8. Goulart, *Over Fifty Years*, pp. 78–83; Waugh, *Comics*, p. 342; Kobler, "Up, Up and Away!" p. 73. One sign of the continuing ubiquity of Superman in American culture is that most readers of this book are probably aware that the infant Superman was sent to Earth by his parents when the planet Krypton exploded. Superman was found and adopted by the Kents, who named him Clark. The adult Superman's alter ego, Clark Kent, worked as a newspaper reporter.

9. Waugh, *Comics*, p. 344; Harvey Zorbaugh, "The Comics: There They Stand," *Journal of Educational Sociology*, 18 (December 1944), pp. 197–98;

Muhlen, "Comic Books," p. 81. Goulart's *Over Fifty Years of American Comic Books* gives background details for the most popular superheroes. The impact of superhero comic books, and their importance to the expansion of the medium, can be judged by the fate of reprint comics such as *Famous Funnies.* In 1936 *Famous Funnies* had an average circulation of 442,000 copies a month. By the end of 1938, after Superman was introduced in *Action Comics,* the figure fell to 361,582. By 1941 circulation was down to 197,247. To reverse this trend the publishers began *Heroic Comics,* and by the end of 1943 the combined circulation for *Famous Funnies–Heroic Comics* had reached 471,898. Meanwhile the circulation of DC's line of comics, excluding *Superman* and *Batman,* which each sold over a million copies bimonthly, had gone from 821,648 in 1939 to 2,144,114 in 1943. Circulation figures are from the Audit Bureau of Circulation *Blue Book.*

10. See *Detective Comics, Inc. v. Bruns Publications, Inc., et al.,* 28 F. Supp. 399 (1939), and 111 F. 2d 432 (1940). For extended discussions of the legal and cultural implications of DC's use of trademark and copyright laws, see Jane M. Gaines, "Superman, Television, and the Protective Strength of the Trademark," in her *Contested Culture: The Image, the Voice, and the Law* (Chapel Hill: University of North Carolina Press, 1991), pp. 208–27; and Neil Harris, "Who Owns Our Myths? Heroism and Copyright in an Age of Mass Culture," in his *Cultural Excursions: Marketing Appetites and Cultural Tastes in Modern America* (Chicago: University of Chicago Press, 1990), pp. 233–49. See also "The Protection Afforded Literary and Cartoon Characters through Trademark, Unfair Competition, and Copyright," *Harvard Law Review,* 68 (1954), pp. 349–63.

11. Goulart, *Over Fifty Years,* p. 78; Kobler, "Up, Up and Away!" pp. 15, 76; Robert Lesser, *A Celebration of Comic Art and Memorabilia* (New York: Hawthorn Books, 1975), pp. 81, 129; and David Longest, *Character Toys and Collectibles: Second Series* (Paducah, Ky.: Collector Books, 1987), p. 155. See also the advertisement for Superman licenses in *Playthings,* 38 (August 1940), inside back cover. Kobler reported that DC's 1940–41 income from all Superman projects was $1,500,000 and from other publications $1,100,000 (p. 76).

12. Siegel and Shuster were unsuccessful in a number of attempts to regain some of the rights they had signed over to DC. See Gaines, "Superman, Television, and the . . . Trademark," p. 211; and Dennis Dooley, "The Man of Tomorrow and the Boys of Yesterday," in Dennis Dooley and Gary Engle, eds., *Superman at Fifty: The Persistence of a Legend* (New York: Collier Books, 1988), pp. 33–34.

13. The destruction of the slum occurred in *Action Comics,* no. 8 (January 1939), and the demolition of the auto plant in no. 12 (May 1939).

14. Cited in Thomas Andrae, "From Menace to Messiah: The History and Historicity of Superman," in Donald Lazure, ed., *American Media and Mass*

Culture: Left Perspectives (Berkeley: University of California Press, 1987), p. 131.

15. Forty-five years later Siegel and Shuster remembered the Nick Williams story as a reaction to a magazine article about Tarzan merchandise. In their memories the story presented licensed Superman products in a positive fashion. But it was a satire. Andrae, "Of Superman and Kids," p. 15; Kobler, "Up, Up and Away!" p. 73. This story was reworked in an early episode of the 1990s television series *Lois & Clark (The New Adventures of Superman)*, in which Superman struggles to find his true self because his fame has resulted in numerous Superman products, such as dolls and soft drinks. An agent straight out of vaudeville approaches Superman with commercial endorsement offers, including one to go to Cleveland. Eventually Superman decides that he controls his own destiny and no manner of commercial product will affect his true self. Nonetheless he agrees to the licensing of his name provided the profits go to charity.

16. Kobler, "Up, Up and Away!" p. 76.

17. The Daisy gun was a light projector that came with a set of Superman slides. Shortly afterward *Action Comics* carried an advertisement for the gun. Superman said, "I want every boy and girl to get my official new Daisy Krypto-Ray Gun." *Action Comics*, no. 42 (November 1941). Similarly, when Paramount released the first of its Superman animated feature shorts, the *Superman* comic book carried a story that used the short as a plot device. The same issue carried an advertisement for the feature short. See *Superman*, no. 19 (November–December 1942).

18. Sterling North, "A National Disgrace (And a Challenge to American Parents)," *Chicago Daily News* (May 8, 1940); reprinted in *Childhood Education*, 17 (October 1940), p. 56; New York State Joint Legislative Committee to Study the Publication of Comics, *Report of the New York State Joint Legislative Committee to Study the Publication of Comics*, legislative document no. 37 (1954), p. 33; Edward DeGrazia, *Censorship Landmarks* (New York: R. R. Bowker, 1969), p. 265; both cited in Steven E. Mitchell, "Evil Harvest: Investigating the Comic Book, 1948–1955" (M.A. thesis, Arkansas State University, 1982), p. 10.

19. "Editorial," *Action Comics*, no. 41 (October 1941); Kobler, "Up, Up and Away!" p. 74. DC's actions paralleled the film industry's establishment of two regulatory agencies—the Motion Picture Producers and Distributors of America, under Will Hays in 1922, and the Production Code Administration in 1934—after criticism of Hollywood's morality. See James Gilbert, *A Cycle of Outrage: America's Reaction to the Juvenile Delinquent in the 1950's* (New York: Oxford University Press, 1986), chap. 10.

20. To be sure, self-reliance is an American virtue, but not one typically urged on the young. The full text suggests that DC evoked self-reliance for children because of anxiety about the coming war. The entire column read:

"In these crucial days each of us, young or old, has responsibilities to be shouldered. The leaders of this great nation of ours are shouldering the responsibility of safe guarding the nation from aggression and guarding our Freedom and Liberty. In much the same way your father must shoulder the responsibility of protecting the home in which you live and your mother cheerfully accepts the responsibility of preserving the family life and all the homely institutions which we hold so dear. Similarly, it is your duty to yourself, your God, your country and your parents to care for yourself in body and mind. You must accept your share of responsibility thereby lessening the weight of responsibility from the shoulders of others. At home, in school on the playground—be Self-Reliant. In so doing you will make all your elders—including me—very proud of you." *Action Comics,* no. 41 (October 1941). Nonetheless, by 1941 self-reliance was a familiar value for many American youths, who had accepted adult responsibilities during the Depression. See Elaine Tyler May, *Homeward Bound: American Families in the Cold War Era* (New York: Basic Books, 1988), pp. 51–57. Josette Frank probably wrote the "Supermen of America" column, because she was the only member of the advisory board to receive a fee from DC. See Mitchell, "Evil Harvest," p. 14.

21. Kobler, "Up, Up and Away!" p. 15. Later installments of the "Supermen of America" page contained coded messages. I suspect that these messages were either plugs for Superman products or aphorisms. Lacking cryptanalytical skills, and a decoder ring, I can only hope that a scholar with a penchant for decoding will someday transcribe them.

22. Geoffrey Perrett, *Days of Sadness, Years of Triumph: The American People, 1939–1945* (Baltimore: Penguin, 1973), pt. 1.

23. For examples of the Sub-Mariner's and Human Torch's early battles with Axis foes, see *Marvel Mystery Comics,* nos. 3 and 4 (January and February 1940), and nos. 16 (February 1941) through 27 (February 1942). For Captain America, see *Captain America,* no. 1 (March 1941). Unlike Superman, Timely's superheroes often killed their opponents.

24. Comic book publishers were not seriously affected by paper restrictions placed on magazines because these were based on total tonnage of paper used rather than on net circulation. Comic book publishers who had blanketed newsstands with large print runs absorbed the paper reductions from returns, which dropped to as low as 3 percent. See Mitchell, "Evil Harvest," pp. 20–21.

25. Zorbaugh, "Comics," pp. 196–98. Most men who served in the war were under thirty-two years old. John Modell cites census figures that show almost 83 percent of males who served in the U.S. armed forces during the war and survived to 1947 were under thirty-two years old in 1945. *Into One's Own: From Youth to Adulthood in the United States, 1920–1975* (Berkeley: University of California Press, 1989), p. 164.

26. The Army distribution figure for *Superman* is computed from John Jamieson's account of the makeup of a typical magazine set and its distribution. Because of varied reporting methods, the Audit Bureau of Circulation *Blue Book* is no help in confirming this figure. John Jamieson, *Books for the Army: The Army Library Service in the Second World War* (New York: Columbia University Press, 1950), pp. 1–3, 128–31, 134–37; Zorbaugh, "Comics," p. 198; Waugh, *Comics*, p. 334. The Library Service replaced *Superman* with *Overseas Comics*, a comic book that reprinted current newspaper comic strips, which King Features produced exclusively for the magazine set.

27. Congress enacted the Soldier Voting Law to facilitate absentee voting by servicemen. Title V of the act forbade government officials from distributing partisan political material. This section caused some commanders to prohibit the distribution of magazines and newspapers through post exchange stores and library services. The establishment of a soldier preference list was designed to overcome this problem. Although individual soldiers remained free to subscribe to what they wanted, the restriction on post exchange stores and library services controlled the most effective means of distributing information. Democratic rights of free speech and a free press were subjected to distribution controls determined by a priori consumption habits. See Jamieson, *Books for the Army*, chap. 15.

28. "What Our Soldiers Are Reading," *Library Journal*, 70 (February 15, 1945), pp. 148–50; Maj. Everett T. Moore cited in Jamieson, *Books for the Army*, pp. 160, 220–21; *National Geographic*, 88 (July 1945), p. 109; Zorbaugh, "Comics," p. 198.

29. Ian Gordon, "Stop Laughing This Is Serious: The Comic Art Form and Australian Identity, 1880–1960" (B.A. honours thesis, University of Sydney, Department of History, 1986), chap. 4. See also John Ryan, *Panel by Panel* (Stanmore, NSW: Cassell Australia, 1979).

30. John Hersey, *Into the Valley* (New York: Alfred A. Knopf, 1943), pp. 74–75, cited in Paul Fussell, *Wartime: Understanding and Behavior in the Second World War* (New York: Oxford University Press, 1989), p. 141; E. J. Kahn, Jr., *The Big Drink: The Story of Coca-Cola* (New York: Random House, 1960), p. 13; Robert B. Westbrook, "'I Want a Girl, Just Like the Girl That Married Harry James': American Women and the Problem of Political Obligation in World War II," *American Quarterly*, 42 (December 1990), pp. 599, 611–12.

31. The multiplicity of subsidiary companies and the inconsistency of circulation reports make it difficult to quantify this statement absolutely. But it is possible to offer a direct comparison between DC's figures and those for another large comic book publisher, Fawcett, for the period ending June 1945. According to the Audit Bureau of Circulation *Blue Book*, DC sales averaged 6.50 million copies a month. Fawcett, its nearest reporting com-

petitor, sold on average 4.25 million copies a month in the same period. Except for 1949 the Marvel group did not report its sales to the Audit Bureau of Circulation. From mid-1944 until 1971, DC did business as the National Comics Group.

32. Henry Morgenthau cited in John Morton Blum, *V Was for Victory: Politics and American Culture during World War II* (New York: Harcourt Brace Jovanovich, 1976), p. 17.

33. For Morgenthau's message see *Batman,* no. 12 (August–September 1942). *Action Comics,* no. 58 (March 1943); *Batman,* no. 15 (February–March 1943). For other war bonds covers, see *Action Comics,* nos. 50 and 86; *Batman,* nos. 12, 17, 18, and 30; *Detective Comics,* nos. 78 and 101; and *Superman,* no. 18.

34. See Modell, *Into One's Own,* p. 166.

35. Perrett, *Days of Sadness,* p. 299; Richard Polenberg, *War and Society: The United States, 1941–1945* (New York: J. B. Lippincott, 1972), p. 30.

36. For an overview of the advertising industry's use of this ideology during World War II, see Charles McGovern, "Selling the American Way: Democracy, Advertisers, and Consumers in World War II" (paper presented at the National Museum of American History, Smithsonian Institution, Washington, D.C., June 23, 1987). Caroline Ware, *The Consumer Goes to War: A Guide to Victory on the Home Front* (New York: n.p., 1942), p. 3, cited by McGovern, "Selling the American Way," p. 13. See also McGovern, "The Political Language of American Advertising, 1890–1940" (paper presented at the annual meeting of the American Studies Association, Baltimore, Md., 1991).

37. May Co. advertisements, *Los Angeles Times* (May 4, 1943), pp. 10, 22.

38. Foreman & Clark advertisement, *Los Angeles Times* (September 9, 1943), p. 9; Bullock's advertisement, *Los Angeles Times* (January 1, 1945), pt. 2, p. 3.

39. Rainer advertisement, *Los Angeles Times* (November 20, 1942), p. 10; Consolidated Vultee Aircraft advertisement, *Los Angeles Times* (March 25, 1943), p. 18.

40. *Popular Science* advertisement, *Los Angeles Times* (September 13, 1943), p. 13; Life insurance industry advertisement, *Los Angeles Times* (September 9, 1943), p. 9. Emphasis in original.

41. Polenberg, *War and Society,* p. 30; Goulart, *Over Fifty Years,* pp. 128–29; Don Thompson, "OK Axis, Here We Come!" in Dick Lupoff and Don Thompson, eds., *All in Color for a Dime* (New Rochelle, N.Y.: Arlington House, 1970), pp. 124–46.

42. *Superman,* no. 14 (January–February 1942) and no. 24 (September–October 1942). DC's production schedule meant that the May 1942 issue of *Action Comics,* which appeared on newsstands in March, was the first produced after the attack on Pearl Harbor. The April 1942 issue

went to press after the attack but was assembled beforehand. In the 1940s comic book covers in general bore little relation to their contents.

43. *Superman,* no. 18 (September–October 1942).

44. *Superman,* no. 23 (July–August 1943); *Batman,* no. 15 (February–March 1943). See also *Superman,* no. 18 (September–October 1942). And see the "For America and Democracy" cover of *All Star Comics,* no. 4 (March–April 1941).

45. One indication of how fortunate this strategy proved is that when the war ended DC extended its domination of the comic book industry, while other companies, such as Marvel, whose heroes had been active on the military front, experienced rapid loss of sales. Les Daniels, *Marvel: Five Fabulous Decades of the World's Greatest Comics* (New York: Harry N. Abrams, 1991), chaps. 2, 3. See also Audit Bureau of Circulation *Blue Book,* 1949.

46. Perrett, *Days of Sadness,* p. 234; Polenberg, *War and Society,* p. 16. I think the illustration depicts grandparents and grandchildren. At the very least the adults pictured are middle-aged.

47. See for instance *Batman,* no. 16 (April–May 1943); no. 18 (August–September 1943); and no. 20 (December 1943–January 1944). All the 1943 issues of *Batman* contained at least one story in which criminals attempted to steal jewels. The April–May 1943 issue had three stories with this theme.

48. *Batman,* no. 22 (April–May 1944).

49. *Action Comics,* no. 48 (May 1942).

50. *Action Comics,* no. 65 (October 1943). Versions of *Brewster's Millions* appeared in 1914, 1921, 1926, 1935, 1945, and 1985. Robert A. Nowlan and Gwendolyn Wright Nowlan, *Cinema Sequels and Remakes, 1903–1987* (Jefferson, N.C.: McFarland, 1989), pp. 102–3.

51. Superman's intervention also proved fortuitous because Roger's cousin Brandon employed gangsters to prevent him from fulfilling the requirements of the inheritance.

52. *Superman,* no. 21 (March–April 1943). *Superman's Christmas Adventure* may well have been used by a number of department stores. Advertising copy was limited to pages where different ads could be substituted. *Superman's Christmas Adventure,* 1944 Bailey Co. promotional comic book. Archives Center, National Museum of American History, Smithsonian Institution, Collection 274, Superman Comic Book Collection, box 1. *Superman,* no. 36 (September–October 1945).

53. Superman and Batman also appeared in stories set in the future in which they stressed the necessity for a "constant vigilance" in defense of American democracy. *Action Comics,* no. 62 (July 1943); and *Batman,* no. 26 (December 1944–January 1945).

54. Muhlen, "Comic Books," p. 81; Steve Mitchell, "The Best Is the

Worst," *Comics Buyers Guide* (July 19, 1985), p. 28; Audit Bureau of Circulation, *Blue Book* (1947).

55. See *National Comics Publications, Incorporated, v. Fawcett Publishers, Inc.*, 93 F. Supp. 349 (1950); and *National Comics Publications, Incorporated, v. Fawcett Publications, Inc.*, 191 F. 2d 594 (1951). Neil Harris discusses these cases in "Who Owns Our Myths," pp. 244–45.

EPILOGUE: THE PERSISTENCE OF COMIC ART AS COMMODITY

1. Fredric Wertham, *Seduction of the Innocent* (New York: Holt, Rinehart and Winston, 1954). For a discussion of the impact of Wertham's book, see James Gilbert, *A Cycle of Outrage: America's Reaction to the Juvenile Delinquent in the 1950's* (New York: Oxford University Press, 1986).

2. For details of the revival of comic books, see Ron Goulart, *Over Fifty Years of American Comic Books* (Chicago: Publications International, 1991), chap. 11.

3. From personal experience I would suggest that researchers looking for behavioral models for the New Left in the 1960s and 1970s should examine the correlation between Marvel comic book reading and particularly infantile activism.

4. For a discussion of camp and pop, see Andrew Ross, *No Respect: Intellectuals and Popular Culture* (New York: Routledge, 1989), chap. 5.

5. Details on the *Batman* television series and Warners' purchase of DC can be found respectively in Lynn Spigel and Henry Jenkins, "Same Bat Channel, Different Bat Times: Mass Culture and Popular Memory"; Eileen R. Meehan, "'Holy Commodity Fetish, Batman!': The Political Economy of a Commercial Intertext;" and Bill Boichel, "Batman Commodity as Myth;" all in Roberta E. Pearson and William Uricchio, eds., *The Many Lives of Batman: Critical Approaches to a Superhero and His Media* (New York: Routledge, 1990). In 1978–79 the price of a regular comic book was forty cents. The circulation of Superman was less than 100,000 copies a month. According to Neil Harris, the royalties from licensing fees for *Star Wars*, a comic-book-like series of movies the first of which was released in 1977, amounted to $60 million by the end of 1978. "Who Owns Our Myths? Heroism and Copyright in an Age of Mass Culture," in his *Cultural Excursions: Marketing Appetites and Cultural Tastes in Modern America* (Chicago: University of Chicago Press, 1990), p. 245.

6. Jenette Kahn, president of DC Comics, quoted in Harris, "Who Owns Our Myths?" p. 236. Otto Friedrich, "Up, Up and Awaaay!!!" *Time*, 131 (March 14, 1988), pp. 66–74.

7. Goulart, *Over Fifty Years*, p. 309; N. R. Kleinfield, "Cashing In on a

Hot New Brand Name," *New York Times* (April 29, 1990), sec. 3, p. 1. According to the April 27, 1992, edition of the television show *Entertainment Tonight,* Batman merchandise from the first film had sales of over $1 billion worldwide by spring 1992.

8. Tom Shales, "TV Previews: 'The Flash': Comic Caper with Zip," *Washington Post* (September 20, 1990), pp. D1, D12; Goulart, *Over Fifty Years,* p. 303.

9. Kleinfield, "Cashing In," p. 1. So ubiquitous were the Power Rangers and children's demand for the dolls, or rather action figures because they are primarily dolls for boys, that an Arnold Schwarzenegger vehicle, *Jingle All the Way,* could be built around the thin plot line of a father's attempt to obtain one (here disguised as Turbo Man) as a last-minute Christmas gift purchase. My evidence for the shift from the Power Rangers to the VR Rangers is a colleague's child's preferences.

10. *Wall Street Journal* (September 10, 1991), sec. C, p. 1; *New York Times* (October 27, 1991), sec. H, p. 37. *Australian* (November 20, 1996), p. 47.

11. For a discussion of children's Saturday morning television and market-ing strategies, see Tom Engelhardt, "The Shortcake Strategy," in Todd Gitlin, ed., *Watching Television* (New York: Pantheon, 1986), pp. 68–110.

12. There is something deliciously ironic in the respectability attached to the Pulitzer Prize being bestowed on a comic. Readers may not agree with me that *The Simpsons* has a critical edge, but I think I am safe in assuming a general awareness of the show's content.

BIBLIOGRAPHY

See tables in the appendix for a list of newspapers examined.

ARCHIVAL AND UNPUBLISHED MATERIAL

Davidson, Sol M. "Culture and the Comic Strips." Ph.D. diss., New York University, 1959.

De Vincent Collection of Illustrated American Sheet Music. Archives Center. National Museum of American History. Smithsonian Institution.

J. Walter Thompson Company Archives. Special Collections Library, Duke University.

Karp, Etta E. "Crime Comic Book Role Preferences." Ph.D. diss., New York University, 1954.

McGovern, Charles. "The Political Language of American Advertising, 1890–1940." Paper presented at the annual meeting of the American Studies Association, Baltimore, Md., October–November 1991.

———. "Selling the American Way: Democracy, Advertisers, and Consumers in World War II." Paper presented at the National Museum of American History, Smithsonian Institution, Washington, D.C., June 23, 1987.

Mrs. Curtis B. Patterson Comic Book Collection. Archives Center. National Museum of American History. Smithsonian Institution.

Mitchell, Steven E. "Evil Harvest: Investigating the Comic Book, 1948–1955." M.A. thesis, Arkansas State University, 1982.

N. W. Ayer Advertising Agency Collection. Archives Center. National Museum of American History. Smithsonian Institution.

Nystrom, Elsa Ann. "A Rejection of Order: The Development of the Newspaper Comic Strip in America, 1830–1920." Ph.D. diss., Loyola University of Chicago, 1989.

Pepsi-Cola Advertising Collection. Archives Center. National Museum of American History. Smithsonian Institution.

Rudolph Dirks Papers. Archives of American Art. National Museum of American Art. Smithsonian Institution.

Swartz, John Alan. "The Anatomy of the Comic Strip and the Value World of Kids." Ph.D. diss., Ohio State University, 1978.

Warshaw Collection of Business Americana. Archives Center. National Museum of American History. Smithsonian Institution.

Winchester, Mark D. "Cartoon Theatricals from 1896 to 1927: Gus Hill's Cartoon Road Shows for the American Road Theatre." Ph.D. diss., Ohio State University, 1995.

Young, William Henry. "Images of Order: American Comic Strips during the Depression, 1929–1938." Ph.D. diss., Emory University, 1969.

MAGAZINES

*Judge,*1887–1900.
Ladies' Home Journal, 1929–1933.
Life, 1887–1900.
Puck, 1887–1900.
Saturday Evening Post, 1929–1933.
Truth, 1893–1896.

COMIC BOOKS

Action Comics, no. 1 (June 1938)–no. 91 (December 1945).
All Star Comics, no. 4 (March–April 1941).
Batman, no. 1 (Spring 1940)–no. 33 (February–March 1946).
Captain America Comics, no. 1 (March 1941)–no. 45 (December 1945).
Detective Comics, no. 27 (May 1939)–no. 106 (December 1945).
Fighting Yank, no. 1 (September 1942).
Marvel Mystery Comics, no. 1 (November 1939)–no. 74 (December 1945).
Sensation Comics, no. 1 (January 1942).
Superman, no. 1 (Summer 1939)–no. 38 (January–February 1946).
Wonder Comics, no. 2 (August 1944).
Wonder Woman, no. 1 (Summer 1944)–no. 13 (Summer 1945).

PUBLISHED SOURCES

Abbott, Lawrence L. "Comic Art: Characteristics and Potentialities of a Narrative Art Medium." *Journal of Popular Culture,* 19 (1986), pp. 155–76.

Adorno, Theodor, and Max Horkheimer. *Dialectics of Enlightenment.* 1944; reprint, New York: Continuum, 1987.

Advertising Research Foundation. *The Continuing Study of Newspaper Reading.* Studies 1–142. New York, 1939–50.

Agnew, Jean-Christophe. "Coming Up for Air: Consumer Culture in Historical Perspective." *Intellectual History Newsletter* 12 (1990), pp. 3–21.

Anderson, Benedict. *Imagined Communities: Reflections on the Origin and Spread of Nationalism.* London: New Left Books, 1983.

Andrae, Thomas. "From Menace to Messiah: The History and Historicity of Superman." In Donald Lazure, ed. *American Media and Mass Culture: Left Perspectives.* Berkeley: University of California Press, 1987. Pp. 124–38.

———. "Of Superman and Kids with Dreams: An Interview with the Creators of Superman, Jerry Siegel and Joe Shuster." *Nemo* (August 1983), pp. 6–19.

Arndt, Walter. *The Genius of Wilhelm Busch.* Berkeley: University of California Press, 1982.

"Aspects of Comic Journalism." *Nation,* 82 (February 22, 1906), pp. 153–54.

"Atrocities of Color Supplements." *Dial,* 40 (February 1, 1906), p. 79.

Bailey, Peter. "Ally Sloper's Half Holiday: Comic Art in the 1880's." *History Workshop,* no. 16 (Autumn 1983), pp. 4–31.

Barcus, Francis E. "A Content Analysis of Trends in Sunday Comics, 1900–1959." *Journalism Quarterly,* 38 (Spring 1961), pp. 171–80.

Barker, Martin. *A Haunt of Fears.* London: Pluto Press, 1984.

———. *Comics: Ideology, Power, and the Critics.* Manchester: Manchester University Press, 1989.

Barkin, Steve M. "Fighting the Cartoon War: Information Strategies in World War II." *Journal of American Culture,* 7 (Spring–Summer 1984), pp. 113–17.

Barrier, Michael, and Martin Williams. *A Smithsonian Book of Comic-Book Comics.* Washington, D.C.: Smithsonian Institution, 1981.

Barth, Gunther. *City People: The Rise of Modern City Culture in Nineteenth Century America.* New York: Oxford University Press, 1980.

Barthes, Roland. *Mythologies.* London: Paladin, 1972.

Bartlett, Norman. "Culture and Comics." *Meanjin,* 13 (1954), pp. 5–18.

Batman from the 30s to the 70s. New York: Crown Publishers, 1971.

Becker, Stephen. *Comic Art in America.* New York: Simon & Schuster, 1959.

Bell, Daniel. "Modernism Mummified." *American Quarterly,* 39 (Spring 1987), pp. 122–32.

Bender, Lauretta. "The Psychology of Children's Reading and the Comics." *Journal of Educational Sociology,* 18 (December 1944), pp. 223–31.

Benjamin, Walter. *Illuminations.* London: Fontana, 1970.

Bennett, Tony, Colin Mercer, and Janet Woollacott, eds. *Popular Culture and Social Relations.* Philadelphia: Open University Press, 1986.

Bent, Silas. *Ballyhoo: The Voice of the Press.* New York: Boni & Liveright, 1927.

Berchtold, W. E. "Men of Comics." *New Outlook,* 165 (April 1935), pp. 34–40; (May 1935), pp. 43–47.

Bergengren, Ralph. "The Humor of the Colored Supplements." *Atlantic Monthly,* 98 (August 1906), pp. 269–73.

Berger, Arthur Asa. *The Comic Stripped American.* Baltimore: Penguin Books, 1974.

Bigsby, C. W. E., ed. *Approaches to Popular Culture.* London: Edward Arnold, 1976.

Blackbeard, Bill, and Martin Williams. *The Smithsonian Collection of Newspaper Comics.* Washington, D.C.: Smithsonian Institution, 1977.

Blum, John Morton. *V Was for Victory: Politics and American Culture during World War II.* New York: Harcourt Brace Jovanovich, 1976.

Blumin, Stuart M. "The Hypothesis of Middle-Class Formation in Nineteenth Century America: A Critique and Some Proposals." *American Historical Review,* 90 (February 1985), pp. 299–338.

Bodnar, John. *Lives of Their Own: Blacks, Italians and Poles in Pittsburgh, 1900–1960.* Urbana: University of Illinois Press, 1982.

———. *The Transplanted: A History of Immigrants in Urban America.* Bloomington: Indiana University Press, 1985.

Bonner, Simon J., ed. *Consuming Visions: Accumulation and Display of Goods in America, 1880–1920.* New York: W. W. Norton, 1989.

"Book Week Audience Hears about Comics." *Publishers' Weekly,* 140 (November 22, 1941), p. 1523.

Boorstin, Daniel. *The Americans: The Democratic Experience.* New York: Random House, 1973.

———. *The Image: A Guide to Pseudo-Events in America.* 1962; reprint, New York: Atheneum, 1987.

Boskin, Joseph. *Sambo: The Rise and Demise of an American Jester.* New York: Oxford University Press, 1986.

"Boston *Herald*'s Abandonment of Comic Supplement." *Nation,* 87 (November 5, 1908), p. 426.

Brantlinger, Patrick. *Bread and Circuses: Theories of Mass Culture as Social Decay.* Ithaca: Cornell University Press, 1983.

Braverman, Harry. *Labor and Monopoly Capital: The Degradation of Work in the Twentieth Century.* New York: Monthly Review Press, 1974.

Brennecke, Ernest. "The Real Mission of the Funny Paper." *Century*

Magazine (March 1924), pp. 665–75.

Brooks, Robert C. "The Art of Wilhelm Busch." *Bookman,* 22 (September 1905), pp. 10–16.

Broun, Heywood. "It Seems to Heywood Broun: The Newspaper Comic Strips." *Nation,* 131 (July 25, 1930), p. 87.

Brown, Josh, et al. "Comic Books and History: A Symposium." *Radical History Review* (1984), pp. 229–52.

Bryson, Norman. "Semiology and Visual Interpretation." In Norman Bryson, Michael Ann Holly, and Keith Moxey, eds. *Visual Theory: Painting and Interpretation.* Cambridge: Polity Press, 1991.

Butsch, Richard, ed. *For Fun and Profit: The Transformation of Leisure into Consumption.* Philadelphia: Temple University Press, 1990.

Canemaker, John. *Felix: The Twisted Tale of the World's Most Famous Cat.* New York: Pantheon, 1991.

———. *Winsor McCay: His Life and Art.* New York: Abbeville Press, 1987.

Cantor, Jay. *Krazy Kat: A Novel in Five Panels.* New York: Alfred A. Knopf, 1988.

Carlson, Peter. "It's an Ad Ad Ad Ad World." *Washington Post Magazine* (November 3, 1991), pp. 14–19, 29–33.

Cohen, Lizabeth. *Making a New Deal: Industrial Workers in Chicago, 1919–1939.* New York: Cambridge University Press, 1990.

"Comic History." *Saturday Review,* 10 (September 16, 1933), p. 108.

"The Comic Nuisance." *Outlook,* 91 (March 6, 1909), pp. 527–29.

"Comic Relief." *Art Digest,* 7 (November 1, 1932), p. 10.

"Comic Stripping: A Review of an Exhibition Held at the George Paton Gallery." *Art Network,* 12 (Summer 1984), pp. 14–15.

"Comic Strips at War." *Look* (November 30, 1943), pp. 51–53.

"The Comic Supplement." *Outlook,* 97 (April 15, 1911), p. 802.

"Comic-ers." *Everybody's,* 33 (July 1915), pp. 71–77.

"The Comics and Their Audience." *Publishers' Weekly,* 141 (April 18, 1942), pp. 1477–79.

Couperie, Pierre, et al. *A History of the Comic Strip.* New York: Crown Publishers, 1968.

Couvares, Francis G. *The Remaking of Pittsburgh: Class and Culture in an Industrializing City, 1877–1919.* Albany: State University of New York Press, 1984.

Craven, Thomas. *Cartoon Cavalcade.* New York: Simon & Schuster, 1943.

"A Crime against American Children." *Ladies' Home Journal,* 26 (January 1909), p. 5.

"Cultivating Dreamfulness." *Independent,* 62 (June 27, 1907), pp. 1538–39.

Curran, James, Michael Gurevitch, and Janet Woolacott, eds. *Mass Communication and Society.* London: Edward Arnold, 1977.

Czitrom, Daniel J. *Media and the American Mind: From Morse to McLuhan.* Chapel Hill: University of North Carolina Press, 1986.

Daniels, Les. *A History of Comic Books in America.* New York: Outerbridge & Dienstfrey, 1971.

———. *Marvel: Five Fabulous Decades of the World's Greatest Comics.* New York: Harry N. Abrams, 1991.

Davis, Natalie Zemon. *Society and Culture in Early Modern France.* Palo Alto: Stanford University Press, 1975.

De Beck, Billy. *Barney Google.* Hyperion Library of Classic American Comic Strips. Westport, Conn.: Hyperion, 1977.

Debord, Guy. *Society of the Spectacle.* Detroit: Black & Red, 1973.

Denning, Michael. *Mechanic Accents: Dime Novels and Working-Class Culture in America.* New York: Verso, 1987.

Dirks, Rudolph. *The Katzenjammer Kids: Early Strips in Full Color.* New York: Dover, 1974.

Dooley, Dennis, and Gary Engle, eds. *Superman at Fifty: The Persistence of a Legend.* New York: Collier Books, 1988.

Dorfman, Ariel, and Armand Mattelart. *How to Read Donald Duck: Imperialist Ideology in the Disney Comic.* Paris: International General, 1975.

Dower, John W. *War without Mercy: Race and Power in the Pacific War.* New York: Pantheon, 1986.

Drachtman, Julian M. "A Prospectus for an American Mythology." *English Journal,* 19 (December 1930), pp. 781–88.

Eco, Umberto. "The Myth of Superman." *Diacritics,* 2 (1972), pp. 14–22.

Editions for the Armed Services, Inc.: A History. New York: Editions for the Armed Services, 1943.

Eisner, Will. *Comics and Sequential Art.* Tamarac, Fla.: Poorhouse Press, 1985.

Erenberg, Lewis A. *Steppin' Out: New York Nightlife and the Transformation of American Culture, 1890–1930.* Chicago: University of Chicago Press, 1981.

Ewen, Stuart. *All Consuming Images: The Politics of Style in Contemporary Culture.* New York: Basic Books, 1988.

———. *Captains of Consciousness: Advertising and the Social Roots of the Consumer Culture.* New York: McGraw-Hill, 1976.

Ewen, Stuart, and Elizabeth Ewen. *Channels of Desire: Mass Images and the Shaping of American Consciousness.* New York: McGraw-Hill, 1982.

Fass, Paula S. *The Damned and the Beautiful: American Youth in the 1920's.* New York: Oxford University Press, 1977.

Faust, Wolfgang. "Comics and How to Read Them." *Journal of Popular Culture,* 5 (1971), pp. 194–202.

Feininger, Lyonel. *The Kin-der-Kids.* New York: Dover, 1980.

Fell, John L. *Film and the Narrative Tradition.* Norman: University of Oklahoma Press, 1974.

Fisher, Budd. *A. Mutt.* Hyperion Library of Classic American Comic Strips. Westport, Conn.: Hyperion, 1977.

Formations of Pleasure. London: Routledge and Kegan Paul, 1983.

"Fortune Survey: The Fortune Quarterly Survey: VIII." *Fortune* (April 1937), pp. 111–12, 185–90.

Fox, Fontaine. *Toonerville Trolley and Other Cartoons.* New York, 1921.

Fox, Richard Wrightman, and T. J. Jackson Lears, eds. *The Culture of Consumption: Critical Essays in American History, 1880–1980.* New York: Pantheon, 1983.

Fox, Stephen R. *The Mirror Makers: A History of American Advertising and Its Creators.* New York: William Morrow, 1984.

Frank, Josette. "What's in the Comics." *Journal of Educational Sociology,* 18 (December 1944), pp. 214–22.

Friedrich, Otto. "Up, Up and Awaaay!!!" *Time,* 131 (March 14, 1988), pp. 66–74.

Frye, Northrop. *Anatomy of Criticism.* Princeton, N.J.: Princeton University Press, 1957.

"Funnies: Colored Comic Strips in the Best of Health at Forty." *Newsweek,* 4 (December 1, 1934), pp. 26–27.

"Funny Strips: Cartoon-Drawing Is Big Business: Effects on Children Debated." *Literary Digest,* 122 (December 12, 1936), pp. 18–19.

Fussell, Paul. *Wartime: Understanding and Behavior in the Second World War.* New York: Oxford University Press, 1989.

Gaines, Jane M. "Superman, Television, and the Protective Strength of the Trademark." In her *Contested Culture: The Image, the Voice, and the Law.* Chapel Hill: University of North Carolina Press, 1991.

Gallup, George Horace. "Guesswork Eliminated in New Method for Determining Reader Interest." *Editor & Publisher,* 62 (February 8, 1930), pp. 1, 55.

———. *Survey of Reader Interest in the Various Sections of Sunday Newspapers to Determine the Relative Value of Rotogravure as an Advertising Medium.* Chicago: Kimberly-Clark Corporation, 1933.

———. "What Do Newspaper Readers Read?" *Advertising & Selling* (March 31, 1932), pp. 22–23.

Gans, Herbert. *Popular Culture and High Culture: An Analysis and Evaluation of Taste.* New York: Basic Books, 1974.

Garnsey, J. H. "Demand for Sensational Journals." *Arena,* 18 (November 1897), pp. 681–86.

Geertz, Clifford. *Interpretation of Cultures: Selected Essays.* New York: Basic Books, 1973.

Gifford, Denis. *American Comic Strip Collections: 1884–1939.* Boston: G. K. Hall, 1990.

———. *The International Book of Comics.* New York: Crescent Books, 1984.

Gilbert, James. *A Cycle of Outrage: America's Reaction to the Juvenile Delinquent in the 1950's.* New York: Oxford University Press, 1986.

Gitlin, Todd, ed. *Watching Television.* New York: Pantheon, 1986.

Godkin, E. L. "A Point in Journalism." *Nation,* 56 (March 23, 1893), pp. 209–10.

———. "Cuts and Truth." *Nation,* 56 (May 4, 1893), pp. 325–26.

Goulart, Ron. *Over Fifty Years of American Comic Books.* Chicago: Publications International, 1991.

Goulart, Ron, ed. *Encyclopedia of American Comics.* New York: Facts on File, 1990.

Graebner, William. "Outlawing Teenage Populism: The Campaign against Secret Societies in the American High School, 1900–1960." *Journal of American History,* 74 (1987), pp. 411–35.

Grafly, Dorothy. "America's Youngest Art." *American Magazine of Art,* 26 (July 1933), pp. 336–42.

Gregory, Winifred. *American Newspapers, 1821–1936.* 1937; reprint, New York: Kraus Reprint Corporation, 1967.

Grimsted, David. *Melodrama Unveiled: American Theater and Culture, 1800–1850.* Chicago: University of Chicago Press, 1968.

Grossman, Gary H. *Superman, Serial to Cereal.* New York: Popular Library, 1976.

"A Growl for the Unpicturesque." *Atlantic Monthly,* 98 (July 1906), pp. 140–43.

Gruenberg, Sidonie Matsner. "The Comics as a Social Force." *Journal of Educational Sociology,* 18 (December 1944), pp. 204–13.

Gutman, Herbert. *Work, Culture and Society in Industrializing America: Essays in American Working-Class and Social History.* New York: Vintage Books, 1976.

Hall, Stuart. "Notes on Deconstructing 'The Popular.'" In Ralph Samuel, ed., *People's History and Socialist Theory.* London: Routledge and Kegan Paul, 1981.

Hancock, Ernest L. "The Passing of the American Comic." *Bookman,* 22 (September 1905), pp. 78–84.

Hancock, La Touche. "American Caricature and Comic Art." *Bookman,* 16 (October 1902), pp. 121–31; 16 (November 1902), pp. 263–74.

Hardison, O. B. *Entering the Maze: Identity and Change in Modern Culture.* New York: Oxford University Press, 1981.

Hardy, Charles, and Gail F. Stern, eds. *Ethnic Images in the Comics.* Philadelphia: Balch Institute for Ethnic Studies, 1986.

Harris, Neil. *Cultural Excursions: Marketing Appetites and Cultural Tastes in Modern America.* Chicago: University of Chicago Press, 1990.

Harvey, Robert. "The Aesthetics of the Comic Strip." *Journal of Popular Culture,* 12 (1979), pp. 640–52.

———. *The Art of the Funnies: An Aesthetic History.* Jackson: University Press of Mississippi, 1994.

Hecht, George J. *The War in Cartoons.* New York, 1919.

Herriman, George. *The Family Upstairs: Introducing Krazy Kat.* Hyperion Library of Classic American Comic Strips. Westport, Conn.: Hyperion, 1977.

———. *Krazy & Ignatz: The Komplete Kat Komics.* Vol. 1: *1916*–Vol. 8: *1923.* Forestville, Calif: Eclipse Books, 1988–91.

Higham, John. "The Reorientation of American Culture in the 1890s." In John Weiss, ed., *The Origins of Modern Consciousness.* Detroit: Wayne State University Press, 1965.

Horn, Maurice, ed. *The World Encyclopedia of Comics.* New York: Chelsea House, 1976.

Horn, Maurice, and Richard Marschall, eds. *The World Encyclopedia of Cartoons.* New York: Chelsea House, 1980.

Horowitz, Daniel. *The Morality of Spending: Attitudes toward the Consumer Society in America, 1875–1940.* Baltimore: Johns Hopkins University Press, 1985.

Hunt, Lynn. *Politics, Culture and Class in the French Revolution.* Berkeley: University of California Press, 1984.

Huyssen, Andreas. *After the Great Divide: Modernism, Mass Culture, Postmodernism.* Bloomington: Indiana University Press, 1986.

Inge, M. Thomas. *Comics as Culture.* Jackson: University Press of Mississippi, 1990.

Jackson, Peter, and Jan Penrose, eds. *Constructions of Race, Place and Nation.* London: UCL Press, 1993.

Jameson, Fredric. "Postmodernism, or The Cultural Logic of Late Capitalism." *New Left Review,* 146 (July–August 1984), pp. 53–92.

Jamieson, John. *Books for the Army: The Army Library Service in the Second World War.* New York: Columbia University Press, 1950.

Jhally, Sut. *The Codes of Advertising: Fetishism and the Political Economy of Meaning in the Consumer Society.* New York: St. Martin's Press, 1987.

Johnson, Lesley. "The Study of Popular Culture: The Need for a Clear Agenda." *Australian Journal of Cultural Studies,* 4 (1986), pp. 1–13.

Johnston, William. "Curing the Comic Supplement." *Good Housekeeping,* 51 (July 1910), pp. 81–83.

Jurgens, George. *Joseph Pulitzer and the New York World.* Princeton, N.J.: Princeton University Press, 1966.

Kaplan, Benjamin, and Ralph S. Brown, Jr. *Cases on Copyright, Unfair Competition, and Other Topics bearing on the Protection of Literary, Musical, and Artistic Works,* 2d ed. Mineola, N.Y.: Foundation Press, 1974.

Kasson, John F. *Amusing the Million: Coney Island at the Turn of the Century.* New York: Hill & Wang, 1978.

Kemnitz, Thomas. "The Cartoon as Historical Source." *Journal of Interdisciplinary History,* 4 (1973–74), pp. 81–93.

Kempkes, Wolfgang. *International Bibliography of Comics Literature.* New York: R. R. Bowker, 1971.

Kielbowicz, Richard B. "Mere Merchandise or Vessels of Culture? Books in the Mail, 1792–1942." *Papers of the Bibliographical Society of America,* 82 (1988), pp. 187–90.

———. "Postal Subsidies for the Press and the Business of Mass Culture, 1880–1920." *Business History Review,* 64 (Autumn 1990), pp. 451–88.

Kitahara, Teruhisa. *Yesterday's Toys.* Vols. 1–3. San Francisco: Chronicle Books, 1989.

Kleinfield, N. R. "Cashing in on a Hot New Brand Name." *New York Times* (April 29, 1990), sec. 3, pp. 1, 6.

Kobbé, Gustav. "The Evolution of Comic Art." *Chautauquan,* 31 (April 1900), pp. 25–32.

Kobler, John. "Up, Up and Away! The Rise of Superman Inc." *Saturday Evening Post,* 213 (June 21, 1941), pp. 14–15, 70–78.

Kobre, Sidney. *The Yellow Press and Gilded Age Journalism.* Tallahassee: Florida State University, 1964.

Koenigsberg, Moses. *King News: An Autobiography.* Philadelphia: F. A. Stokes, 1941.

Kunzle, David. "Goethe and Caricature: From Hogarth to Töpffer." *Journal of the Warburg and Courtauld Institutes,* 48 (1985), pp. 165–88.

———. *History of the Comic Strip.* Vol. 1: *The Early Comic Strip.* Berkeley: University of California Press, 1973.

———. *History of the Comic Strip.* Vol. 2: *The Nineteenth Century.* Berkeley: University of California Press, 1990.

———. "World Upside Down: The Iconography of a European Broadsheet Type." In Barbara A. Babcock, ed., *The Reversible World: Symbolic Inversion in Art and Society.* Ithaca: Cornell University Press, 1978.

Lasch, Christopher. *The Culture of Narcissism: American Life in an Age of Diminishing Expectations.* New York: W. W. Norton, 1979.

———. "Mass Culture Reconsidered." *Democracy,* 1 (October 1981), pp. 7–22.

Leach, William R. "Transformation in a Culture of Consumption: Women and Department Stores, 1890–1925." *Journal of American History,* 71 (September 1984), pp. 319–42.

Lears, T. J. Jackson. "The Concept of Cultural Hegemony: Problems and Possibilities." *American Historical Review,* 90 (June 1985), pp. 567–93.

———. *Fables of Abundance: A Cultural History of Advertising in America.* New York: Basic Books, 1994.

———. *No Place of Grace: Antimodernism and the Transformation of American Culture, 1880–1920.* New York: Pantheon, 1981.

———. "Uneasy Courtship: Modern Art and Modern Advertising." *American Quarterly*, 39 (Spring 1987), pp. 133–54.

Lee, Alfred McClung. *The Daily Newspaper in America*. New York: Macmillan, 1937.

Lehman, Harvey C., and Paul Witty. "The Compensatory Function of the Sunday Funny Paper." *Journal of Applied Psychology*, 11 (June 1927), pp. 202–11.

———. *The Psychology of Play Activities*. New York: A. S. Barnes, 1927.

Leiss, William. *The Limits to Satisfaction: On Needs and Commodities*. Toronto: Toronto University Press, 1976.

Lent, John. *Comic Art: An International Bibliography*. Drexel Hill, Pa.: n.p., 1986.

Lesser, Robert. *A Celebration of Comic Art and Memorabilia*. New York: Hawthorn Books, 1975.

Levine, Lawrence W. *Highbrow/Lowbrow: The Emergence of Cultural Hierarchy in America*. Cambridge, Mass.: Harvard University Press, 1988.

Little, Arthur H. "If the Egg-Talk Sounded Tall, Consider Talk of Men!" *Printers' Ink* (September 7, 1933), pp. 61–64.

Longest, David. *Character Toys and Collectibles*. Paducah, Ky.: Collector Books, 1984.

———. *Character Toys and Collectibles: Second Series*. Paducah, Ky.: Collector Books, 1987.

Lourie, S. D. "Comic Strips." *Forum*, 79 (April 1928), pp. 527–36.

Lowenthal, Leo. *Literature, Popular Culture and Society*. Englewood Cliffs, N.J.: Prentice-Hall, 1961.

Lupoff, Dick, and Don Thompson, eds. *All in Color for a Dime*. New Rochelle, N.Y.: Arlington House, 1970.

Lynd, Robert, and Helen Merrell. *Middletown: A Study in Modern American Culture*. New York: Harcourt Brace and Jovanovich, 1929.

MacCabe, Colin. *High Theory/Low Culture*. New York: St. Martin's Press, 1986.

McCardell, Roy L. "Opper, Outcault and Company: The Comic Supplement and the Men Who Make It." *Everybody's Magazine*, 12 (June 1905), pp. 763–72.

McCay, Winsor. *Little Nemo*. Franklin Square, N.Y.: Nostalgia Press, 1974.

———. *Winsor McCay's Dream Days*. Hyperion Library of Classic American Comic Strips. Westport, Conn.: Hyperion, 1977.

McCloud, Scott. *Understanding Comics*. New York: Harper Perennial, 1994.

McCracken, Grant David. *Culture and Consumption: New Approaches to the Symbolic Character of Consumer Goods and Activities*. Bloomington: Indiana University Press, 1988.

MacDonald, Dwight. "Masscult and Midcult." In his *Against the American Grain*. 1962; reprint, New York: Da Capo, 1983.

McDonnell, Patrick, Karen O'Connell, and Georgia Riley de Havenon. *Krazy Kat: The Comic Art of George Herriman.* New York: Harry N. Abrams, 1986.

McGovern, J. B. M. "Important Phase of Gutter Journalism: Faking." *Arena,* 19 (February 1898), pp. 240–53.

McKendrick, Neil, John Brewer, and J. H. Plumb. *The Birth of a Consumer Society:The Commercialization of Eighteenth Century England.* Bloomington: Indiana University Press, 1982.

McManus, George. *Bringing Up Father.* Hyperion Library of Classic American Comic Strips. Westport, Conn.: Hyperion, 1977.

———. *Jiggs Is Back.* Berkeley: Celtic Book Company, 1986.

"Make Comics Educational." *Survey,* 26 (April 15, 1911), p. 103.

Manning, Frank E., ed. *The Celebration of Society: Perspectives on Contemporary Cultural Performance.* Bowling Green, Ohio: Bowling Green University Popular Press, 1983.

Marble, Annie Russell. "The Reign of the Spectacular." *Dial,* 35 (November 1, 1903), pp. 297–99.

Marchand, Roland. *Advertising the American Dream: Making Way for Modernity, 1920–1940.* Berkeley: University of California Press, 1985.

Marquis, Alice Goldfarb. *Hopes and Ashes: The Birth of Modern Times.* New York: Free Press, 1986.

Marschall, Richard. *America's Great Comic Strip Artists.* New York: Abbeville Press, 1989.

Mason, George. "Satan in the Dance Hall." *American Mercury* (June 1924), pp. 177–80.

May, Lary. *Screening Out the Past: The Birth of Mass Culture and the Motion Picture Industry.* New York: Oxford University Press, 1980.

Meikle, Jeffrey L. *Twentieth Century Limited: Industrial Design in America, 1925–1939.* Philadelphia: Temple University Press, 1979.

Mergen, Bernard. "Children's Play in American Autobiographies, 1820–1914." In Kathryn Grover, ed., *Hard at Play.* Amherst: University of Massachusetts Press, 1992.

Milton, Jennie. "Children and the Comics." *Childhood Education,* 16 (October 1939), pp. 60–64.

Modell, John. *Into One's Own: From Youth to Adulthood in the United States, 1920–1975.* Berkeley: University of California Press, 1989.

———. "Patterns of Consumption, Acculturation and Family Income in Late Nineteenth Century America." In Tamara K. Hareven and Maris A. Vinovskis, eds. *Family and Population in Nineteenth-Century America.* Boston: Little, Brown, 1978.

Modleski, Tania, ed. *Studies in Entertainment: Critical Approaches to Mass Culture.* Bloomington: Indiana University Press, 1986.

Mott, Frank Luther. *American Journalism: A History of Newspapers in the United States through 250 Years, 1690–1940.* New York: Macmillan, 1941.

Muhlen, Norbert. "Comic Books and Other Horrors." *Commentary,* 7 (January 1949), pp. 80–86.

Mukerji, Chandra, and Michael Schudson, eds. *Rethinking Popular Culture: Contemporary Perspectives in Cultural Studies.* Berkeley: University of California Press, 1991.

Murrell, William. *A History of American Graphic Humor.* Vol. 2: *1865–1938.* New York: Macmillan, 1938.

Nelson, Roy Paul. *Comic Art and Caricature.* Chicago: Contemporary Books, 1978.

"New Art in the Making." *Art News,* 31 (January 7, 1933), p. 8.

Norris, James D. *Advertising and the Transformation of American Society, 1865–1920.* New York: Greenwood Press, 1990.

North, Sterling. "A National Disgrace (And a Challenge to American Parents)." *Childhood Education,* 17 (October 1940), p. 56.

Nunley, John W. *Caribbean Festival Arts: Each and Every Bit of Difference.* St. Louis: St. Louis Art Museum, 1988.

Nye, David E. *Image Worlds: Corporate Identities at General Electric, 1890–1930.* Cambridge, Mass.: MIT Press, 1985.

Nye, Russel. *The Unembarrassed Muse: The Popular Arts in America.* New York: Dial Press, 1970.

Olney, Martha L. *Buy Now, Pay Later: Advertising, Credit, and Consumer Durables in the 1920s.* Chapel Hill: University of North Carolina Press, 1991.

Opper, Frederick Burr. *Happy Hooligan.* Hyperion Library of Classic American Comic Strips. Westport, Conn.: Hyperion, 1977.

———. *Happy Hooligan: Home Again.* New York: American-Journal-Examiner, 1906.

O'Sullivan, Judith. *The Art of the Comic Strip.* College Park: University of Maryland, Department of Art, 1971.

———. *The Great American Comic Strip: One Hundred Years of Cartoon Art.* Boston: Bulfinch Press, 1990.

Outcault, Richard F. *Buster Brown.* Hyperion Library of Classic American Comic Strips. Westport, Conn.: Hyperion, 1977.

———. *Buster Brown and His Chum Tige.* New York: F. A. Stokes, 1915.

———. *Buster Brown and His Pets.* New York: Cupples & Leon, 1913.

———. *Buster Brown at Home.* New York: F. A. Stokes, 1913.

———. *Buster Brown, Early Strips in Full Color.* New York: Dover, 1974.

———. *Buster Brown, His Dog Tige and Trouble.* New York: New York Herald Co., 1903.

———. *Buster Brown Hunts His Mama's Purse.* New York: New York Herald Co., 1903.

———. *Buster Brown Plays Cowboy.* New York: Cupples & Leon, 1907.

———. *Buster Brown, Tige and the Bull.* New York: Cupples & Leon, 1907.

———. *Buster Brown's Pranks.* New York: F. A. Stokes, 1905.

Pearson, Roberta E., and William Uricchio, eds. *The Many Lives of Batman: Critical Approaches to a Superhero and His Media.* New York: Routledge, 1990.

Pedrick, Mary Garwin. "Comic Sunday Supplements." *Good Housekeeping,* 50 (May 1910), pp. 625–27.

Peiss, Kathy. *Cheap Amusements: Working Women and Leisure in Turn of the Century New York.* Philadelphia: Temple University Press, 1986.

Pennell, Elizabeth Robbins. "The Modern Comic Newspaper: The Evolution of a Popular Type." *Contemporary Review,* 50 (October 1886), pp. 509–23.

———. "Our Tragic Comics." *North American Review,* 211 (February 1920), pp. 248–58.

Perrett, Geoffrey. *Days of Sadness, Years of Triumph: The American People, 1939–1945.* Baltimore: Penguin, 1973.

Piersen, William. *Black Legacy.* Amherst: University of Massachusetts Press, 1993.

Pieterse, Jan Nederveen. *White on Black: Images of Africa and Blacks in Western Popular Culture.* New Haven: Yale University Press, 1992.

Pinsky, Maxine A. *Greenberg's Guide to Marx Toys.* Vol. 1: *1923–1950.* Sykesville, Md.: Greenberg Publishing, 1988.

Polenberg, Richard. *War and Society: The United States, 1941–1945.* New York: J. B. Lippincott, 1972.

Pope, Daniel. *The Making of Modern Advertising.* New York: Basic Books, 1983.

Price, Burr. "Comics Go Big Business." *World's Work,* 60 (August 1931), pp. 35–37.

"The Protection Afforded Literary and Cartoon Characters through Trademark, Unfair Competition, and Copyright." *Harvard Law Review,* 68 (1954), pp. 349–63.

Rader, Benjamin. "The Quest for Subcommunities and the Rise of American Sport." *American Quarterly,* 29 (Fall 1977), pp. 335–69.

Radway, Janice. *Reading the Romance: Women, Patriarchy, and Popular Literature.* Chapel Hill: University of North Carolina Press, 1984.

Rasula, Jed. "Nietzsche in the Nursery: Naive Classics and Surrogate Parents in Postwar American Cultural Debates." *Representations* (Winter 1990), pp. 50–77.

Reitberger, Reinhold, and Wolfgang Fuchs. *Comics: Anatomy of a Mass Medium.* Boston: Little, Brown, 1972.

Rieff, Philip. *The Triumph of the Therapeutic: Uses of Faith after Freud.* New York: Harper & Row, 1966.

Robbins, Trina. *Paper Dolls from the Comics*. Forestville, Calif.: Eclipse Comics, 1987.

Robinson, Jerry. *The Comics: An Illustrated History of Comic Strip Art*. New York: G. P. Putnam's Sons, 1974.

Roediger, David. *The Wages of Whiteness: Race and the Making of the American Working Class*. New York: Verso, 1991.

Rosenberg, Bernard, and David Manning White, eds. *Mass Culture: The Popular Arts in America*. Glencoe, Ill.: Free Press, 1957.

———. *Mass Culture Revisited*. New York: Van Nostrand Reinhold, 1971.

Rosenzweig, Roy. *Eight Hours for What We Will: Workers and Leisure in an Industrial City, 1870–1920*. New York: Cambridge University Press, 1983.

Ross, Andrew. *No Respect: Intellectuals and Popular Culture*. New York: Routledge, 1989.

Rovin, Jeff. *The Encyclopedia of Super Villains*. New York: Facts on File, 1987.

———. *The Encyclopedia of Superheroes*. New York: Facts on File, 1985.

Ryan, John K. "Are the Comics Moral?" *Forum*, 95 (May 1936), pp. 301–4.

Ryan, Mary P. "The Projection of a New Womanhood: The Movie Moderns in the 1920s." In Jean E. Friedman and William G. Shade, eds. *Our American Sisters: Women in American Life and Thought*. Boston: Allyn & Bacon, 1976.

Savage, William W. *Comic Books and America, 1945–1954*. Norman: University of Oklahoma Press, 1990.

Sawyer, J. H. "Buster Brown Advertises Shoes." *Judicious Advertising*, 8 (March 1910), pp. 27–30, 89.

Schudson, Michael. *Advertising, The Uneasy Persuasion: Its Dubious Impact on American Society*. New York: Basic Books, 1984.

———. *Discovering the News: A Social History of American Newspapers*. New York: Basic Books, 1978.

Seldes, Gilbert. *The Seven Lively Arts*. New York: Harper Brothers, 1924.

Shales, Tom. "TV Previews: 'The Flash': Comic Caper with Zip." *Washington Post* (September 20, 1990), pp. D1, D12.

Shelton, William Henry. "The Comic Paper in America." *Critic*, 39 (September 1901), pp. 227–34.

Sheridan, Martin. *Comics and Their Creators*. Boston: Ralph T. Hale, 1942.

Silberman, Alphons, and H. D. Dyroff, eds. *Comics and Visual Culture*. New York: K. G. Saur, 1986.

Singal, Daniel Joseph. "Toward a Definition of American Modernism." *American Quarterly*, 39 (Spring 1987), pp. 7–26.

Sloan, David E. E., ed. *American Humor Magazines and Comic Periodicals*. New York: Greenwood Press, 1987.

Smith, Katherine Louise. "Newspaper Art and Artists." *Bookman*, 13 (August 1901), pp. 549–56.

Snyder, Robert W. *The Voice of the City: Vaudeville and Popular Culture in New York*. New York: Oxford University Press, 1989.

Sokolsky, George M. *The American Way of Life*. New York, 1939.

Sones, W. W. D. "The Comics and Instructional Method." *Journal of Educational Sociology*, 18 (December 1944), pp. 232–40.

"Sounding the Doom of the 'Comics.'" *Current Literature*, 45 (December 1908), pp. 630–33.

Sterrett, Cliff. *Polly and Her Pals*. Hyperion Library of Classic American Comic Strips. Westport, Conn.: Hyperion, 1977.

"The Story of Pop: What It Is and How It Came to Be." *Newsweek* (April 25, 1966), pp. 56–61.

Stote, Amos. "Figures in the New Humour." *Bookman*, 31 (May 1910), pp. 286–93.

Stowe, David. "Uncolored People: The Rise of Whiteness Studies." *Lingua Franca*, 6 (September–October 1996), pp. 69–77.

Strasser, Susan. *Satisfaction Guaranteed: The Making of the American Mass Market*. New York: Pantheon, 1989.

"Superman Scores." *Business Week* (April 18, 1942), pp. 54–56.

Susman, Warren. *Culture as History: The Transformation of American Society in the Twentieth Century*. New York: Pantheon, 1984.

Swanberg, W. A. *Citizen Hearst: A Biography of William Randolph Hearst*. New York: Charles Scribner's Sons, 1961.

Swift, Lindsay. "Atrocities of Color Supplements." *Printing Art*, 6 (February 1906), pp. 343–45.

Taylor, William R. "The Launching of Commercial Culture: New York City, 1860–1939." In John Hull Mollenkopf, ed. *Power, Culture, and Place: Essays on New York City*. New York: Russell Sage Foundation, 1988.

Tedlow, Richard S. *New and Improved: The Story of Mass Marketing in America*. New York: Basic Books, 1990.

Thompson, Don, and Dick Lupoff, eds. *The Comic-Book Book*. New Rochelle, N.Y.: Arlington House, 1973.

Thompson, E. P. "Time, Work-Discipline, and Industrial Capitalism." *Past and Present*, 38 (1967), pp. 56–97.

———. *Whigs and Hunters: The Origins of the Black Act*. New York: Pantheon, 1975.

Thompson, Jesse. "What a Decade of Depression Has Done to Advertising Copy." *Advertising & Selling* (August 1939), pp. 17–20, 74.

Thompson, Jim. *Bad Boy*. 1953; reprint, New York: Mysterious Press, 1988.

Thompson, Lovell. "Not So Comic." *Atlantic Monthly*, 167 (January 1941), pp. 105–7.

"To Improve the Comic Supplement." *Outlook*, 97 (April 15, 1911), p. 103.

Toll, Robert C. *Blacking Up: The Minstrel Show in Nineteenth Century America*. New York: Oxford University Press, 1974.

———. *The Entertainment Machine: American Show Business in the Twentieth Century.* New York: Oxford University Press, 1982.

Töpffer, Rodolphe. *Enter the Comics.* Lincoln: University of Nebraska Press, 1965.

Trachtenberg, Alan. *The Incorporation of America: Culture and Society in the Gilded Age.* New York: Hill & Wang, 1982.

Umbreit, Kenneth B. "A Consideration of Copyright." *University of Pennsylvania Law Review,* 87 (1939), pp. 932–53.

U.S. Copyright Office. *Cartoons and Comic Strips.* Circular R44. Washington, D.C.: Library of Congress, Copyright Office, 1981.

Varnedoe, Kirk, and Adam Gopnik. *High & Low: Modern Art and Popular Culture.* New York: Museum of Modern Art, 1990.

Wagner, Geoffrey. *Parade of Pleasure: A Study of Popular Iconography in the USA.* London: Derek Verschoyle, 1954.

Waterhouse, Richard. "The Internationalisation of American Popular Culture in the Nineteenth Century: The Case of the Minstrel Show." *Australasian Journal of American Studies,* 4 (July 1985), pp. 1–11.

Watts, Steven. "Walt Disney: Art and Politics in the American Century." *Journal of American History,* 82 (June 1995), pp. 84–110.

Waugh, Coulton. *The Comics.* 1947; reprint, Jackson: University Press of Mississippi, 1990.

Weitenkampf, Frank. "Inwardness of the Comic Strip." *Bookman,* 61 (July 1925), pp. 574–77.

Wertham, Fredric. *Seduction of the Innocent.* New York: Holt, Rinehart and Winston, 1954.

West, Richard Samuel. *Satire on Stone: The Political Cartoons of Joseph Keppler.* Urbana: University of Illinois Press, 1988.

Westbrook, Robert B. "'I Want a Girl, Just Like the Girl That Married Harry James': American Women and the Problem of Political Obligation in World War II." *American Quarterly,* 42 (December 1990), pp. 587–614.

"What Our Soldiers Are Reading." *Library Journal,* 70 (February 15, 1945), pp. 148–50.

White, David Manning, and Robert H. Abel, eds. *The Funnies: An American Idiom.* New York: Free Press, 1963.

Wiebe, Robert H. *The Search for Order, 1877–1920: The Making of America.* New York: Hill & Wang, 1967.

Wigand, Rolf T. "Toward a More Visual Culture through Comics." In Alphons Silberman and H. D. Dyroff, eds. *Comics and Visual Culture.* New York: K. G. Saur, 1986.

Williams, Raymond. *Problems in Materialism and Culture: Selected Essays.* London: Verso, 1980.

Williams, Rosalind. *Dream Worlds: Mass Consumption in Late Nineteenth Century France.* Berkeley: University of California Press, 1982.

Williamson, Judith. *Decoding Advertisements: Ideology and Meaning in Advertising*. London: Marion Boyars, 1978.

Winchester, Mark D. "Hully Gee, It's a War!!! The Yellow Kid and the Coining of 'Yellow Journalism.'" *Inks*, 2 (November 1995), pp. 22–37.

Witek, Joseph. *Comic Books as History: The Narrative Art of Jack Jackson, Art Spiegelman, and Harvey Pekar.* Jackson: University Press of Mississippi, 1989.

Witty, Paul. "Some Uses of Visual Aids in the Army." *Journal of Educational Sociology*, 18 (December 1944), pp. 241–49.

Wolf, S. C. J. "Tribute to Comic Strip Artists." *Literary Digest*, 117 (April 7, 1934), p. 51.

Wyeth, E. R. "Children, Comics and the Cold War." *Meanjin*, 13 (1954), pp. 397–400.

The Yellow Kid: A Centennial Celebration of the Kid Who Started the Comics. Northampton, Mass.: Kitchen Sink Press, 1995.

Young, Stark. "Krazy Kat." *New Republic*, 11 (October 11, 1922), p. 175.

Zorbaugh, Harvey. "The Comics: There They Stand." *Journal of Educational Sociology*, 18 (December 1944), pp. 196–203.

Zurier, Rebecca. "Hey Kids: Children in the Comics and the Art of George Bellows." *Print Collectors' Newsletter* (November–December 1987), pp. 196–203.

Zurier, Rebecca, Robert W. Snyder, and Virginia M. Mecklenburg. *Metropolitan Lives: The Ashcan Artists and Their New York*. New York: W. W. Norton, 1995.

INDEX